Music Therapy

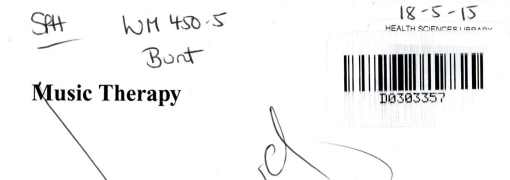

Music therapy is recognised as being applicable to a wide range of healthcare and social contexts. Since the first edition of *Music Therapy: An art beyond words*, it has extended into areas of general medicine, mainstream education and community practice. This new edition revises the historical and theoretical perspectives and recognises the growing evidence and research base in contemporary music therapy.

Leslie Bunt and Brynjulf Stige document the historical evolution of music therapy and place the practice within seven current perspectives: medical, behavioural, psychodynamic, humanistic, transpersonal, culture-centred and music-centred. No single perspective, individual or group approach is privileged, although the focus on the use of sounds and music within therapeutic relationships remains central. Four chapters relate to areas of contemporary practice across different stages of the lifespan: child health, adolescent health, adult health and older adult health. All include case narratives and detailed examples underpinned by selected theoretical and research perspectives. The final two chapters of the book reflect on the evolution of the profession as a community resource and the emergence of music therapy as an academic discipline in its own right.

A concise introduction to the current practice of music therapy around the world, *Music Therapy: An art beyond words* is an invaluable resource for professionals in music therapy and music education, those working in the psychological therapies, social work and other caring professions, and students at all levels.

Leslie Bunt is Professor in Music Therapy at the University of the West of England, Bristol. He is a Primary Trainer in Guided Imagery and Music and a freelance conductor. Leslie's current practice and research interests focus on music therapy and adult cancer care, and his previous books include *The Handbook of Music Therapy*, co-edited with Sarah Hoskyns (Routledge, 2002).

Brynjulf Stige is Professor in Music Therapy at the Grieg Academy, University of Bergen, Norway. He was founding editor of the *Nordic Journal of Music Therapy* and founding co-editor of *Voices: A World Forum for Music Therapy*. His previous books, including *Invitation to Community Music Therapy*, co-authored with Leif Edvard Aarø (Routledge, 2012), have explored relationships between music therapy, culture and community.

Music Therapy

An art beyond words

Second edition

Leslie Bunt and Brynjulf Stige

LONDON AND NEW YORK

Second edition published 2014
by Routledge
27 Church Road, Hove, East Sussex, BN3 2FA

and by Routledge
711 Third Avenue, New York, NY 10017

Routledge is an imprint of the Taylor & Francis Group, an informa business

First edition published by Brunner-Routledge 1994

British Library Cataloguing in Publication Data
A catalogue record for this book is available from the British Library

Library of Congress Cataloging-in-Publication Data
Bunt, Leslie, author.
  Music therapy : an art beyond words / Leslie Bunt and Brynjulf Stige. –
Second edition.
      pages cm
  Includes bibliographical references and index.
  1. Music therapy. I. Stige, Brynjulf, author. II. Title.
  ML3920.B85 2014
  615.8′5154–dc23   2013042864

ISBN: 978-0-415-45068-3 (hbk)
ISBN: 978-0-415-45069-0 (pbk)
ISBN: 978-1-315-81798-9 (ebk)

Typeset in Times
by Keystroke, Station Road, Codsall, Wolverhampton

Printed and bound in Great Britain by
TJ International Ltd, Padstow, Cornwall

Contents

Acknowledgements

One of the privileges of being a music therapist is the opportunity to work musically with people who have much to teach about courage, endurance and beauty. Our warmest thanks go to all the patients and participants from whom we have been learning over the years. There is also a large group of colleagues and friends who deserve our gratitude. The community of music therapy – the 'invisible college' we talk about in Chapter 9 – has been an extremely important source of inspiration for us. We thank the many students we have worked with over the years.

Special thanks go to Brian Abrams, who read the whole manuscript and gave us invaluable feedback on the potential relevance and usefulness of this book. We also want to express our special thanks to the other music therapy colleagues who have read and commented on various chapters of the manuscript: Simon Gilbertson, Denise Grocke, Bob Heath, Sarah Hoskyns, Jane Lings, Katrina McFerran, Hanne Mette Ridder, Daphne Rickson, Gro Trondalen, Cathy Warner and Barbara Zanchi. Thanks to all for constructive critique and suggestions. We are especially grateful to Barbara Zanchi and Simon Gilbertson for providing case narratives and additional material. Thanks to Kate Cullen for compiling the index. We thank members of our families and friends for their continual support, especially Susan Pontin, who read every word of the whole manuscript more than once and contributed greatly in the stylistic integration of our two voices. Laura Bunt commented constructively on a final draft of a chapter, Torgeir Stige helped us with the two figures in Chapter 8 and Christopher Gray answered one of our scientific questions. Our appreciation goes to the editorial team at Routledge, Joanne Forshaw and Susanna Frearson, for their patience and trust. Finally but not least, we thank our readers, who may be the beginner music therapist or the curious enquirer. Our imagined dialogues with you have helped us retain focus and have nurtured reflections on what music therapy is and could be.

Introduction

Formation and form

Exposition: the vision that informed the first edition

Music therapy is a relatively new profession. It is being increasingly recognised at a time when there has never been such a variety of music available to so many people. These two statements summarised the situation in 1994 when the first edition of this book was published. The first statement remains true even though the changes and developments in the past twenty years have been enormous. The second statement is truer than ever. Music's availability in contemporary society creates many new possibilities for music therapy but also new responsibilities.

Most people today have access to music. We may go regularly to listen to music in concert halls, jazz clubs or opera houses, or at folk or rock festivals. We may perform music as members of a local choir, band or orchestra. Music of all styles is also available at the push of a button in the comfort of our own homes or increasingly, in this digital age, as we move about our daily business, not only listening to our own preferred music but also being exposed to background music in cafés and shops. Music is likewise very much a feature of our experience of the cinema and it plays a major part in the advertising industry. Increasing ease of travel opens up opportunities to meet people from all corners of the globe, to listen to, take part in and learn about more music from different cultures, including from oral-based traditions. Since the publication of the first edition, the invention of the internet has made it easier to explore music from all over the world. We would need more than our one lifetime to become familiar with a small fraction of all of this music.

Our preferences for music are based in culture yet are individual, relating to our personal and musical histories. And we seldom meet people who report no liking for any kind of music whatsoever. What are the connections between us and music? The answers are many and include the pleasure gained from listening; the warmth and sense of togetherness from being part of a group making music; the stimulus and satisfaction from regular practice and rehearsal; the intellectual delight of exploring the intricacies of musical forms and structures; the physical energy released within our bodies by both playing and listening to music, inspiring us often to move and dance. At the root of all these reasons lies the fact that music links with our innermost emotional, spiritual and most private selves, and yet is also a social experience. Music helps us to feel more human: what is essential about our humanity can be found in our music. We have these private responses but music can also bring us into very close and immediate contact with the people around us, connecting us with both the past and the immediate future. Without our involvement as either listener or player there would be no music. We are the necessary factor in giving rhythmic, melodic and harmonic meaning to the varying frequencies, durations and intensities that make up the physical world of sound.

A central theme of both editions is that these needs, connections and uses of music can form an important contribution to present-day health and social care. A child may have a language problem or an adult may be depressed. In a music therapy session the potential exists for the person to become an integrated part of the music – to move, during the time playing or listening, into a world beyond the verbal and physical. People of all ages can become engaged in exploring a wide range of musical activities: participating in an improvisation; listening to and talking about music; performing in a band or choir; creating or re-creating a song or piece of instrumental music. Music is very flexible and music therapists can adapt it to connect with people of all ages and abilities, helping them to make use of music in individual or group settings.

How much has music to offer a child or adult with a learning disability or impairment of any kind? Can music help people overcome or cope with mental health issues? Does singing help a person with dementia? What is it about music that can be used as a form of health promotion, or a healthy antidote to the contemporary pressures of life?

Transition: considerations and collaboration

The profession of music therapy has developed considerably since the first edition. Areas of practice and different kinds of activities continue to evolve. The therapy space is opening up as therapists become increasingly aware of the social and community contexts in which music therapy is practised. Music therapists are being called upon to explore different kinds of music, including those produced by advanced computer technology. There are demands to provide evidence and to account for the impact of any period of therapeutic work. These have led, over the past few decades, to a growth in research and publications incorporating a wide range of methodologies.

Leslie and Brynjulf first met in 1986 and have been in regular contact since the mid-1990s. In preparing the second edition, Leslie wanted to maintain the overall form and layout of the 1994 version, particularly the emphasis on case narratives, and to update the text with some of the significant developments in practice, research and theory-building. This new writing partnership between Leslie and Brynjulf evolved through a series of meetings at various international events and subsequent dialogues. We explored and debated our shared values about music therapy and established some core themes that we hoped to make more explicit in this new edition. We did not wish to privilege any one specific approach to music therapy practice but were conscious of wanting to include more cultural and social aspects.

Development: music therapy in a new key

In this second edition, several ideas and perspectives discussed in the first edition will be highlighted and developed further: how people of all ages with different needs make active use of music; how relationships and transactions are developed through music; how the ecology of human development requires awareness about its social, cultural, spiritual and political contexts. 'Ecology' here refers to the reciprocal influences between individuals and their environments.

The notion of lifespan development offers an alternative to traditions that focus mostly on human development in childhood. A lifespan perspective allows for an outlook where possibilities for growth in every phase of life are considered. To work with adults in music therapy, for instance, goes beyond repairing what might have once gone awry. A lifespan perspective invites us to examine challenges, for which people need inner and outer resources. These resources can be explored ecologically. In facing a developmental challenge the question is not just whether the individual is ready but whether the whole resource system is strong enough. If the system is strong, challenges can lead to personal growth, whether the person is 2, 22 or 82. In a weak resource system, if the challenges are too many or too large, they might convert to risks and lead to ill health, impaired quality of life and reduced coping. The range and intensity of challenges, our access to resources and our capacity to use them constructively in collaboration with others determine what paths we will be taking and whether or not we will need or want professional support.

The ecological perspective that informs our writing does not exclude those that are narrower or more focused. We seek to present a range of perspectives and traditions within music therapy, but will not favour individual or small group treatment as the main modes of practice. We will also discuss practices that are more collaborative or communal in their approach, with an additional focus on learning and health promotion. For music therapists there are many reasons to be interested in positive health and health promotion, as the chapters of this book will illuminate in various ways. When a person's ill health is the focus, we wish to differentiate between 'illness' and 'disease' or 'disorder'. For the purpose of this text we define 'illness' as what people experience and 'disease' or 'disorder' as what healthcare professionals diagnose and treat. There is also a third dimension, namely the social role of not being in good health, as perceived by a community. These processes overlap, interact and separate in complex ways, as we will explain in more detail in Chapter 7. Music therapists also work with children and adults with disabilities and with people and communities that are disadvantaged.

Given the range of practices and contexts in contemporary music therapy, we do not apply one generic term for the people benefiting from the services of music therapists. In some texts the term 'client' is used, but it is not appropriate in all contexts. We have therefore chosen to use 'patient' in medical contexts, 'student' or 'child' in schools, 'participant' in more community-oriented practices, and so on. We use 'patient/participant' when the range of contexts is crucial, 'player' when the creative musical interaction of music therapy is highlighted, or simply 'person'. Of course, the music therapist is participant and player too, and often works not only with individual persons but also with groups and communities. We have tried to represent a broad international field of music therapy writers while at the same time we are, of course, coloured by our own respective British and Scandinavian backgrounds. We introduce music therapists with their full name and thereafter by their surname. Writers from other disciplines are described by their profession where relevant.

Recapitulation: outline of the new edition

The first three chapters correspond to the first three chapters of the earlier edition: Chapter 1, 'The growth of music therapy'; Chapter 2, 'Music therapy examples and perspectives' (changed title); and Chapter 3, 'Sound, music and music therapy'. Chapters 4–7 have evolved from the earlier Chapters 4–6. Each of these will include a small number of selected case narratives from practice, some maintained from the first edition and some new. These will be underpinned by a selection of revised theoretical and research-based reflections. The key areas chosen to represent current music therapy practice are as follows: Chapter 4, 'Music therapy and child health'; Chapter 5, 'Music therapy and adolescent health' (a completely new chapter); Chapter 6, 'Music therapy and adult health'; and Chapter 7, 'Music therapy and older adult health' (another new chapter). These practice-oriented chapters prepare the ground for the two final chapters on the profession and discipline.

We make no apologies for being selective about which areas of practice to describe and will attempt to point readers to other areas of practice not discussed in detail. Our vision for this introductory text is not to be comprehensive but to reveal the range of the discipline and profession and to instigate reflections on possible future developments. The original Chapter 7, 'Music therapy as a resource for the community', maintains its emphasis on professional and community issues and now becomes Chapter 8, 'The profession of music therapy: a resource for the community'. Some features of the earlier final chapter, 'Music therapy as a synthesis of art and science: Orpheus as emblem', have been maintained, with the emphasis now being on how music therapy is developing as a discipline. The new title of Chapter 9 is 'The discipline of music therapy: towards an identity of hybridity?'. Finally, our two voices will separate as we reflect on the journey taken together in preparing and writing the book; in a brief Epilogue we will speculate on whether music therapy can be justifiably described as 'an art beyond words', the book's subtitle for both editions.

We hope that this new edition still upholds the introductory nature of the original. We view practice as central, and present a range of as many case narratives as possible. Our intention is for all theoretical and research-based reflections to underpin practice, the imagined sounds of people making music never being too far away from the page. Overall we hope that there will be something in this introductory text for all those who are interested in this rapidly developing profession and discipline and all those who continue to be fascinated and affected by this wonderful enigma we call music.

1   The growth of music therapy

Introduction

Music has been used extensively throughout history as a healing force to alleviate illness and distress, but only in relatively recent times has music therapy begun to evolve as its own profession and discipline. What has evolved is a modern and research-based practice in the service of human health, together with new and inclusive ways of relating to music. This double identity of music therapy, as both a health profession and discipline and a music profession and discipline, contributes to the enormous diversity that characterises contemporary music therapy. This opening chapter will trace the emergence of music therapy, summarise some further historical and cultural reference points, explore some definitions, survey different areas of activity and practice, and reflect on the evolution of music therapy as a new professional discipline.

The United States was the first country to develop music therapy as a modern profession and discipline. There were early European initiatives such as the Austrian music therapy training established in Vienna in 1959[1] but we will begin with developments in the United Kingdom and United States to illustrate some of the processes that made possible the establishment of music therapy as a modern profession.

The emergence of music therapy in the United Kingdom and the United States

Into the richly diverse world of music entered a mid- to late-twentieth-century phenomenon: the professional music therapist. There were historical antecedents for this emergence. William B. Davis has documented the activities of the Guild of St Cecilia, founded in 1891 by Canon Frederick K. Harford, himself an accomplished musician, to play music to a large number of patients in London hospitals. Groups of singers and instrumentalists playing muted violins and harp performed

---

1 Mössler (2011).

in rooms adjoining the patients' wards. The musicians were encouraged not to see or talk to the patients. The Guild gained the support of leading reformers of the day, including Florence Nightingale, and received a great deal of attention. Grand plans were made, including providing groups of musicians for other provincial cities and experimenting with the use of sedative and stimulatory music and ways to relay live music to groups of hospital patients via the telephone. There was an exchange of correspondence in the *Lancet* and the *British Medical Journal* indicating some early apparent success stories, with patients reporting reduction of pain while the music was being played and staff commenting on the calming and stimulating effects.[2]

In spite of these positive stories the Guild folded under the pressure of criticism from the musical and medical press, in particular relating to the temporary nature of any effects, lack of funds and Harford's own ill health.[3] Davis and Kate E. Gfeller have traced the development of similar associations in the United States during the early years of the twentieth century. These included the singer Eva Vescelius's creation in 1903 of the National Therapeutic Society of New York, whose belief was 'that the object of music therapy was to return the sick person's discordant vibrations to harmonious ones'.[4]

In these early years of the twentieth century, music was used in hospitals mainly to boost morale, as a general aid to convalescence and as an entertaining diversion.[5] Physicians invited musicians to play to large groups of patients, assuming that music might activate 'metabolic functions' and relieve mental stress.[6] Listening to music could provide an aesthetic experience of quality and was regarded by many as a humane way of occupying patients' time. Anecdotal accounts of music's inherent worth abound in the early literature on music in medicine.[7] Medical doctor Edward Podolsky cites, for example, the case of a schizophrenic musician being administered daily 'doses' of Chopin. Davis and Gfeller refer to the musician and nurse Isa Maud Ilsen prescribing Schubert's *Ave Maria* for the treatment of insomnia.[8] There seems to have been a general consensus that exposure to music could do nothing but good. As we will see when discussing contemporary practices, theories and research, this assumption is misguided. Music can be used for a variety of purposes, such as self-care and community-building, but also for self-harm and torture. This is one of the reasons

2 See Harford (2002a, b, c) (one article from the *Lancet* and two from the *British Medical Journal*, originally published in 1891 and republished in the *Nordic Journal of Music Therapy*'s series of classic articles). See also Tyler (2002) for discussion of Harford's work.
3 See Davis (1988) on music therapy in Victorian England and also Alvin (1975) and Edwards (2007).
4 Davis and Gfeller (2008: 27–8). See also Edwards (2007: 186).
5 Blair (1964: 26).
6 Feder and Feder (1981: 115).
7 Note the interesting development in the titles of these books: Van de Wall, *Music in Institutions* (1936); Licht, *Music in Medicine* (1946); Schullian and Schoen, *Music and Medicine* (1948); Podolsky, *Music Therapy* (1954).
8 Podolsky (1954: 18) and Davis and Gfeller (2008: 28). These early examples were of listening to music and did not include the full range of direct musical participation.

why there is a need for professional knowledge and academic research on relationships between music and health.[9]

The large influx into hospitals of Second World War veterans was significant for the development of music therapy as a modern discipline and profession. The medical authorities, in the United States in particular, wanted to develop services for these returning veterans. Musicians began to be employed regularly in hospital teams. But the medical and scientific communities were not so easily convinced by the early anecdotal stories of patients being reached by music when they responded to little else. Musicians were challenged to verify and systematise their work, to assess the influence of music and to examine the outcome and impact of any musical intervention in specific treatment plans. Physician and musician George W. Ainlay reports that until the 1940s and 1950s there appeared to be a general lack of understanding of music's value, apart from its general aesthetic and cultural aspects, from both physicians and musicians.[10] The musicians quite understandably lacked training in such assessment procedures and background medical and psychological knowledge.

The scene was now set for the development of training courses for musicians wanting to develop their skills in this specific use of music. Some early key dates in the United States were as follows:

- 1944: Michigan State University: first curriculum established;
- 1945: National Music Council formed a music therapy committee;
- 1946: Kansas University: first full academic course taught;
- 1950: National Association of Music Therapy (NAMT) formed;
- 1971: American Association of Music Therapy (AAMT) formed.[11]

The NAMT and AAMT united into a single body in 1998, renamed the American Music Therapy Association (AMTA).[12] The AMTA is committed to the advancement of education, training, professional standards, credentials and research in support of the music therapy profession. Professional competencies, proposed in 1999 by a commission set up by the AMTA, defined the basic levels of skills required to practise, the most recent revisions occurring in 2009.[13]

The history of any profession also links to the pioneering visions of key personalities. In the United States these included Ruth Boxberger, the first executive of the NAMT; Everett Thayer Gaston, director of the first music therapy training at Kansas University; and music therapists and writers Edith Boxill, William Sears and Florence Tyson. Recently some of the writings of these

9 The claim that music participation and listening is innately helpful has been made even within the professional literature but has been scrutinised critically by several authors, for example Edwards (2011a), Gardstrom (2008) and McFerran and Saarikallio (in press).
10 Ainlay (1948: 322–51).
11 For further historical details, see Fleshman and Fryrear (1981), Gaston (1968), Goodman (2011) and Michel (1976).
12 www.musictherapy.org.
13 Ibid.; Goodman (2011: 29).

important pioneers have been brought together in edited volumes.[14] In the United Kingdom the pioneers included the concert cellist and teacher Juliette Alvin and also the composer and pianist Paul Nordoff, who collaborated with the special education teacher Clive Robbins.[15] Rachel Darnley-Smith and Helen Patey have positioned these developments in the United Kingdom within their historical context, referring to some exploratory work carried out in the 1940s in which musicians and medical personnel researched, for example, the effects of different genres of recorded music on patients.[16] In the United Kingdom some early key dates were as follows:

- 1958: Society for Music Therapy and Remedial Music formed by Alvin and renamed the British Society for Music Therapy (BSMT) in 1967;
- 1968: Guildhall School of Music and Drama, London: first full-time postgraduate course taught by Alvin;[17]
- 1974: Goldie Leigh Hospital, south London: first course taught by Nordoff and Robbins;[18]
- 1976: Association of Professional Music Therapists (APMT) formed, with Angela Fenwick as the first chair.[19]

During the 1980s and 1990s new courses were set up, mostly by former students of Alvin and Nordoff and Robbins, and in other parts of the country.[20] In 1995 the Nordoff Robbins Centre began the first full-time taught Master's-level music therapy training.[21] From 2006 all music therapy trainings were required to be at Master's level, and possibilities for studying for a PhD in music therapy have been increasing steadily. In 2008, plans began for the development of a new organisation uniting the BSMT and APMT, the charitable with the professional, and in 2011 a new organisation, the British Association for Music Therapy (BAMT), was formed.[22]

A further historical indicator is the growth of professional status and recognition. In April 1980 the issue of appropriate pay and conditions of service was addressed in the United Kingdom's parliamentary House of Commons. This was

14 See Boxill (1997), McGuire (2004; on the legacy of Tyson) and Sears (2007). For historical research on music therapy, see also Solomon (2005).
15 Nordoff and Robbins (1971, 2007). Paul Nordoff was American but Nordoff and Robbins developed their early pioneering work in the United Kingdom.
16 Darnley-Smith and Patey (2003: 13).
17 The Guildhall course was set up originally in cooperation with the BSMT and is currently validated by City University, London (www.gsmd.ac.uk).
18 This course is currently based within the Nordoff Robbins Music Therapy Centre in North London and since 1984 has been validated by City University (www.nordoff-robbins.org.uk).
19 Other committee members included Mary Priestley, Esme Towse, Auriel Warwick and Tony Wigram.
20 For further details, see Darnley-Smith and Patey (2003: 15–23) and Wigram *et al.* (1993).
21 Historical detail kindly verified by Pauline Etkin, who directed Nordoff Robbins Music Therapy from 1991 to 2013.
22 www.bamt.org.

the result of growing pressure from the APMT and support from colleagues on the need for a separate identity for the profession. A discussion paper had been in circulation that assumed music therapy could be subsumed under the umbrella profession of occupational therapy. While wishing to work alongside other allied health professionals, music therapists felt strongly that their emerging profession needed its own independent structure. The following question was put by the Hon. Ian Mikardo MP before the Rt Hon. Dr Gerard Vaughan MP, the then Secretary of State for Social Services:

> [I]s he aware that this relatively small group of professional workers, who make an important contribution to therapeutic treatment, are the only public service employees who have no real negotiating machinery? Their wages are fixed unilaterally by their employers. Is it not time that this nineteenth-century Dickensian anomaly was got rid of, and that we moved into the twentieth century?[23]

The 'anomaly' was eventually discarded in 1982 by the award of a career and grading structure for music and art therapists by the Department of Health and Social Security.[24] This placed music therapists alongside speech therapists, physiotherapists and occupational therapists, for example, as recognised members of a health and social care profession in the United Kingdom. The profession was no longer to be regarded as an ad hoc group or to come under the structure for occupational therapists. Since 1982 there have been further developments in the United Kingdom. The profession was awarded state registration in 1997 alongside art and drama therapy. Initially the registration came from the Council for Professions Supplementary to Medicine (CPSM) but since 2002 the Health Professions Council (HPC) has been the legislative body.[25] In 2012 the Council was renamed the Health Care Professions Council (HCPC) and it maintains a register of all therapists who have completed approved training courses and who maintain their practice through continuous professional development. The HCPC protects the public and gives legal protection to the registered title of music therapist.[26]

In the United States, similar developmental stages can be observed. Music therapy trainings have been established in about seventy universities, some at Bachelor's level and some at Master's; PhD possibilities exist in several universities through interdisciplinary collaboration. Temple University in Philadelphia has established a strong specialised PhD education in music therapy.[27] Since 1986 the Certification Board for Music Therapists (CBMT) has been accredited by the

---

23 Hansard 29 April 1980: Art and Music Therapists (Pay): 6.
24 DHSS Memorandum: PM (82) 6.
25 www.hpc-uk.org.
26 Bunt and Hoskyns (2002: 11–12).
27 Other opportunities for PhD study in music therapy exist elsewhere, for example the international programme at Aalborg University, Denmark.

National Commission for Certifying Agencies. Currently the CBMT is the organisation responsible for certifying music therapists to practise.[28]

Paths of development in contemporary music therapy

In many countries around the world the 1960s and 1970s were pioneering decades for music therapy, while the 1980s and 1990s opened up a period for the professionalisation of services and the formalisation of education and research. After 2000 there was an exponential development of music therapy research. Stige has proposed that in order to understand the emergence of contemporary music therapy, we need to take into account the modernisation of societies, including processes such as differentiation and rationalisation. Differentiation here refers to how aspects of life, such as health care, develop their own spheres of discourse and practice. Rationalisation refers to the way in which activities are organised through formalised regulation, usually informed by reason and science.[29]

The growth of music therapy is based not only on the initiatives and hard work of visionary pioneers but also in conditions created by society. Hence, we should expect the developments of music therapy in different countries to have some common characteristics due to shared processes of modernisation as well as differences due to idiosyncratic conditions. The emergence of music therapy in a country such as Norway can exemplify this. There are similarities with the stories told above about the development of music therapy in the United States and the United Kingdom. Music therapy emerged from initiatives in practice before associations and training programmes were established and before further possibilities for research and education at Master's and PhD level were created. But there are also significant differences in relation to the socio-cultural aspects of music therapy. As in many countries, early music therapy pioneers in Norway were often based in charitable endeavours and idealism. As music therapy gradually became organised and professionalised, it developed in more socially engaged directions. In the 1960s the first pioneers of music therapy in Norway started to organise meetings and seminars, welcoming inspiration from international pioneers such as Nordoff and Robbins. In the 1970s, music therapy associations were established and systematic work began to set up a training course in Oslo. The first group of Norwegian students began their music therapy education in 1978, with Even Ruud, Unni Johns and Tom Næss as the three main lecturers.[30] This move towards professionalisation coincided with the ideological changes just referred to. The vision was no longer charity in the service of ill-fated individuals but a welfare society in which the rights of people with disabilities were respected. Ruud's early writings often described a vision of music therapy contributing to a more just society with equal access to music.[31] These changes in

---

28 www.cbmt.org.
29 Stige (2003/2012: 187–188).
30 Stige and Rolvsjord (2009).
31 See, for example, Ruud (1980).

Norwegian music therapy in the 1970s were probably not unrelated to changes in Norwegian society, for example when it came to support of the arts. At this time there was a shift in government policy, with more support for popular and folk-art activities and more awareness about every person's right to participate in culture and society. This prepared the ground for the strong community music therapy tradition that started to emerge in Norway, not least after the establishment in 1988 of the music therapy training that is now located in Bergen.[32]

In short, compared to the early developments in the United States and United Kingdom, the growth of music therapy in Norway was much less based in responses to the medical needs of those in hospital and much more on the cultural rights of everyone in society. The differences that we can see between the developments of music therapy in different countries suggest that we should be careful in claiming that there are given phases or patterns of development to a profession and discipline. The metaphor 'paths of development' seems to capture something significant: there may be some common elements but each nation's 'path' towards the establishment of music therapy as profession and discipline is still in many ways unique.[33]

Music therapy is currently an international phenomenon. Developments in South America, Africa, Asia and Australia are as vital as those in the United States and Europe. The location of world congresses up to the time of writing goes some way to indicate the global evolution of music therapy. The first world congress took place in Paris in 1974, with 400 attendees from twenty countries. The locations since have been Buenos Aires (1976), Puerto Rico (1981), Paris (1983, when there were two events), Genoa (1985), Rio de Janeiro (1990), Vitoria-Gasteiz (1993), Hamburg (1996), Washington, DC (1999), Oxford (2002), Brisbane (2005), Buenos Aires (2008) and Seoul (2011), where over 1,200 music therapists, trainers, researchers and students from forty-six different countries presented hundreds of papers in various formats.[34] If we take into consideration the growth of music therapy in countries such as India, China, Korea and Japan, we can assume that in the future there will be more world congresses in Asia. And when will we see the first world congress in Africa? The organisation of a world congress involves collaboration between a local organising committee, an international scientific committee and the World Federation of Music Therapy.[35]

In several parts of the world, countries have grouped together to form larger organisations, for example the South American Music Therapy Confederation. In 1990 the European Music Therapy Confederation was formed. One of its aims is

---

32 'Community music therapy encourages musical participation and social inclusion, equitable access to resources, and collaborative efforts for health and wellbeing in contemporary societies'; Stige and Aarø (2012: 5).
33 We borrow the metaphor from Aigen's (1998) study of developmental processes in the Nordoff Robbins approach to music therapy.
34 See the interview series charting the history of the world congresses (www.voices.no) and online availability of books of abstracts and/or congress proceedings from several of the events mentioned above.
35 www.wfmt.info.

for therapists trained in one country within the European Union to have their qualifications recognised in another member state and potentially be able to work in a country other than the one in which they trained.[36] Increased access to the internet has been of enormous advantage to a profession at whose heart is the notion of communication. Associations and groups have constructed websites enabling the sharing of information (see, for example, the online open-access journal *Voices*).[37]

Further historical and cultural reference points

We begin here a brief excursion into further historical and cultural reference points by noting the ubiquitous and powerful influence of music. In his book *The Singing Neanderthals*, archaeologist Steven Mithen cannot imagine a time or culture when people did not sing or dance, children play musical games, mothers hum to their babies or communal singing take place to commemorate important events. As he aptly notes, 'Without music, the prehistoric past is just too quiet to be believed.'[38]

It is often pointed out that music is the oldest art form associated with helping the ill, not forgetting that the separation of various art forms such as dance, music and drama to a large degree is a modern construction. Davis and Gfeller comment that music was used in early nomadic hunter-gatherer communities to entreat the gods and ward off evil spirits. Here, they suggest, were the beginnings of a magical and religious belief in the supernatural capacity for music used in healing rituals to influence physical and mental health.[39] Many of the music therapy pioneers cited such uses of music in tribal medicine alongside mythological sources and biblical references, an oft-quoted example being David playing his harp to the troubled Saul, to provide some historical perspective.[40] More rational approaches to the use of music in healing emerged in different civilisations: Rolando Benenzon noted that the use of music to influence the human body was first mentioned in writing in Egyptian medical papyri dating back to 1500 BCE.[41]

The historian Peregrine Horden argues that the written sources of the pre-classical civilisations of Mesopotamia and Egypt are too fragmented for any real investigation of beliefs and practices. He suggests that the historical study of music therapy should start with the four major traditions of literate and learned medicine: Graeco-Roman, Arabian, Indian and Chinese. All of these literate traditions include various notions of musical therapy.[42] We will give some glimpses of the European tradition.

36 www.emtc-eu.com.
37 www.voices.no.
38 Mithen (2006: 4).
39 Davis and Gfeller (2008); Mithen (2006). For overviews of music and healing traditions, see Gouk (2000) and Boyce-Tillman (2000).
40 Soibelman (1948). See also Alvin (1975), Boyce-Tillman (2000), Licht (1946) and Schullian and Schoen (1948).
41 Benenzon (1981: 143).
42 Horden (2000: 43).

An empirical stance to medicine informed the philosophers of ancient Greece, usually combined with colourful speculations grounded in specific schools of thought. Here can be observed the development of rational concepts of order, proportion and harmony within music, coexisting with more metaphysical and speculative descriptions. Pythagoras (born 569 BCE) laid the foundations for our Western understanding of musical proportions, pitch and interval relationships with his experimentations on the one-string monochord. As physician, Pythagoras is reported to have explored how various combinations of melodies played on the lyre, or sung, could influence a range of moods. These reports are placed alongside his more philosophical speculations linking these human vibrations and connections to a mystical contemplation of universal resonances, planetary movements and the 'music of the spheres'.[43] We can observe how rational and philosophical explorations in the ancient world existed beside the more magical, unrestrained and purging aspects of the use of music in various healing rites to alleviate disorder.[44]

Other ancient ideas that have interested music therapy commentators include reference to vibrations of music being able to influence the healthy balance needed between the four 'humours' (blood, phlegm, yellow bile and black bile).This theory originated in Greek antiquity, becoming even more important in Europe during the Middle Ages and retaining its influence even until the eighteenth century.[45] Music took on a further secular role during the Renaissance. The discoveries of the anatomists were to promote a scientific and physiological basis to medicine. However, the older beliefs that evil was inherent in illness, especially mental illness, could not be suppressed by these new developments. Of relevance to the emergence of music therapy was the increased use of music as an individual and fundamentally human act of expression.

In an overview of the use of music in healing, historian Penelope Gouk notes that tracing the origins of the discipline of music therapy to ancient Greece and the European Renaissance is symptomatic of the historical moment when the music therapy profession was beginning to gain ground but that such 'ethnocentric and elitist assumptions are no longer tenable'.[46] She made this comment in relation to Schullian and Schoen's 1948 collection *Music and Medicine*, describing it as one that also gives pride of place to the Western medical model of care as opposed to other, more 'traditional' systems.[47] In a similar way, Horden notes how some music therapy commentators have called on this European past to give validation to the present, taking it 'as axiomatic that the past can be interpreted in much the same light as the present'.[48] Clearly, the ideas from antiquity were part of a

---

43 For a collection of some classical sources, see Godwin (1986), in particular Iamblichus of Chalcis's summary of Pythagoras. And see Wigram *et al.* (2002: 17–28).
44 Feder and Feder (1981).
45 Wigram *et al.* (2002: 24–5).
46 Gouk (2000: 3).
47 Schullian and Schoen (1948).
48 Horden (2000: 21). See also Gouk (2000: 173–94).

cosmology and society that are different from the beliefs and conditions that characterise most people's lives today. These older ideas cannot be transplanted directly onto our times.

It is clear from the compilations by Gouk and Horden that there is less sense of historical continuity than is often proposed and that music therapists can learn much by exploring the use of music in non-Western medical and healing traditions. Carolyn Kenny and Joseph Moreno have contributed to the increasing awareness within music therapy about these traditions and the value of myths and rituals.[49] When interpreting contemporary cultures different from our own, we cannot make comparisons in any direct or unproblematic way, as similarly observed by Horden, because conditions, traditions and worldviews vary considerably.

These observations suggest that adequate learning from historical and cultural reference points requires critical examination of the assumptions that guide our own practice and scholarly ideas. The forerunners and pioneers of modern music therapy followed such paths only to a limited degree. They often turned to science for what they considered a new and objective beginning in the history of music therapy. The physiological and emotional effects of music began to be recorded. Davis and Gfeller cite the earliest reference to music therapy to appear in print in the United States when in 1789 an anonymous article, 'Music physically considered', was published in the *Columbian Magazine*.[50] The author outlined the use of music for influencing various 'emotional conditions', observing 'that a person's mental state may affect physical health'.[51] This article recommended that specialised training was necessary.

Jumping ahead, interest in the effects of music on health continued in Parisian medical life in the mid-nineteenth century, as exemplified by a treatise of Dr Hector Chomet, 'The influence of music on health and life', which discussed the preventive uses of music.[52] However, the lack of sustained and rigorous experimentation can be observed in many of the early uses of music in medicine. It was still apparent during the middle years of the twentieth century and led to a warning by the physician Sidney Licht that is still relevant today:

> Musicians must be cautioned to consider that their sincere efforts may result only in discrediting music, as a therapeutic agent. As a result its acceptance on the basis of such merits as it may possess may be undeservedly delayed because of antagonism aroused by extravagant claims made in its behalf.[53]

A body of physiologically based research measuring the effects of music on specific patient groups played a large part in the emergence of modern music therapy in the United States. Such research led to the possibilities of a medical

---

49 Kenny (1982/1988, 1989, 2006) and Moreno (1988).
50 Davis and Gfeller (2008: 22).
51 Ibid.
52 Cited by Alvin (1975: 48).
53 Licht (1946: 18).

model providing a reference point for the emerging discipline and profession. Many music therapists also turned to behaviour therapy and the direct observation and documentation of external behaviours. This so-called 'first force' in psychology contributed a great deal to the growing acceptance of music therapy from the 1950s to the 1970s, particularly in the United States. Psychoanalysis and the work of Freud and Jung and their successors (the 'second force') provided another major reference point.

During the latter part of the last century the 'third force' of an approach rooted in humanistic and existential philosophy began to wedge its way between the two pillars of behaviour therapy and psychoanalysis. Many music therapists would agree that their work embraces such humanistic goals as 'helping individuals to realize their potentials'.[54] Lars Ole Bonde notes that the work of the psychologist Abraham Maslow links the humanistic approach to that of the transpersonal, often regarded as the 'fourth force'.[55] The theorist Ken Wilber furthers our understanding of the transpersonal, 'focusing on the vast field of spiritual, non-ordinary experience and knowledge in Eastern and Western philosophy and psychology'.[56]

Kenneth Bruscia has argued that culture-centredness could be considered a 'fifth force' in music therapy, a challenge to our uncontextualised generalisations about the nature of music, therapy and music therapy.[57] Several colleagues have similarly argued that we need to develop more music-centred perspectives.[58]

There are both advantages and disadvantages in forming close relationships with existing frames of reference, as we shall see in Chapter 2 when we explore these different 'forces' in relation to music therapy. But to escape any frame of reference is hardly a possibility. Since the publication of the first edition in 1994 a series of important publications has furthered the evolution of music therapy and placed this emergent discipline and profession not only within prevailing psychological and therapeutic approaches but also within larger cultural, social and musical developments and patterns. This is in line with Gouk's proposal for more consideration of cultural contexts and interdisciplinary approaches, and Horden's invitation to music therapists to explore wider social contexts for greater understanding of practice.[59]

What is music therapy?

The question of what music therapy is, is one that seems to fascinate people but it is notoriously difficult to find a definition that will suit everyone. We can begin by describing how music therapy provides an opportunity for anybody to make a relationship with a trained music therapist through which his or her needs can be

---

54 Feder and Feder (1981: 43).
55 Bonde (2001).
56 Ibid.: 178–9.
57 Bruscia (2002: xv).
58 Aigen (2005, 2014); Ansdell (2013); Garred (2006); Lee (2003).
59 Gouk (2000: 3); Horden (2000: 16).

addressed. The music is not an end in itself but is used as a means to an end. As the American music therapy pioneer Don Michel points out, any definition of music therapy is not self-evident; it is not as though music therapists are helping people's music, in the way that speech and language therapists aid speech and language development.[60] However, some argue strongly that music therapists *are* in fact helping people's music; only if music is also an end can it be emotionally and aesthetically meaningful for the person and successfully appropriated for other purposes. Various music-centred and ecological perspectives on this have been developed by, for example, Kenneth Aigen in the United States and Gary Ansdell in the United Kingdom.[61]

How we describe music therapy depends upon our intention and purpose in a given situation. Music therapy students and musicians from all traditions may be interested to learn more of how the music is adapted to suit the needs of different people. Here discussion might focus on compositional and improvisational techniques and the range of music used, including the use of songwriting and receptive (listening) techniques. Budget-holders within commissioning agencies debating whether to set up a music therapy post often need convincing evidence of the efficacy of music therapy. Is there any research evidence relating to the given context? Here discussion might be directed towards some of the therapeutic outcomes or impact of the work, including any limitations or contraindications.

Music offers a versatile space for people to establish contact with each other. In music therapy we observe how people use the music and what might affect the flow of interactive communication. Pamela Steele reminds music therapists of their major responsibility to listen: 'Perhaps the most primary service which we offer our patients within the space and time of the therapeutic environment is our willingness and ability to listen.'[62] She develops the notion of attendance, previously discussed by Kenny: 'Attendance implies a mutual interchange, an alert, resourceful, caring, vigilant patience and guidance. It represents an attitude, a way of being.'[63]

More formal definitions of music therapy have changed in emphasis over the years as the emerging profession has adapted to different needs, contexts and cultural shifts in attitudes towards the nature of health. In the early development of the profession a standard definition in the United Kingdom was Alvin's from 1975: 'Music therapy is the controlled use of music in the treatment, rehabilitation, education and training of children and adults suffering from physical, mental or emotional disorder.'[64] The word 'controlled' implies that the music is used in a clear and focused manner but the definition as a whole makes for a somewhat therapist-centred approach, as if the therapy is 'done to' people. Terminology goes in and out of fashion, linked to the philosophical, ethical and moral perspectives of

60 Michel (1976: vii).
61 Aigen (2005, 2014); Ansdell (2013).
62 Steele (1988: 3).
63 Kenny (1982/1988: 3).
64 Alvin (1975: 4).

the day. There would be some discomfort among contemporary music therapists in using some of the terms in Alvin's definition.

The term 'therapeutic aims' is central to a definition published in 1980 by the NAMT in the United States, when music therapy was defined as 'the use of music in the accomplishment of therapeutic aims: the restoration, maintenance and improvement of mental and physical health'.[65] Many definitions from the United States during this period refer to influencing changes in behaviour, for example 'The therapist uses music, in a therapeutic environment, to influence changes in the patient's feelings and behaviour.'[66]

Rather than referring to therapist-centred interventions 'done to' people, many authors stress that music therapy takes place within the creative context of a developing relationship. The focus is now moving to other aspects drawn from the original Greek meaning of *therapeia*, namely the human qualities of caring, attending and serving. We can see different emphases continuing to dominate discussions at both national and international levels, the two elements of music and therapy each having its own knowledge base even before we begin to explore the complexities, boundaries and overlaps when bringing the two worlds together. How and where different emphases are placed is also complex.

Additionally, there are different international standards regarding music therapy training. This affects our definitions as well. Some courses only train postgraduate professional musicians of a certain maturity who have some working experience with a range of client groups; other courses take students straight from school on first degree programmes. The internationally expanding nature of the profession makes it even more important to discover areas of common ground and to support the natural evolution of any international standards and codes of practice, as already mentioned in relation to developments in Europe. Different countries will develop different definitions of music therapy according to their own musical and cultural histories and particular patterns of care. The very notion of therapy could be viewed as an over-individualised concept, and the situation becomes even more complex once we explore how music is used as part of traditional healing rituals.[67] Music therapists are responding to these challenges in a number of ways, partly by clarifying the limits of their practice and partly by expanding and redefining it.

Redefining music therapy

The complexities of definitions have preoccupied music therapists throughout the early history of the profession, and the need for a thorough overview led Bruscia in 1989 to write an entire book on the subject. Just less than a decade later he published a second edition, the many developments and applications of practice during the intervening years providing him with a rich range of material for

---

65 Cited in Bruscia (1998a: 272).
66 Fleshman and Fryrear (1981: 59).
67 Moreno (1988).

making changes and additions to his original text. In 1989 he offered this working definition: 'Music therapy is a systematic process of intervention wherein the therapist helps the client to achieve health, using musical experiences and the relationships that develop through them as dynamic forces of change.'[68] Even though the second edition of *Defining Music Therapy* is thoroughly revised, Bruscia changed only one word in his later definition, substituting the verb 'promote' for 'achieve'.[69] This replacement communicates a shift in perspective, inspired by Antonovsky's salutogenic orientation.[70] In 1998 Bruscia views health as a contextualised process rather than the state of the individual and he describes it as 'the process of becoming one's fullest potential for individual and ecological wholeness'.[71]

In the first edition of this book Bunt offered his own working definition, employing the term 'well-being', which highlights the experiential dimension of health. An updated version of this definition is offered here. Two changes have been made: the words 'patient/participant' and 'spiritual' have been added, the former pairing to clarify the range of medical and social contexts of music therapy practice, the latter being added after a presentation when an audience member commented that the original definition lacked this important aspect:

> Music therapy is the use of sounds and music within an evolving relationship between patient/participant and therapist to support and encourage physical, mental, social, emotional and spiritual well-being.[72]

Most definitions of music therapy try to capture a description of professional practice. A definition of music therapy which embraced broader societal perspectives was developed by Ruud, who suggests that music therapy is aimed at 'increasing people's possibilities for action'. This view is based on a sociological understanding of health challenges. Health, if understood as 'possibilities for action', is challenged not only because of individual problems but also because of structural barriers in society. Music therapists sometimes work with people whose difficulties might be 'interwoven with the material and economic structure of society, or whose problems are shaped more by their own attitudes and reflections, as well as by the attitudes of others, rather than by their individual or objective biological constitution'.[73]

New definitions will continue to surface as music therapy interacts with changes in society. The redefining of music therapy is not just the activity of scholars sitting at their desks but is enacted by the whole profession working practically in various

---

68 Bruscia (1989: 47).
69 Bruscia (1998a: 20).
70 Aaron Antonovsky was an Israeli medical sociologist who argued that the health professions have been too focused on pathology and need to focus more on how people manage stress and stay well (salutogenesis); see Antonovsky (1979.)
71 Bruscia (1998a: 22).
72 For the same definition, see Bunt and Hoskyns (2002: 10–11). See also Bunt (2001, 2002).
73 Ruud (1998: 51–2).

contexts. As we will discuss later in this chapter and throughout the book, music therapy's growth from pioneering practice to university education, professional practice and research has gradually led to the development of a new discipline. We therefore need definitions and reflections on its identity. Stige has previously proposed this definition: 'Music therapy as discipline is the study and learning of the relationship between music and health.'[74]

As we will discuss in Chapter 2, the relationships between music and health may be understood and explored in different theoretical frameworks. When it comes to the development of music therapy as its own potentially separate discipline, the situation is far from straightforward. As at the start of any new profession, searches are made among related and more established disciplines for common reference points. The range of disciplines underpinning music therapy includes social anthropology, musicology, ethnomusicology, history, psychology, neurology, sociology and medicine. Music therapists also refer to philosophy and mythology and are aware of the inspiration of other art forms from within the humanities, such as poetry and the visual arts. This list is not comprehensive. Music therapy is obviously an emerging discipline with links to the sciences, arts and humanities, as we will discuss in the final chapter of the book.

Activities in music therapy

As several of the definitions above underline, music therapy is very often understood as a relational practice in which activities are collaborative processes linked to a situation, and not separate interventions performed by the therapist. What happens in these collaborative processes?

In some countries, such as the United Kingdom, improvisation established itself quite early as a major activity in music therapy. Here, music helps to release feelings or to articulate in a musical gesture a feeling for which words are often inadequate, providing a different perspective and at times some resolution of what is hurting and painful. And when words are not possible, because of some kind of impairment or disability, improvisation provides an alternative means of communication, a means of individual voices being heard. People can articulate in musical form feelings and impulses that can be uplifting and very expressive, and also those that, in other forms, could be quite alarming or destructive.

There is such a diverse range to the styles of improvisation in music therapy that in 1987 Bruscia compiled a whole text on the subject, *Improvisational Models in Music Therapy*. He refers to the 'inventive, spontaneous, extemporaneous, resourceful' nature of improvising in music therapy: 'It involves creating and playing simultaneously.'[75] Sometimes the end result of an improvisation may be more akin to what Bruscia describes as simple 'sound forms', where the emphasis is on the process rather than the final artistic musical product. Music therapists are

74 Stige (2002: 198).
75 Bruscia (1987: 5).

trained to adapt to a vast range of sound and musical forms that make up improvisations created by people of all ages.

Bruscia discusses the use of improvisation in assessment, treatment and evaluation.[76] There is reference to the debate relating to the balance of musical and verbal content within sessions. He also observes that there are two basic groupings to the various improvisational approaches. On the one hand there is an emphasis on structured improvisations, usually directed by the therapist, and on the other a more free-floating approach. A structured or directed session seems to have a clear beginning, middle and end with moves towards and away from a central focus. In the other kind of free-floating or so-called non-directive session the emphasis appears to be more patient centred, with fluctuating changes of direction moment by moment. Bruscia suggests that there is a general tendency for group practice to favour the more structured approach, and individual practice the more free-floating one, although there are many variations, gradations and exceptions.

Tony Wigram was a gifted improviser and music therapy trainer, and his book on improvisation is a highly practical resource which includes a useful CD of worked examples.[77] In the book's introduction, Bruscia places Wigram's contribution in the line of earlier writings, including those by Alvin, Nordoff and Robbins, and Mary Priestley, another music therapy pioneer. Wigram's book provides ideas for both individual and group work and includes examples for pianists at different levels as well as material for exploration not only on the piano. In concluding his foreword, Bruscia writes:

> If therapy is about finding preferred alternatives that clients have not been able to discover on their own, then it seems self-evident that therapists have to be personal experts at exploring alternatives, their own as well as their clients'. To teach therapists to improvise, then, is to teach them how to find alternative ways of being in the world: and to teach therapists how to improvise with others is to teach them how to explore and live in the alternatives of others.[78]

Another collaborative process is songwriting, and in Australia, for instance, it has grown into a major activity in music therapy. In his foreword to Felicity Baker and Wigram's edited compilation on songwriting, Ruud notes how songwriting has potential in many music therapy contexts and for therapists working within various therapeutic perspectives: 'Songwriting provides an aesthetic context inviting clients to explore, within a new play-frame, their own life, their possibilities, their losses and their aspirations.'[79] In this text, music therapists describe

---

76 The first 'units' of this text focus on some major approaches of improvisational music therapy, including Nordoff Robbins ('Creative Music Therapy'), Alvin ('Free Improvisation Therapy') and Priestley ('Analytical Music Therapy').
77 Wigram (2004).
78 Bruscia (2004: 18).
79 Ruud (2005a: 10).

different ways of writing songs alongside their adult and child participants. Baker and Wigram define songwriting as '[T]he process of creating, notating and/or recording lyrics and music by the client or clients and therapist within a therapeutic relationship to address psychological, emotional, cognitive and communication needs of the client.'[80]

Wigram joined his colleague Denise Grocke for the third of this series on activities in music therapy,[81] this time focusing on listening to music in a range of contexts and using different approaches.[82] In her foreword to this text, Cheryl Dileo points out how listening is found within music therapy across the whole lifespan, with applications relevant for wide-ranging healthcare needs.[83] Grocke is an experienced researcher, practitioner and trainer in the specialist receptive approach known as the Bonny Method of Guided Imagery and Music (BMGIM).[84] There are many examples presented of how listening approaches can be combined with relaxation inductions or imagery. They can be used with or without verbal discussion and with other artistic forms such as creative writing or drawing. The text contains many practical guidelines for using different genres of music in diverse contexts with recommendations for both individual and group work. Ethical considerations and levels of competencies in relation to the approaches and contexts are highlighted.

In addition to improvisation, songwriting and listening, a music therapist may also be involved in movement sessions, in arranging music for different instrumental combinations, in inviting people to sing along to popular songs or in recording music performed by individuals or groups. Some music therapists would also consider verbal reflection a music therapy activity, the weaving in and out of music and words creating an unbroken musical flow to sessions. How music therapists practise depends upon their chosen perspective, and a particular musical activity is very much linked to situation and context. One significant aspect of this is the cultural background and preferences of both patient/participant and therapist. In some contexts, playing in a rock band might be the best way of motivating and helping participants; in other contexts, music theatre or opera could create space for exploration and elaboration of personal as well as societal issues.[85] Popular genres such as rap are increasingly used in music therapy and invite creative combinations of improvisation, songwriting, performance and recording.[86] In the

80 Baker and Wigram (2005: 16).
81 Note that while we refer to improvisation, songwriting and listening as 'activities', a range of alternative terms are used in the literature, such as 'methods' and 'experiences'.
82 Grocke and Wigram (2007).
83 Dileo (2007).
84 For more information about the BMGIM, visit www.ami-bonnymethod.org. Note that the book by Grocke and Wigram does not equip students to apply the BMGIM, for which there are separate trainings.
85 For example, for a discussion of music therapy as freedom practice inside and outside prisons, see Tuastad and O'Grady (2013).
86 See Hadley and Yancy (2012).

future, music technology will almost certainly shape music therapy activities much more often than is the case today.[87]

The most prominent activities in music therapy in the beginning of the twenty-first century will not necessarily remain so during the coming decades. What matters most is not the most prevalent activity but what matches the needs and possibilities of people and places. The fact that some music therapists have started to explore when and how musical performances might be appropriate illustrates this point.[88] Most music therapists would argue that what they do is only important if *how* they do it, *where* and *when* are all taken into careful consideration. Typical values characterising the music practices of music therapists are inclusiveness and acceptance. Activities are adjusted to each group and person; timing and location are crucial aspects.

Areas of music therapy practice

Areas of practice are shaped not only by the possibilities of the profession but also by the needs and structures of a society. If we look back over the development of music therapy in the United Kingdom during the past half-century we see that two main areas of practical work have been with adults with learning disabilities and with adults with mental health issues (adult psychiatry).[89] Again there are historical reasons for this, given that some of the first fully trained music therapists began to find employment in the large institutions responsible for the care of these two groups. Music therapy was found to be a point of contact for many residents living in institutions, especially those with long-term problems, such as profound physical and learning disabilities or chronic schizophrenia. Large proportions of the residents had lived in the hospitals for many years. Individuals and groups of adults were often referred to music therapy on the assumption that exposure to music and the attentive presence of a caring therapist could do nothing but good (a problematic assumption, as is discussed on p. 6).

Gradually, systematic reasons for referral were identified. Music therapists began to evolve assessment and evaluation procedures. In the area of learning disabilities it became increasingly clear that music therapy could help support and develop such areas as physical skills, cognitive potential, motivation, speech and language skills, pre- and non-verbal expression, social skills, choice-making and independence. In adult psychiatry some of the noted areas were changes in mood, releasing of tension, expression of feelings, social interaction in a group and development of self-esteem. Music could be a medium through which feelings could be articulated and shared, thus providing a different point of access for any necessary verbal elaboration. Music therapy was seen to be contributing more than

---

87 See Magee (2014).
88 See Ansdell (2005a, 2010a).
89 'Mental health' and 'psychiatry' are at times used interchangeably. If the terms are differentiated, 'psychiatry' is often connected to the medical model of pathology while 'mental health' is a more interdisciplinary and broader concept.

the general enrichment of a person's quality of life. Here are the beginnings of specific contributions to therapeutic models of health and social care.

Other areas of practice soon evolved: the child with wide-ranging learning difficulties, including speech and language and other cognitive and emotional difficulties; the child and adult on the autistic spectrum; the child or adult with visual or hearing impairments; the older person, including people with both neurological and mental health issues; the adult offender. Nowadays a music therapist might work in healthcare or community settings with children, adolescents, adults or older adults. It is becoming apparent that music therapy is being perceived as a professional speciality with broad areas of practical application for people of all ages.

In the second edition of *Defining Music Therapy*, Bruscia defines an '*area* of practice' as what is 'in the foreground of concern for the client, the therapist, and clinical agency'.[90] Of particular relevance, Bruscia argues, are the 'priority health concern' for client and agency, the goal(s) of the music therapist and the 'nature of the client–therapist relationship'. On the basis of these criteria, Bruscia identified six areas of practice: Didactic, Medical, Healing, Psychotherapeutic, Recreational and Ecological.[91]

Such a characterisation of practice is of interest as to some degree it cuts across populations defined by diagnosis. This might be important if we want to challenge the assumption that problems are only located in the individual. We can take the area of didactic practices as an example. Bruscia defines these as 'focused on helping clients gain knowledge, behaviors, and skills needed for functional, independent living and social adaptation'.[92] Such practices are relevant not only for people categorised as having learning disabilities; people with medical conditions or mental health challenges, for instance, might benefit from a music therapy programme through which they can learn new skills of relevance for their possibility to thrive in everyday life.

Relationships between individual and environment are made especially prominent in the area of practice that Bruscia labels ecological:

> The ecological area of practice includes all applications of music and music therapy where the primary focus is on promoting health within and between various layers of the sociocultural community and/or physical environment. This includes all work which focuses on the family, workplace, community, society, culture, or physical environment, either because the health of the ecological unit itself is at risk and therefore in need of intervention, or because the unit in some way causes or contributes to the health problems of its members. Also included are any efforts to form, build, or sustain communities through music therapy.[93]

90 Bruscia (1998a: 157).
91 Ibid.: 157–8.
92 Ibid.: 159.
93 Ibid.: 229.

The inclusion of an ecological area of practice in Bruscia's classification highlights some characteristics that might be relevant for our understanding of music therapy more generally. Practice is characterised by complexity and contingency and is never merely a 'doing' of something. It evolves as we, as humans, actively relate to a situation. Consequently, any fixed characterisation of areas of practice is bound to be challenged. Instead of thinking of areas of practice as fixed and boundaried territories, we could think of them as more or less open fields where agents collaborate in the use and production of resources.[94]

The evolution of a new professional discipline

Any therapeutic profession has an ethical and moral responsibility to research the potential impact of the work. What are the links between therapeutic objectives, the music therapy process and eventual outcomes? Parents will often ask how music therapy can specifically help their child. If we go to a therapist and embark on a period of intensive personal therapy, we want to have some indication of what may be expected to happen during the process and to have some understanding of the therapist's theoretical orientation. At a practical level we also want to know what we are getting for our money. Budget-holders are reluctant to part with funding unless there is a clear indication that employing a music therapist will contribute in a specific way to the patients for whom they are administering funds. These external factors are even more acute in times of economic restraint, accountability and requirement for providing cost-effective services. Members of the profession need to find ways to respond to the current international emphasis on evidence-based practice. In addition, several music therapists, as we shall see in Chapters 8 and 9, have argued that we need to define a research agenda through which societal questions such as people's access to music in everyday life, inequities in health, marginalisation and discrimination are addressed.

Developments in music therapy research have made enormous strides in the years between the publication of the first and second editions of this text. In the 1994 edition, comparison of two early surveys of publications in both US- and UK-based music therapy journals and publications indicated an identical ranking order of categorisation of the articles, namely descriptive, philosophical, experimental and historical, with a comparable range of percentage scores. The categories were based on the original US survey.[95] The dearth of published research during the first stages of the profession was as predicted. As more clinical work has become available for analysis, more systematic research and potential theory-building are developing. As in any new profession, competent practice

---

94 For further discussion of this claim, see Stige (2003/2012).
95 Jellison (1973: 114–29). Examples within Jellison's categories were (a) philosophical – analysis, criticism, speculation; (b) historical – reviews, surveys of past information; (c) descriptive – current music therapy status: case studies of individuals and groups; descriptions of work settings and training programmes; indicators of the growth of the profession; and (d) experimental – results of structured research, presentation of research plans.

commonly precedes the development of research and the emergence of a new discipline.

Articles of a more historical nature were ranked in the lowest position in all these early American and British surveys. Most emphasis in the surveyed articles was on describing current practice, methods of training, places of work and the expression of different viewpoints. All this work will in time become the historical past of the profession. 'The music therapy profession is young but as it matures and creates its own "past," accurate historical documentation may increase to analyze the past in order to interpret the future.'[96]

Jane Edwards commented in 2005 that the *Journal of Music Therapy* set a standard for music therapy research when it was established in the United States in 1964.[97] She presented an additional seven journals, alongside their dates of publication, that incorporate music therapy in their title and are published in English: the *Canadian Journal of Music Therapy* (1973), *Music Therapy* (1981–96), *Music Therapy Perspectives* (1982), the *British Journal of Music Therapy* (1987), the *Australian Journal of Music Therapy* (1990), the *Nordic Journal of Music Therapy* (1992) and the *Annual Journal of the New Zealand Society for Music Therapy* (1994).[98] Since Edwards' 2005 chapter, *Voices: A World Forum for Music Therapy* and *Approaches: Music Therapy and Special Music Education* have established themselves as online peer-reviewed journals.[99] There are also some interdisciplinary journals that publish many music therapy articles, such as *Music and Medicine*, *Arts in Psychotherapy*, *Arts and Health* and *Music and Arts in Action* (MAIA). There are also several national peer-reviewed music therapy journals in a range of languages. Together, all these journals contribute to the current international standing of music therapy research. Furthermore, many music therapists publish in the journals of disciplines such as psychology and psychiatry. This enhances interdisciplinary communication and critique. Peer-reviewed journals and international conferences constitute arenas for exchange, debate and reflection, and therefore contribute substantially to the development of music therapy as a discipline.

Kenny has used a lifespan framework to describe the evolution of music therapy.[100] During its infancy and young childhood the profession was learning basic rules for survival, acquiring all the necessary tools of the trade and working hard to set up jobs for newly trained therapists. As was recounted earlier, the ground was set by the pioneering vision, teachings and determination of the 'parents' of the next generation of therapists, trainers and researchers. After initial steps had been taken and more work established, it was natural that the search for further acceptance and identity required the formation of professional associations. Further standards for efficient and clinical practice led to increased professional

96 Ibid.: 7.
97 Edwards (2005a: 20).
98 Ibid.: 21.
99 www.voices.no; http://approaches.primarymusic.gr/.
100 Kenny (1988).

recognition and establishment of career structures. Such welcomed moves were paralleled by the underpinning of practice by theories drawn from medical and psychological approaches (see Chapter 2). Music therapists began to form a sense of identity as both a profession and an evolving discipline (see Chapters 8 and 9) as more training courses and posts were set up. In adolescence there was much research and exploration, experimenting with various approaches to the work and research designs, as if in an attempt to see whether the various clothes and styles would fit. In 1988 Kenny pointed out that music therapy in the United States was moving into mature adulthood, the stage when a deepening understanding results in attempting to stand on one's own. At that time there was even the prediction of a mid-life crisis brewing, with re-evaluations of the past and searches for new meanings and directions.

The metaphor Kenny introduced is appealing because it suggests both that the context for the evolution of music therapy changes continuously and that we should not take it for granted that music therapy will continue to grow into eternity. So far in this chapter, perhaps we have described this development too much as steady linear progress. We need frameworks for thinking about the evolution of music therapy that embrace the contingencies, controversies and vulnerabilities that are part of the history. Any lifespan view of development is multidimensional and multidirectional. There is no fixed route; we all have the potential to change and grow. As an individual moves through childhood and the adult years there is a shifting perspective on self, on others and on the surrounding society. For all of us there are recurring themes and physical ups and downs that interact with life events. We all have our personal stories that constantly change and re-form as we respond differently to events around us.

The metaphor of lifespan development suggests that there might be occasions to celebrate. In the first edition it was reported that in the United Kingdom the BSMT could be proud of its first thirty years of life and the APMT of entering its late teenage years. At that stage in the United Kingdom there was more encouragement of differing styles of work, approaches and opinions. Clinical work and research questions were being presented in a climate that was more open than before to mutual respect and debate. Like American colleagues at a similar stage in development, music therapists in the United Kingdom were at a point where they were beginning to gain sufficient confidence to evolve their individual styles and research methods without constantly looking over their shoulders for guidance or referring to other traditions. The evolution of the discipline was beginning to be explored.

Nowadays, after two further decades, there is quite a lot to celebrate in many countries. Similar patterns are occurring worldwide with the expansion of music therapy training, practice, associations and research across all continents. There has been a steady increase in the publication, availability and translation of new texts, and opportunities for dialogue and debate at national and international meetings and conferences. The internet has created even more opportunities for communication and exchange. As music therapy develops on its life's journey, we can observe further areas of debate and questions that not only are germane to our profession but also can be part of ongoing dialogue with other creative arts therapists, allied health professionals and music in health practitioners. (We shall discuss these areas further in Chapter 8.)

The lifespan image of development also suggests that if music therapy does not keep reinventing itself, or if the conditions change dramatically, decay and death are possibilities. Alternatively, the cycle might begin to repeat itself with the growth and natural evolution of new ideas and patterns. New specialities and movements within music therapy could then be interpreted in at least two perspectives: as fragmentation of the field or as attempts to reinvent or invigorate it.

We will close our reflections on the lifespan metaphor of development by adding some comments on music, the tool of our trade. Music can be used at different stages of life to suit different needs. Music is in constant ebb and flow. Music therapists are able to observe children and adults creating all kinds of musical gestures. An adult may be very familiar with the basic parameters of music but in free improvisation may dip back through earlier experiences to capture again some of the early sensuous delight in the sounds. Beethoven is an example of a composer who offers opportunities for a lifespan perspective. If we look at the string quartets we can see how the various changes throughout the series can meet our needs as we get older. There is a great deal written about the last quartets as the culmination of a life dedicated to composing, works full of the wisdom and spiritual insight of maturity. Yet this wisdom also has the feel of the rapt innocence of childhood, with some song-like melodies of the utmost yet profoundest simplicity. In later years we may also find the youthful energy of the early quartets invigorating and inspiring. The very fact that people with dementia can often recall more of their childhood than of recent events may be part of this whole cyclical process of beginnings and endings. Long-term memory still remains intact. Our sense of hearing is both the first to develop and, very often, the last to leave us.

Poets and playwrights have used many metaphors to describe this lifespan process. Images from the natural world have been used to describe the journey: for example, the flow of a river, the daily movement of the sun, the changing seasons. These images may perhaps be interpreted to suggest very different futures for the discipline. How we use music can be beautifully represented in the image of the spiral, a shape so fundamental to life. There are many variations: the homes of snails and sea creatures, our inner organs of hearing and the natural forms of whirlpools and hurricanes.[101]

Concluding points

At the start of this chapter we referred to exchanges in the *British Medical Journal* and the *Lancet* in relation to Harford's work with the Guild of St Cecilia in 1891. At the end of the chapter we refer to a recent article, again in the *Lancet*. In June 2012 *Lancet Neurology* published a piece by David Holmes entitled 'Music

---

101 McGlashan (1976: 102–3).

therapy's breakthrough act'. This related to the role music therapy played in the rehabilitation of US Congresswoman Gabrielle Giffords, who had sustained serious left hemisphere brain damage after an assassination attempt. According to Holmes's report, music therapy had gradually helped Giffords to move from not being able to speak to singing brief parts of songs and eventually 'a whole repertoire of tunes'. Speech rhythms began to be articulated in short phrases. We do not want to overplay this single case but it is interesting that Holmes predicted that the media attention given to this story could contribute to further recognition of the potential of music therapy.[102]

In this opening chapter we have charted the emergence of music therapy as a profession and as an evolving discipline. We have explored some of the ways in which music therapy has been defined and redefined. We have briefly identified some of the historical and cultural reference points, activities and areas of practice. An overarching theme has been that of lifespan development, but no steady growth can be taken for granted. Music therapy will have to reinvent itself and adjust to new conditions of development in order to survive and thrive, although we are both very much of the opinion that, with an emphasis on creating an open attitude to the ways in which music therapy might develop, there is a healthy future ahead for the profession and discipline. We are left with some perennial questions:

- How will music therapists be able to acknowledge and nurture their dual identity as health workers and musicians?
- How will music therapists engage with societal issues such as inequities in health and in access to music?
- What part can music therapy play in helping people to gain or regain contact with each other through music?
- Given music's capacity to engage a sense of both personal and group identity, can music be used in the twenty-first century in the time-honoured sense of being a means of local, social and community-based integration?

We would like to conclude this first chapter with the thought that the emergence of the professional music therapist could not have happened at a more crucial time in relation to changes in society and in music itself, both during the middle years of the twentieth century and today.

---

102 Holmes (2012: 486–7).

2 Music therapy examples and perspectives

Introduction

How is music therapy practised? What actually happens in a session, and what does it all mean? This chapter starts with a description of a child's individual session, which can be viewed from a variety of professional and developmental perspectives. Some features are common to other forms of therapeutic interventions and some more specific to music therapy. A description of a session with a group of adults follows. These two examples will place into context the rest of the chapter, in which tools for thinking about music therapy will be discussed. Seven different perspectives will be introduced: medical, behavioural, psychodynamic, humanistic, transpersonal, culture-centred and music-centred. Each perspective is presented with broad brushstrokes before a closing discussion on ways of using and combining theoretical perspectives in practice. Further elaboration and developments of theoretical perspectives will underpin examples in subsequent chapters.

The opening two examples illustrate the primacy of practice in music therapy. This is not to say that music therapy is always practice driven. At times, new and inspiring ideas emerge from theoretically based dialogues with members of other disciplines. Theory and practice are not in this sense polarised. The reflective practitioner will be informed by theory to support practice, even when it might appear far from the actual present moment of creative interaction in the therapy space. It is worth noting that the theoretical perspectives presented in this chapter might differ in how the relationships between theory and practice are construed. In some the balance might be towards adjusting practice to fit a scientific theory; in other situations, theories are not so central to an intervention but are appropriate for further reflection and description of what is taking place.

An individual session

John was attending a child assessment centre with his parents for an assessment period.[1] During the assessment, John and his parents were seen by a team of

---

1 All names in the case examples throughout the book have been changed unless specific permission has been given to use a first name. Other details within the descriptions have been altered to maintain anonymity and confidentiality.

specialists: a speech and language therapist, an educational psychologist, a physiotherapist, an occupational therapist, a child psychotherapist, a social worker and a music therapist. At the end of the assessment period all the therapists met with the parents at a case conference chaired by the consultant paediatrician.

John is 3½. His parents are concerned that he is not talking. The parents are also worried because John appears to be withdrawn at times, finding it difficult to make contact with the other children and adults around him. He does not seem interested in exploring the activities presented to him during some of the assessment sessions. The occupational therapist observes John tapping a table and suggests that music therapy might be an appropriate medium for observing a wide range of his behaviours and assessing his communication skills. John is referred to music therapy and then attends his music therapy assessment sessions with his mother. This is a description of his second session. The setting is a small room. The therapist is at the piano with a drum and cymbal standing to the side. This arrangement is the same as for the first session, when John played for the most part on these two instruments.

John comes in, moves quickly to the drum and cymbal, takes up the drumsticks that are offered him and starts to play. The contact with the instruments is immediate. He plays in short, sharp, loud bursts of sound. The therapist explores a variety of musical ideas to meet and try to match some of the excitement and short bursts of energy that John is generating. Music based on alternating intervals of fourths and fifths in the bass with clear, short melodies that are played or sung seem to attract John's attention and to support and sustain his drumming. It is as if these short ideas are musical calls or reflective echoes of his playing. His name continues to be called in short vocal phrases while attention is drawn to the situation with a musical commentary: for example 'Hello, John. John is playing his drum.' The combined music is loud and the phrases become longer and more sustained. John vocalises freely, with repeating streams of 'da, da, da . . .'. The vocal sounds contain some basic rhythmic patterns and are closely con-nected to his loud drum playing. He points to another stick, using the vocal call of 'da'. More sustained contact is established and there are the beginnings of an interaction through the music.

John drops the sticks on the floor and takes a bit of time picking them up, bending from the waist as an alternative to getting down on his hands and knees. He returns to the drum and cymbal and starts up the excited 'da' playing and vocalising again. He plays the cymbal by itself and this builds for about twenty seconds as a sustained outburst. Up to this point he has made rather indiscriminate use of both cymbal and drum. This loud, resonant cymbal sound is matched by the therapist with high-cluster piano chords. Here John's whole body is in constant motion, synchronising with the sounds he is making by moving from head to foot. He slows the music down, using larger arm movements on the cymbal. The therapist sings longer phrases and introduces long, sustained vowel sounds. John leaves his playing area of the drum and cymbal and comes across to the piano. He looks straight towards the therapist and sings long 'ees' and 'ahs', gradually adjusting these vowel-based vocal sounds to the tonality of the music being improvised. His face becomes very animated, with much smiling.

The therapist has a strong feeling that John is trying hard to communicate and that he finds a spontaneous sense of release in his worlds of sound and music. There is a strong sense of connection.[2]

John jabs out with one stick to make one single sound on the drum. This suddenly interrupts the close vocal contact and takes the music off in a new direction. The therapist tries to reflect the feeling behind this gesture and responds with a short and loud piano chord; John replies with a single sound. The therapist plays two connected sounds; John plays three, then one again. An interactive turn-taking game begins, akin to a conversation in sound and reminiscent of 'call and response' patterns. There is much laughter and sense of explorative play.

There has clearly been a shift from the tentative, fragmented start of the session to this point where there is more mutual understanding and shared meaning. It seems that John and the therapist are able to start up musical ideas and immediately to persuade the other to join or imitate the gesture and mood. All this happens without the therapist saying many words.

The session continues for a further ten minutes, ending after around twenty-five minutes. The second half of the session contains an alternation of the fast, rhythmic 'da' activity and the slower, vowel-like vocalising and playing. These two areas seem to be two distinct musical moods. John moves in ever-increasing circles away from the area of the drum and cymbal and from where his mother is sitting. He appears to grow in confidence. He uses the limited space to move and dance. The music continues to engage his body totally; even when away from the two main areas of musical activity, he has been moving and dancing in relation to the music he is making or hearing. At one point John adapts immediately in response to a change introduced by the therapist from a fast four-beat to a slower, rocking three-beat tempo. During this second part of the session John's playing becomes

2 Italics are used in this narrative to add more reflective comments.

increasingly organised and there is more awareness of the therapist's music. At one point, for example, he imitates a soft sound gesture on the cymbal. John's music is more sustained, with fewer fleeting changes of mood. He is able to move at a slower pace and at one point becomes much stiller and claps gently in time to a slow tempo.

By the end of the session it is clear that contact was made via the music and this was sustained for increasing lengths of time as the session unfolded. The vocalising was both exciting (the consonant-based 'da') and intimate (the vowel-based sounds). It appeared that John had expressed many of his feelings in his music and had communicated them to the therapist. There was a sense of joint communication, moving towards a shared partnership, with the therapist not just providing a mirror that could reflect back John's every gesture and mood: the therapist was able to find some music that would pick up, help to articulate, elaborate John's ideas and feelings and play them back to him in a musical form. He in turn was picking up some of the therapist's ideas and was becoming increasingly able to incorporate them into his own playing. Here was a kind of musical playground where some of John's needs could be observed, spontaneously played out, met and potentially explored through the music.

This one session can provide us with more than just information about John's musical play, significant though that is. It can help us to observe the way he interacts with another person and to discover some of his specific needs and resources. Music is an all-embracing form, providing a rich source of information that can be viewed from a range of different standpoints, or through different 'lenses', to adopt a metaphor used by Mercédès Pavlicevic and many others.[3] We observed John physically moving and dancing about the room, organising himself in space and time and manipulating the instruments. We heard him making a variety of vocal sounds in response to a range of musical stimuli. We commented about his level of attention, which led to assumptions about his concentration during the session. We noted his social skills and the way he related to an unfamiliar adult. We made intuitive judgements about the quality of his interactions and the range of feelings he was expressing and trying to communicate. We noted his level of motivation to participate and the way in which he picked up another person's ideas. Music can therefore help us understand a great deal about the physical, intellectual, emotional and social needs of a child.

Can we now reconstruct a hypothetical meeting when the film of this session is watched by other members of the multidisciplinary team? We can speculate how

3 Pavlicevic (1997: 5).

the session might be viewed and questioned from within the broad theoretical, developmental and practical frameworks of the different disciplines. For example, what might the speech and language therapist glean from the session? She notates phonetically the various sounds John makes during the session, observing the range of vowel and consonant sounds, the pitch and contour of the sounds. She notes that the short 'da' sound occurs when John is very actively involved, both playing excitedly and dancing; the more melodious and sustained vowel sounds occur when he is less active and closer to the therapist. She tracks the way sounds are picked up from the two players in the room and used in a non-verbal interaction. She is interested in when and how the sounds occur, in the variety and complexity of the sounds. She notes how John appears to understand what is expected of him in this setting and that the space is a place for making all kinds of sounds and music. The session has given her more evidence of the sounds he can make, his level of expression, and indicators of his general level of verbal understanding. The music therapist can use these observations to explore how in future sessions the rhythmic and melodic aspects of music can provide a stimulus for evoking, extending and organising John's vocal sounds in both synchronous and interactive play.

A group session

The context for this open group session is an admissions ward in a general hospital's psychiatric unit. It is a short-stay ward for people in acute phases of disorders such as schizophrenia and bipolar disorder. The setting is an airy day room on the ward. It is eleven in the morning. A space is cleared at the end of the room and, before the session can start, the therapist asks whether the television can be turned off. The setting is not ideal but is the most comfortable and contained space on the ward. Members of the nursing staff announce the start of the music therapy group and invite patients to move into the room. Some patients have attended for previous sessions but, because it is a short-stay acute unit, some new attendees can be expected.

In this kind of setting, with a changing population on the ward, each group session needs to be considered in its own right as a contained, unique experience. An overall aim is to find a musical means of meeting as many individual needs as possible within the group at that particular moment in time. In this group experience the music therapist is in a privileged position as an attendant listener, witness, facilitator and catalyst enabling this creative process to begin, take shape and grow. The session has a loose overall framework of an opening, middle and closing section. Some musical structures will be set up, particularly at the start, in the hope of fostering a sense of trust and security. Within such boundaried structures there is freedom to improvise and explore.

The group is scheduled to run for an hour and a quarter, yet the nature of the setting and of the patients' illnesses necessitates that people are free to come and go as they wish. Staff are requested not to interrupt the session if at all possible. These boundaries of time and space are set from the very outset to further a sense of trust and safety for expressing feelings. These feelings may develop in any direction, one of the features of improvised music being that it unfolds moment by moment. It is stressed that there is no question of a right or wrong way to play an instrument. Strong feelings may be expressed on the instruments and there is a further boundary which excludes physically violent behaviour directed either to one another or to the instruments.

A music therapy trainee and the therapist have brought to the group a variety of tuned and untuned percussion instruments. The selection is from all over the world and includes Chinese gongs and cymbals, Indian bells, African 'talking' drums and West Indian bongo drums, as well as a large xylophone and more familiar Western-style percussion instruments. There are also some rather unusual and potentially humorous blowing instruments, along with the necessary hygienic wipes. Some of the instruments produce a beautiful sound by the slightest means; others are more challenging and require finer control and dexterity.

The arrival of the instruments attracts some tentative interest and curiosity. The instruments are placed on the carpet and small tables at the centre of a circle of a dozen chairs. By this stage a group of eight patients has assembled: five women and three men. The initial feelings picked up from many in the group are ones of tiredness and tension. Heaviness and lack of motivation are sensed and, from some patients, the feeling that they have come to the group to give it a try, some kind of temporary diversion. Members of the group are quietly invited to explore the instruments and to use one or two of their own choices as a way of introducing themselves to the group. The therapist tries to communicate that not playing is also totally acceptable, everyone needing differing lengths of time to become acquainted with the instruments. Some patients choose to play: others introduce themselves verbally. A few spontaneous comments occur about the quality of each sound, whether the sound is acceptable or too jarring. Some people find the sounds of the shaking instruments too intrusive and harsh; others report personal associations or memories that are evoked by the instruments.

After the introductions on the instruments (the therapist and trainee also taking part), the therapist sets up a basic heartbeat pulse on a drum, checking with the members of the group that this pulse is neither too fast nor too slow. Several members find it too fast and the tempo is altered. The patients are invited to join in if they wish and some members add their own unique pattern in turn and continue to play. Some people join in after a while; some do not play. The piece gradually builds up organically to a loud climax. Some patients comment about the effects of the different instruments, their likes and dislikes and the physically arousing nature of getting louder. An invitation is given to change instruments. The same structure is repeated with the additional complexities of playing faster or slower, individual members of the group being encouraged to change the tempo as they wish. Spontaneous comments are made relating to the excitement of playing fast and the difficulty of controlling slower speeds. As often happens, as the music goes faster it becomes naturally and spontaneously louder, and correspondingly softer when slower. One patient feels rather embarrassed and shares with the group that she would be happier playing with eyes closed. The musical structure is repeated, this time with the invitation to close eyes if this feels safe and comfortable, concentrating on internal listening. This structure, with an emphasis on pulse and rhythm, energises some patients and they become more active.

There is a growing sense that the patients are becoming more relaxed and the therapist wonders whether people would feel comfortable playing some music for each other, a kind of musical dialogue. The proposed structure is modelled by the therapist, who observes one patient, intuitively absorbing an impression of this person, and plays a short pattern of sounds on some bongo drums as a personal message. She replies to the therapist on her instrument, adding rhythmic and melodic patterns of her own. She then plays for another member of the group. This activity provides an opportunity for individual members to express a variety of feelings. Each dialogue is completely different.

Up to this point the energy levels have appeared to be rather low, and many people also appear to be quite anxious. There is not a great deal of talk, and what talk there is tends to relate to the individual sounds and the music being made. By this stage most patients have explored some of the instruments, both for themselves and with tentative beginnings of interacting with others. Some people change instruments again before combining the instruments in a short improvisation. This begins spontaneously and is a gentle kind of tentative exploration. For a second piece the theme of 'climbing a hill' is suggested by one patient as an image on which the whole group can focus. Another patient feels that the theme is too difficult and would require too much effort to rise above how she is feeling. Somebody else chooses a whistle and says that he wants to fly high like a bird at the top of the hill. The music starts out of comparative silence with slow, long and heavy sounds, taking a long time to reach any level of speed or excitement. The music moves gradually towards a momentary climax and ends with a loud outburst of activity. After the improvisation, all the patients relate in turn where the music has taken them – inner individual fantasies articulated as part of the group's shared musical journey. Some comment how they feel still not far from the bottom of the hill; the patient who chose the whistle is still very much at the top, soaring away excitedly with the birds. Another patient suggests that a gradual return is made to base camp as the theme for a second improvisation. Other instruments are chosen for this return journey. The group improvises again, each member starting from where they have left off at the end of the first improvisation. The music becomes slower and ends in a calmer mood. There is a shared discussion on how each member negotiated the return to base camp. The session ends with this moment of quiet reflection as the group disperses for lunch.

In summary, we can note some specific features of a music therapy group such as the one just described. A range of instruments is offered and the choice of what to play is not imposed; there is a freedom of active choice-making within the limits of availability. The emphasis is on interactions and connections through sounds. Music-making can be highly motivating, aesthetically satisfying, physically rewarding and a deeply sensuous experience, or it can be challenging and frightening. A musical gesture can immediately influence the behaviour of another person and have a direct effect on the nature and direction of any improvised music. Improvised music-making has the potential to bring people together on equal terms in how and what is expressed, and likewise, it can highlight the differences between group members. Music can be an expressive enactment of aspects of a person's emotional, social, intellectual, physical and spiritual life, enabling insights to be gained into areas of strength and difficulty. Music can be regarded in many ways as a metaphor or symbol; we invest musical events with meaning, inner images becoming manifest in articulated outer forms and outer forms becoming internalised. When people make all kinds of music together the combined result can still be meaningful, unlike the confusion of meaning if we all talked at once. The journey of discovery is both a private and a shared one, involving trust, learning processes, joint negotiations, shared meanings and the dynamic processes that are at the root of any relationship.

   In the initial exploration in this example, each patient is free to explore private connections with their own instruments. The use of the heartbeat pulse early in the session was intended as a means of providing a sense of supportive holding and containment, any music played by the patients thus being held in a kind of structured musical security net. As the group develops, there is further opportunity for some interactive musical activity with a less directive approach from the therapist as the patients became more familiar with the instruments and suggest musical activities themselves. These brief comments illustrate the need, when appropriate, to underpin practice with theory. For example, the phrase 'supportive holding and containment', used earlier in the paragraph, is often associated with a psychodynamic perspective. We need to understand the choice of perspective to fully grasp what is being described.

Tools for thinking about music therapy

How can the music therapist begin to communicate the main features about the journey of a music therapy process to other members of the multidisciplinary team? Can the themes be articulated in language that both is comprehensible to other professions and adequately represents the music therapy process?

An early and influential reflection on the theories that inform music therapy was developed by Ruud in the 1970s in *Music Therapy and Its Relationship to Current Treatment Theories*. He focused on theories from medicine and psychology, adding that music therapy should also embrace sociological perspectives.[4] A very different argument was developed by Aigen in 1991. He argued that music therapists should develop 'indigenous theories' based in the study of music therapy practice, rather than importing theories from other disciplines.[5] In 1995 Ansdell suggested a flexible approach in which theories could evolve from the integration of borrowed theory and more indigenous understandings.[6] *Readings on Music Therapy Theory*, edited by Bruscia, reveals the range of theory development strategies in contemporary music therapy.[7]

At this point we introduce seven theoretical perspectives that reflect the evolution of music therapy as a professional discipline, understanding that we have to be selective for reasons of space.[8] We will first present perspectives that informed music therapists from the establishment of the modern profession and discipline in the 1940s and 1950s, namely medical perspectives (see Chapter 1). Five other 'forces' of thought that, according to Bruscia, have influenced the development of music therapy will then be introduced, namely the behavioural, psychodynamic, humanistic, transpersonal and culture-centred.[9] Behavioural perspectives were influential very early on in the development of American music therapy, while the psychodynamic and the humanistic perspectives gradually became more influential from the 1960s and 1970s, not least in Europe. In the 1980s and 1990s a transpersonal emphasis gained a stronger foothold within the profession and since 2000 culture-centred perspectives have become influential. To end the chapter a seventh group that has become more visible since 2000 will be introduced, namely music-centred perspectives.[10]

---

4 Ruud (1978/1980).
5 Aigen (1991).
6 Ansdell (1995).
7 Bruscia (2012).
8 Some music therapists would, for example, stress how music therapy has been informed by theories in music education; see Darrow (2008).
9 Bruscia (2002). Note that the order of the establishment of these five 'forces' differs slightly between music therapy and psychology.
10 Each of the seven perspectives is a kind of tree with many branches, so it would perhaps be more precise to talk about 'groups of perspectives'. For the sake of simplicity we will stick to 'perspectives'.

The sequence of seven perspectives that reflects the evolution of ideas within the music therapy literature does not necessarily imply that the earliest perspectives have been left behind. Medical perspectives in music therapy, for example, have always been present and have even been revitalised lately, as witnessed in the revolution of knowledge on neuroscience and music. Similarly, no claim is being made for a synchronous match between the evolution of theoretically oriented literature and the evolution of practice: for example, even though advanced theoretical elaborations of music-centred perspectives in music therapy emerged quite recently, Nordoff and Robbins had already pioneered such practices in the late 1950s. Additionally, the tools we use when thinking about music therapy cannot be segregated from the cultural assumptions that people bring into sessions. When focusing on various theoretical perspectives it is easy to overlook the significance of actual social contexts and of the contributions of patients/participants to music therapy practices.

Music therapy in medical perspectives

In the early development of music therapy, much emphasis was placed on physiological research and the formulation of biologically based reference points in attempting to explain the influence of, for the most part, listening to music. Many physicians were among the early advocates of music therapy, and it is understandable, given the fact that music therapists wanted to gain access to a medically dominated treatment culture, that early researchers began to explore any potential physiological connections and music's effects on autonomic responses.

Medical perspectives suggest that treatment strategies are based on scientifically proven evidence about the effects of a particular intervention on a particular range of symptoms. The 'lens' through which we need to look, at least when medical perspectives are framed within biomedical terminology, will focus on physiological, 'measurable and predictable' responses.[11] Are there any observable causal links between a range of symptoms, the application of specific music therapy strategies and the resultant outcomes? In 1954 an American medical doctor, George E. Arrington, summarised the work at that time, noting measurable changes when subjects were listening to music in such areas as metabolism, breathing, pulse rate, levels of fatigue, attention, rate of activity, muscle reflexes and electrical conductivity of the body.[12] Some of this early physiologically based research can be criticised for focusing on immediate results from one-off experiments. Often only a small range of pre-recorded music is presented for listening and many of the reactions may relate simply to the amount of pleasure or displeasure aroused by the piece. But clearly something is happening on a physiological level, as we are all aware when listening or taking part in any kind of musical activity.

11 Ruud (1978/1980: 2).
12 Arrington (1954: 264–73).

One way in which music can be viewed as influencing physiological function at a fundamental level of response comes from isolated reports in the music therapy literature of comatose patients regaining consciousness after listening to music.[13] In direct contrast there is also documented evidence of the very rare condition of musicogenic epilepsy when a particular piece of music, a melody, a harmonic passage or even the sound of bells can induce fits and temporary loss of consciousness.[14] Musicians and music therapists need to be mindful of the power of music to influence such deep levels of functioning.

Music can be used 'before, during or after' medical procedures, for example in the reduction of stress and anxiety, as a means of distraction or as an aid to relaxation.[15] This is an area that sometimes is called 'music medicine', and doctors, nurses and other health professionals also carry out this kind of work. The use of music, for example, for pain control, both pre- and post-operative, has been gaining international interest during recent years.[16] There appears to be a body of evidence to support such a physiological base to music therapy and the use of music in these medical contexts. Much of the early work can now be replicated using more sophisticated measuring equipment and experimental designs that are robust enough to account for the many individual differences and variables involved.

In Chapter 6 we shall refer to Michael Thaut's extensive body of research on the connections between rhythmic auditory perception and motor skills, development and integration, a further indication of deep physiological attunement to certain musical parameters. In accordance with the principles of a medical perspective, Thaut has developed what he calls 'a scientific model of music in therapy and medicine'.[17]

Other music therapists are continuing to build bridges with members of the medical community, while also maintaining that music therapy includes a relational and psychosocial dimension. As with the work of David Aldridge and his team, many researchers explore not only the physiological features of music therapy in these medical contexts but also some of the complex interactions on mood, emotions and other psychological aspects.[18] As we shall see in Chapter 6, there is growing acceptance of the relational and psychosocial role of music therapy in the rehabilitation and neurorehabiliation processes.[19]

It is very difficult to isolate the physiological from the psychological and the emotional. As Ruud indicates, physiological responses to music possibly create the kind of body state that is necessary for emotional arousal, and our emotions are not independent from cognitive and socio-cultural processes.[20]

---

13 See an example of the work of Dagmar Gustorff presented as chapter 7 in Ansdell (1995).
14 Critchley and Henson (1977: chapters 19 and 20). See also Sacks (2007).
15 Bruscia (1998a: 195–6); and see, for example, Dileo (1999), Loewy and Spintge (2011), Spintge and Droh (1992) and other articles in the journal *Music and Medicine*.
16 For a review, see Bernatzky *et al.* (2011).
17 Thaut (2000).
18 Aldridge (1996).
19 For a review on music therapy and physical rehabilitation, see Weller and Baker (2011).
20 Ruud (1978/1980).

Music therapy in behavioural perspectives

An exploration of music therapy's connections to behaviour therapy develops naturally from the discussion of the medical perspectives, given the shared emphasis on scientific understanding. Clifford Madsen and his colleagues regarded music therapy as 'a method of behavioral manipulation' clearly 'falling within the purview of the behavior modification movement'.[21] Madsen was one of the American music therapy pioneers and it is not surprising that one of the directions followed by the emergent profession was to consider music therapy as a kind of science of behaviour.

The act of music-making can be viewed as a positive reinforcement for many people. As we noted in the examples, people of all ages are able to stay with music for long periods without becoming over-stimulated and exhausted. There are obvious exceptions in cases when there are particular problems. Great care is needed when working with some autistic children, for example, not to over-stimulate an often already highly aroused child. Learning procedures are clearly involved in both short- and long-term music therapy processes. In the sessions described near the start of the chapter we can surmise that John and the adults learned more about how to use the instruments and get the most from them as the sessions progressed. People are engaged in constant processes of discovery while making music, since music offers such endless opportunities for creating new and interesting ideas. It is also possible to link both short- and long-term aims for therapeutic intervention with specific activities and individual and group needs.

The early stimulus–response model of behaviour therapy developed into an approach when the behaviour under observation was related both 'to the setting conditions in which it occurs and . . . to the consequences of the behaviour in those conditions'.[22] Psychologist Derek Blackman discusses how, according to Skinner and the radical behaviourists, environmental factors also play their part in influencing mental and social life, noting, for example, that we cannot understand a person and their actions without a close observation of their contact and interactions with others. There is a reciprocal process in wanting to reinforce those who reinforce us, and social reinforcement refers to a situation in which one person's actions are reinforced, positively or negatively, by another's pleasure or displeasure.

There are many examples in the early music therapy literature of very successful interventions that were clearly based within a behaviour therapy framework and that helped considerably to establish music therapy practice as a profession. Rigorously controlled studies, based on statistical and comparative evidence, examined the effects of music on small aspects of carefully defined behaviour.[23] A development of behaviour therapy can be seen in the current use of cognitive

21 Madsen *et al.* (1968: 70).
22 Blackman (1980: 102).
23 See the CD-ROM, published in 2004 by the former National Association of Music Therapy, of research articles from the *Journal of Music Therapy*. See also Standley (1991).

behaviour therapy (CBT). Short-term courses of cost-effective CBT enable the patient to explore relationships between patterns of thinking and emotions and to alter or modify in the present a previously held and often irrational or distorted way of thinking or viewing the world.[24] A music therapy example could be in helping an adult move from the fixed rigidity of an obsessive and isolated beating pattern to a more fluid and flexible way of playing and interacting. In this way we may be mirroring a process in cognitive therapy, namely the substituting of more positive planning for the automatic cognitive processes that may overwhelm a person under duress.

Within a behaviour therapy framework a music therapist would need to address such systematic questions as: What is the observable behaviour that needs changing? What are the settings where this behaviour is observed? Does this behaviour need increasing or decreasing (and would this be appropriate)? If the behaviour is causing problems, what situations are currently reinforcing such behaviour and thus preventing changes from occurring? What new system of reinforcement can be introduced and applied to alter the behaviour? How can the consequences be observed and analysed?

A major strength of a behavioural approach is that no claims are made other than those relating to the clearly stated objectives. The approach cannot be criticised for being too anecdotal or subjective. On the other hand, the approach may be viewed as rather mechanistic. By definition it is reductive and predictive, with causal relationships being set up between behaviour, intervention and therapeutic outcome. If we relate this to music therapy we observe that specific responses are linked to specific musical events, interventions and eventual outcomes. This approach has been criticised for the focus on clearly observable small bits of behaviour in undue isolation (the 'symptom rather than cause' argument) and the apparent neglect of any focus on purpose, choice and consciousness.[25] Many music therapists consider that such an emphasis excludes the richness and complexities of cultural processes, or the more private and inner states often regarded by them as central to the work.

Music therapy in psychodynamic perspectives

The discipline of psychoanalysis, pioneered by Freud near the end of the nineteenth century, was to provide the twentieth century with a radically new theory of mind and personality, exploring the area of the unconscious. Before we outline the reception and use of this tradition within music therapy, clarification of some terms might be helpful. Psychoanalysis refers to the primarily verbal individual analysis pioneered by Freud and his close associates, while psychodynamic therapy is a broader term referring to therapeutic practices that make connections

24 CBT derives from the work of Beck and his colleagues; see Dryden and Branch (2012) and Scott (2011).
25 Ruud (1978/1980: 40–1).

between conscious and unconscious processes. Psychotherapy embraces therapies that have as their focus links between the therapeutic process and the mind (psyche) and in which the emphasis is on the relationship between client/patient and therapist. Psychotherapy can therefore be based in perspectives other than the psychodynamic ones we discuss here.[26]

In his psychoanalytic theory Freud developed a typology of *id* (the world of instinctual drives), *ego* (with its sense of reality-checking, balancing and mastering) and *super-ego* (akin to the world of conscience and morality).[27] The group improvisations can be viewed as an acceptable form to contain some of the more id-based primitive instincts. The patients were beginning to monitor their playing and how it related to others in the group (the involvement of more ego and super-ego processes). We could interpret this as the ego acting more as a regulator of the admittance of 'primary process' material – what Freud would regard as irrational and illogical – into everyday 'secondary process' thinking – the more rational and logical. The patients in the group were able to organise internal impulses through the active processes of variation and repetition into pleasure-giving musical structures. The ego is able to make sense of, and be in control of, all the stimuli.

Psychodynamic principles of music therapy were pioneered by such music therapists as Benenzon in Latin America, Eschen in Germany, Lecourt in France, Priestley in the United Kingdom and Tyson in the United States.[28] Priestley's approach, for example, is often called Analytical Music Therapy and involves periods of both verbal and musical interaction, as well as interpretative interventions. Both patient and therapist are involved as participants in an interactive, simultaneous music therapy process. This kind of mutual participation immediately separates out the actively involved music therapist from the more traditional listening role of the analyst. It brings music therapy closer to the more intersubjective psychotherapeutic approaches where the worlds of patient and therapist overlap in the arena of the therapeutic space.[29] Later theorists in the psychodynamic tradition developed such relational and interpersonal perspectives, Alvarez, Kohut, Stern and Winnicott being among the theorists who have inspired many music therapists. In the music therapy resources to which we now turn, the influence of these authors is prominent.

Today, two compilations of music therapy literature are central resources for psychodynamic perspectives: Bruscia's *The Dynamics of Music Psychotherapy* and Susan Hadley's *Psychodynamic Music Therapy: Case Studies*.[30] Hadley neatly summarises some of the common assumptions brought by therapists working

---

26 For an introduction to psychodynamic psychotherapy, see Bateman *et al.* (2010).
27 For an introduction to Freud, see Storr (1989/2001).
28 Benenzon (1981); Eschen (2002); Lecourt (1991); McGuire (2004; on Tyson); Priestley (1975/2012, 1994). There will be more discussion on the work of Priestley and other therapists working within the psychodynamic framework in Chapter 6.
29 See Hobson's introduction to a more a more dialogical approach to psychotherapy (1985/2000).
30 Bruscia (1998b); Hadley (2003).

within these perspectives. She points out that if we accept this psychodynamic 'lens', we acknowledge that '[h]uman behavior, broadly construed, is determined by the psyche' and that we 'interact and relate to the world with varying levels of consciousness (unconscious, preconscious and conscious layers)'. According to this frame of thought, the way we interact with each other can be traced back to our earliest patterns of behaviour with significant others. We tend to keep on repeating these well-rehearsed patterns. In any therapeutic encounter, both parties 'bring to the . . . relationship their own unique patterns of relating to the world, based on their own pre-dispositions and life experiences (transference, countertransferences and defenses)'.[31]

These last three terms parenthesised by Hadley are constructs that are fundamental for viewing the work through this lens. Transference refers to the patient reliving aspects of past significant relationships within the therapeutic relationship and context, generally through transferring a complex matrix of both positive and negative aspects of these earlier relationships and patterns onto the therapist. Hence the need in the early tradition of psychoanalysis for the therapist to stay out of the picture frame as much as possible – the notion of the 'blank screen' onto which these transferences can be projected. The therapist 'counters' the transference through a myriad of unconscious reactions towards the patient, the so-called countertransference.[32] According to psychodynamic theory, we all need a range of 'defences' to survive in the world and to protect the ego, the way we respond to different situations arising from earlier experiences and relationships. Examples of defences are projection, introjection, denial, splitting, repression, displacement and intellectualisation.[33] Sometimes music-making can also be a defence mechanism, protecting the self from being overwhelmed.[34]

It is apparent that to work within this approach necessitates being informed by one or more of the psychodynamic schools of thought. We have briefly touched on pointers from the deterministic, reductive and medically based Freudian model to later theoretical developments that focus on interpersonal and relational aspects of human development. Musical interaction and the presence of musical instruments in the musical space add further potential for exploration of both positive and negative transference phenomena, with the instruments and even music itself taking on the projections of different symbolic content (see Chapter 4 for further discussion in relation to the writings of, among others, Winnicott and Stern).

Music therapy in humanistic perspectives

Many therapies cluster under the 'umbrella' term 'humanistic'. Some are offshoots of psychoanalysis and existentialism; others are less orthodox.[35] There is an

31 Bruscia (1998b: xxiii, xxiv); Hadley (2003: 12).
32 See Priestley (1994) for an exposition of the different kinds of countertransference.
33 For an explanation of 'thirty-two ego defenses', see Bruscia (1987: 146).
34 Racker (1965).
35 Feder and Feder (1981: 43).

emphasis on helping people realise their full potential and on 'growth' rather than 'treatment'.[36] Psychotherapist and psychologist John Rowan points out that an underlying premise of the approach (also known as the 'human potential movement' or the 'self-awareness movement') is that at our core we human beings are essentially 'OK' – although this is not to ignore the darker aspects of human nature.[37] Therapists working within a humanistic approach claim to be concerned with areas that have not been so explicitly highlighted by the psychoanalysts and behaviour therapists, for example respect and positive regard for individuals and their unique differences; 'wholeness', integrating mind, body and spirit; development of purpose and personal intention; freedom of choice; self-growth, or self-actualisation, particularly in relation to others; creativity;[38] peak experiences; self-esteem; authenticity and autonomy.[39]

Within a humanistic approach, a main feature is on experiencing present feelings in the 'here and now'. There is less analysis of behaviours that have as their mainspring earlier, deeply rooted patterns or examination of bits of behaviour. The therapist is more often regarded as a catalyst or facilitator and not as an expert to be consulted by a potentially dependent patient. A more collaborative process of joint negotiation exists and there is less emphasis on interpretation by the therapist. Abraham Maslow was a pioneer in humanistic psychology with his work on self-actualisation and hierarchy of needs; two other major practitioner pioneers in this field were Fritz Perls (Gestalt therapy) and Carl Rogers (person-centred therapy and counselling).[40] Rogers' core factors of empathy, genuineness and regarding everyone positively ('unconditional positive regard') can be viewed as being part of any therapeutic relationship.

The work of many music therapists seems to fall naturally within a humanistic framework. A music therapist could be seen as aiming to encourage creativity and self-expressive behaviour and to maximise growth and potential, often as part of an evolving group process. In his discussion of the work of Nordoff and Robbins, Ruud underlines how they regard music therapy as a 'growth process' for the participating child, an idea closely related to humanistic perspectives. Even though Ruud also claims that the approach of Nordoff and Robbins transcends any theoretical framework, he does point to relationships between their practice and the writings of humanistic psychologist Clark E. Moustakas.[41]

In his criticism of behavioural music therapy, Ruud argued that this approach necessarily involves objectification of the client and therefore is incompatible with the mutual search for personal growth that characterises humanistic music therapy.[42] He was instrumental in introducing the music therapy community to the

---

36 Ibid.: 43, 43–9 for further discussion and introduction to the work of some pioneering therapists.
37 Rowan (1998: 1–3).
38 May (1975).
39 Ruud (1978/1980: 63–86).
40 Maslow (1968); Perls (1969); Rogers (1951/2003, 1961/1976).
41 Ruud (1978/1980: chapter 4); and see Moustakas (1970).
42 Ruud 1978/1980: chapter 5).

philosophy of dialogue developed by Martin Buber, an Austrian-born existentialist philosopher who distinguished between the 'I–Thou' and the 'I–It' relationship, the first being personal and mutual, the second objective and less intimate.[43] Later, Buber's dialogical perspective became the frame for some of Rudy Garred's writings.[44]

Ruud also relates the humanistic tradition of music therapy to a 'philosophy of recognition', as developed by the critical theorist Axel Honneth, and proposes that

> we need to broaden our understanding of recognition from not only being valid for a two-part relationship, but to operate also at a societal level. Recognition . . . is not only fundamental to the primary relationship between the infant and the caretaker, but can be included in a critical perspective, where social inclusion and human rights play an important role.[45]

Humanistic perspectives encourage therapists to take interest in the strengths and possibilities of each person, but if this approach is not combined with social awareness, Ruud argues, a humanistic approach with its positive regard for individuals does run the risk of promoting self-centred individualism.

Music therapy in transpersonal perspectives

Words are often inadequate to describe the timeless and more numinous qualities of music that enable listeners and players to move beyond the person-bound confines of time and space into more limitless areas of consciousness. The area of the transpersonal extends the other emphases on the body and mind to incorporate the spirit.[46] Notions referring to spiritual experiences, transpersonal perspectives and transcendence will be used interchangeably here, even though some authors might distinguish between these terms. Rowan regards the psychiatrist Stanislav Grof's definition of the transpersonal as the 'most succinct', namely: 'experiences involving an expansion or extension of consciousness beyond the usual ego boundaries and beyond the limitations of time and/or space'.[47] Gestalt therapist Petrūska Clarkson explores how such an 'extension' of the 'ego boundaries', a kind of letting go, is a feature of a transpersonal relationship within a therapeutic encounter. 'It is rather as if the ego of even the personal unconscious of the psychotherapist is "emptied out" of the therapeutic space, leaving space for something numinous to be created in the "between" of the relationship.'[48]

Psychiatrist Roberto Assagioli, in the development of psychosynthesis, is one of the first psychoanalysts to explore the relationships between the personal and

43 Buber (1958).
44 Garred (2006).
45 Ruud (2010: 35).
46 Maslow (1968: iii–iv); Rowan (1998: 14–15).
47 Rowan (1993: 6–7) citing Grof (1979: 155).
48 Clarkson (1994: 42).

transpersonal selves.[49] He integrates the Freudian typology of id, ego and super-ego with the Jungian relationship between an individual and a more collective unconsciousness.[50] He also makes a further connection between an individual's sense of 'Conscious Self' and a 'Higher Self', referred to by Rowan as the 'Transpersonal Self'.[51]

Is there a kind of striving in music to move beyond the self to touch or embrace the spiritual? Is this reflected in the way Bruscia positioned 'transpersonal music' at the centre of his 'six dynamic models of music therapy', as approached 'through the aesthetic realm'?[52] All the other 'models' itemised by Bruscia – that is, music being 'subjective', 'objective', collective' or 'universal' in nature and experience – are 'superimposed' by the 'aesthetic' and the 'transpersonal'. For Bruscia the transpersonal is viewed as an area that transcends all of these other 'models', breaking down the more artificially constructed boundaries.

When music enters this in-between liminal space there is potential for moving beyond the present constraints of time and space.[53] Much that takes place in making music is beyond words, existing in those borderline places between inner and outer, self and other, music and words. On many occasions in the case examples in this book, we shall observe some of music's capacities to move the listener and player beyond the personal, beyond everyday preoccupations and into the world of the imagination, to different states of consciousness and different time-frames and perspectives. Improvising and making music together are also part of a joint and collective encounter that can create a music space full of shared and flowing resonance.

Aldridge said in 1995 that music therapists might feel they were taking risks by using terms like 'spirituality' and 'hope': such terms are not frequently used in scientific disciplines such as medicine. Aldridge argues, however, that palliative care, for example, is one area where there is more breadth of understanding of healthcare needs. In this area the medical literature discusses spiritual needs, and Aldridge argues that there should be similar consideration within the literature of music therapy. He advocates an acknowledgement of what he calls the spirit of humankind: 'It is a careful, sober consideration of spirituality that I want to elaborate upon here, linking the promotion of hope to working creatively with music.'[54]

Over recent decades there has been a growing acceptance of the place of the spiritual and transpersonal within music therapy practice and discourse. For example, at the Music Therapy World Congress held in Oxford in 2002, one of the three key areas for 'Dialogue and Debate' was 'Music, Spirituality, Healing'.

---

49 For an introduction to psychosynthesis, see Assagioli (1965/1990).
50 For an introduction to Jung, see Storr (1973/1991).
51 Assagioli (1965/1990); Rowan (1993: 40–1).
52 Bruscia (1998a: 133–4, 149–51); and see Wigram *et al.* (2002: 41–2).
53 See Ruud (1998: 121–34) for one of the first discussions in the literature on 'liminal states' in relation to improvisation and Guided Imagery and Music.
54 Aldridge (1995: 103).

This area was placed alongside the two other main sections of 'Music, Culture, Social Action' and 'Music, Meaning, Relationship'.[55] In the same year a compilation entitled *Guided Imagery and Music*[56] highlighted spiritual and transpersonal dimensions, for instance in a chapter by Brian Abrams. The chapter reviews the literature on the transpersonal dimensions of the Bonny Method, and he outlines requirements for an indigenous theory on transpersonal BMGIM phenomena.[57]

In *How Music Helps*, Ansdell presents an ecological perspective that includes moments of transcendence which give us meaning and perspective. The music therapy situation could be used as a ritual or quasi-ritual occasion on which patients/participants bring their worlds together, so to speak. When people today say that they are spiritual rather than religious, this can signal, Ansdell argues, an ecological sensibility of sorts: there is a sense of feeling part of, or wanting to feel part of, some larger whole which transcends the narrow limits of the self.[58] Such experiences may be closely linked both to art and to personal encounters – and, for some people, to nature too.

Music therapy in culture-centred perspectives

Culture is integral to human existence. As psychologist and biologist Colwyn Trevarthen and other researchers on human interaction have underlined, a child needs to absorb culture. Humans have a biological disposition for interest in social interaction and shared meaning-making, which means that as soon as we are born, we start on a trajectory of cultural learning and participation.[59] Culture-centred music therapy explores the implications of this for practice, theory and research. Basic tenets include the idea that music is not primarily a stimulus but a situated activity; nor is culture primarily a set of conditions, but a resource for the dynamic interplay between self and society.[60]

Ideas related to the socio-cultural nature of music therapy were pioneered by such colleagues as Kenny and Ruud in the 1980s and they have become more prominent since 2000, partly in tandem with the emergence of international discourses on community music therapy, feminist music therapy and resource-oriented music therapy.[61] In psychology, similar perspectives were pioneered by Russian psychologists such as Lev Vygotsky in the early twentieth century, and

---

55 See World Federation of Music Therapy (2002).
56 Bruscia and Grocke (2002).
57 Abrams (2002).
58 Ansdell (2013).
59 Trevarthen (1995). Pavlicevic and Ansdell (2009) elaborate on this theme in a discussion of how 'communicative musicality' (the human innate capacity for non-verbal communication, see Chapter 4) is necessary but not sufficient in the development of collaborative music-making (or 'musicking'; see Chapter 3).
60 Stige (2002).The term 'situated' suggests that contexts matter, that what an activity affords depends upon the relationships created in each situation.
61 See, for example, Hadley (2007), Pavlicevic and Ansdell (2004), Rolvsjord (2010) and Stige and Aarø (2012).

socio-cultural theory traditions have emerged in a range of disciplines during the past decades.[62]

In a culture-centred case study within the context of mental health, Stige has argued that culture-centred music therapy in many ways is person-centred: the participants' biopsychosocial needs are explored collaboratively and in contextual terms where culture is understood as a resource for action.[63] This view highlights the interaction between our internal worlds and the external world, and between individual and community. Consequently, human interdependence is understood not as a challenge to autonomy but as a basis for it.

Culture-centred perspectives emphasise the relational nature of music therapy within ecological thinking.[64] In biology, *ecology* refers to the reciprocal influences between organisms and their environments. In music therapy and many other disciplines the term has become prominent in depicting relationships between an individual and the socio-cultural environment. Here distinctions such as 'intrapersonal' and 'interpersonal' become blurred. The claim that mind and culture complement each other is made by Russian-American psychologist Urie Bronfenbrenner, who explains how 'microsystems' (the activities, roles, and relationships experienced by the developing person) interact to form 'meso-systems' (the interrelations between two or more 'microsystems'). 'Exosystems' and 'macrosystems' are broader and higher levels of organisation that also interact with the other levels. Bronfenbrenner argued that the various levels can be understood as nested: lower levels are embedded in higher levels.[65]

All human practices can be understood ecologically: changes at the level of the individual have implications for various social systems and vice versa.[66] In culture-centred music therapy the developing person is seen as active in shaping the conditions of his or her development. Or to put it differently, person and context constitute each other in transactional processes.[67] Music as social participation (the possibility of taking part and making a difference) is therefore of crucial interest in this perspective.[68] The term *agency* can be used to illuminate this, referring to the capacity of human individuals and groups to act and promote change. As humans we may have an inherent capacity for agency, but the form it takes depends on the resources available in the social milieu where we develop. Action requires access to resources, and agency therefore operates within constraints. Agency allows for the possibility that people can use and produce resources in ways that exceed personal limitations and the hindrances of established social systems.[69] Music can

---

62 See, for example, Kitayama and Cohen (2007).
63 Stige (2011).
64 See Abrams (2012).
65 Bronfenbrenner (1979, especially 16–42).
66 Ansdell (2013); Stige and Aarø (2012).
67 Sameroff and MacKenzie (2003) build on this tradition in their perspective on human development. They argue that research based on a transactional perspective discovers that the developing person changes other people's expectations and behaviour, which in turn are changed by the altered context.
68 Stige (2006).
69 Giddens (1984).

be considered a 'structuring resource' that enables agency; it can often be used to mobilise other resources as well at both a personal and a social level.[70]

Reflecting on the relationship of culture-centred perspectives to more established 'forces' of thought within the discipline, Bruscia has articulated the following vision:

> One of the lessons we are learning as a profession is that one new idea does not necessarily replace or surpass previous ideas; rather, each new idea enters into an already existing culture of ideas, where all ideas begin to interact. Thus, when a new idea is introduced, the entire culture is fertilized: existing ideas are influenced by the new idea, and the new idea is influenced by its integration into the existing culture. Thus, culture-centered thinking does not replace or surpass the behavioral, psychodynamic, humanistic, or transpersonal forces of thought; rather, it catalyzes them to be more culture-sensitive; in return, the established forces challenge culture-centered thinkers to somehow integrate existing values into their thinking. The developmental process is more holistic than linear, so that there is a place for every idea of continuing relevance.[71]

This vision encourages a theoretical debate to which we will return towards the end of the chapter: to what degree could and should various perspectives on music therapy be combined? Culture-centred music therapy naturally invites this debate because the perspective is based on ideas synthesised from several disciplines.

Music therapy in music-centred perspectives

Music is the common denominator in music therapy. The perspectives that we have presented so far originated in disciplines other than music and were then received and recontextualised as music therapy theory. How far can we assume that these perspectives provide a sufficient understanding of musical processes and outcomes in music therapy? This is one of the many pertinent questions asked by advocates of music-centred perspectives.

Aigen is perhaps the author who most explicitly has employed and defined the term 'music-centred' through the publication of *Music-Centered Music Therapy* in 2005, while there is a range of related theoretical contributions that have emerged since 2000. When Aigen introduces the origins and foundations of music-centred music therapy, he refers to the concepts of 'music in therapy' versus 'therapy in music' and pursues the latter direction, which indicates that music is considered the primary agent and medium of change.[72] The term 'therapy in music' was first coined in a publication by Nordoff and Robbins in 1965, and Aigen explains that

---

70 Krüger and Stige (in press -a).
71 Bruscia (2002: xvi).
72 A related distinction was introduced by Bruscia, namely 'music in therapy' versus 'music as therapy' (1987: 8–9).

these two pioneers were interested in 'the art of music as therapy'.[73] Music-centred perspectives focus on how 'musical expressions and experience are the actual domains the therapist seeks to act *on* rather than just act *through*', Aigen explains.[74]

Aigen was an early advocate of indigenous theory in music therapy and in many respects his writings about music-centred music therapy represent a continuation of this theme.[75] His early texts on indigenous theory could be read as a warning against importing theory from disciplines other than music, while his later writings carefully underline that it is the use, not the origin, that decides whether theoretical perspectives can be considered indigenous or not: '[T]he strategy of considering the label *indigenous* as one that describes how an idea is used rather than where it originates makes room for incorporation of ideas from nonmusical areas of inquiry into legitimate indigenous theory.'[76] Aigen then proceeds to use cognitive linguist George Lakoff and philosopher Mark Johnson's schema theory (or metaphor theory) of the embodied mind[77] as a tool for describing what he considers the inherent clinical value of musical experience:

> For example, when a music therapist employs a goal such as *increasing impulse control*, this implies a metaphoric understanding of human actions as being directed by a physical force that requires containment and/or redirection, much as a dam holds back the force of a body of water. Schema theory holds that our experience of music is similarly mediated by the same metaphoric structures that operate in other areas of human functioning and that music may have a unique role in creating these structures of experience.[78]

Aigen also uses musicologist Victor Zuckerkandl's dynamic theory of tone[79] to describe relationships between structures of music and structures of experience, for example how qualities of tones and melodies reflect different levels of tension and balance. Another music-centred advocate, Lee, to an even larger degree focuses on the importance of musical structures and employs the metaphor of the 'architecture of aesthetic music therapy'.[80] In short, these authors argue that if music makes a difference, we should be interested not only in what the difference is but also in what the music is.

The challenge for all attempts at describing relationships between the structures of music and those of experience is to avoid mechanistic explanations that certain structures affect individuals in predictable ways (see Chapter 3). Some music-centred theorists have therefore carefully elaborated more relational and contextual

---

73 Nordoff and Robbins in 1965, as quoted in Aigen (2005: 47).
74 Aigen (2005: 49).
75 Aigen (1991).
76 Aigen (2005: 32).
77 Lakoff and Johnson (1980).
78 Aigen (2005: 165).
79 Zuckerkandl (1956).
80 Lee (2003).

perspectives. Garred has developed a dialogical perspective on music therapy primarily based on the philosophy of Buber but also on the work of Stern and other interaction theorists.[81] Ansdell has developed an ecological perspective on how music helps, and underlines how our experiences of music are situated in a context. He suggests that it is our situated musical experiences that enable us to create 'musical worlds' where we can maintain and negotiate identity and personhood, build relationships and community, and experience moments of meaning and transcendence.[82]

Although the music therapists referred to in this section build mostly on the Nordoff Robbins tradition, music-centred ideas can frame other approaches.[83] The relational and ecological perspectives advocated by some authors of this tradition of thinking also have strong connections to humanistic and culture-centred perspectives.

Concluding points

If we look back at the two examples at the beginning of the chapter, to what degree do they fit with the theoretical perspectives we have outlined? We could explore John's individual session through the 'lens' of a behavioural perspective, for example. Through this 'lens' we can observe that his very act of playing the drum can incorporate an in-built reward system. At a simple level of description, John plays the drum, and the sound comes back to him as his sound. He has made the sound, the sound appears to give him pleasure and he repeats the experience. The effect of one pleasurable musical gesture contains a reinforcing effect, so this one gesture stimulates and elicits the next. There is also the additional reinforcing effect and reward of the adult supporting, encouraging and responding to these gestures. The therapist can also choose to support and encourage certain behaviours and not others. In John's session the behaviour being encouraged was sustained contact on an instrument. The therapist gave John a great deal of positive reinforcement by joining him in the sounds he made, feeding back to him instantaneously and elaborating on his musical ideas. We could apply the behaviour therapist's taxonomy of cues, rewards, tokens, contingencies, goals and positive and negative reinforcers to this process. John had a reward both from the instrument itself and from the therapist's response. During this pleasurable musical process there were observable changes in his behaviour.

There would be disagreement, however, about how to describe the most promi- nent aspects of this session. Bruscia has argued strongly that it is unacceptable for a music therapist to stay rigidly within one theoretical perspective, because a person's needs as well as changes in context will require flexibility in thinking.[84] Katrina McFerran has advocated a similar theoretical openness and flexibility

81 Garred (2006).
82 Ansdell (2013).
83 Aigen (2005), for example, refers to both the Nordoff Robbins and the BMGIM traditions.
84 Bruscia (2002, 2011).

about work with adolescents.[85] Other theorists have to a larger extent highlighted the meta-theoretical and practical difficulties in integrating theoretical perspectives; different perspectives may be conceptually incompatible. For instance, some of the perspectives we have discussed could be said to be based on a mechanistic metaphor (focusing on the human organism responding to stimuli) while others are based on a contextual metaphor (focusing on the interaction between humans and their environments).[86] Even so, there is clearly a move towards connecting several of the perspectives outlined here. Outside music therapy, Allan N. Schore, for example, is integrating neuroscience and psychotherapy through his pioneering work on 'affect regulation'. There are wide-ranging implications here for clinical areas such as recuperation from trauma as well for explaining some of the neurobiological changes that occur within both patient and therapist in a psychotherapeutic encounter.[87] Similarly, Trevarthen integrates biological and more relational perspectives when he reflects on what therapists, including music therapists, can learn from research on communication with infants.[88] From inside music therapy, new perspectives have emerged that integrate ideas from several of the perspectives described in this chapter. One case in point is Diego Schapira's 'plurimodal' approach, with its person-centred and holistic orientation based in a psychodynamic perspective.[89] Another is Randi Rolvsjord's approach to 'resource-oriented music therapy', which includes elements of humanistic, culture-centred and music-centred thinking (and ideas from positive psychology).[90]

There are also ideas that resemble each other across different theoretical perspectives, for example the 'iso principle'. An early music therapy pioneer within the medical perspective, the American psychiatrist Ira Altshuler, was very interested in the physiological responses to music and evolved a principle he labelled the 'iso principle' which is still at the heart of much current music therapy practice. 'Iso', based on the Greek,

> simply means 'equal'; that is, that the mood or the tempo of the music in the beginning must be in 'iso' relation with the mood or tempo of the mental patient. The 'iso' principle is extended also to volume and rhythm.[91]

This principle can be applied to both individual and group work. In the group example at the beginning of the chapter, we remember how the members took some time to find a way of feeling comfortable making music together. The therapist needed to observe carefully the speed and mood of the opening musical gestures made by the members. The therapist searched for musical ideas to

85 McFerran (2010).
86 An influential philosophical text on the metaphors that inform various worldviews was written by Pepper (1942).
87 Schore (1994, 2012).
88 Trevarthen (2003); and see Chapter 4.
89 Schapira (2003).
90 Rolvsjord (2010).
91 Altshuler in Arrington (1954: 31).

discover a musical common denominator that would help to bring the group gradually together, to find some sense of group cohesion via the music. Some music therapists would refer to Altshuler's 'iso principle' when describing these processes, while others might use Rogers' more humanistic notions of empathy and 'unconditional positive regard' or Stern's concept of 'affect attunement'.[92]

Some music therapists think of the seven perspectives that we have presented here as competing explanations and feel that they need to choose one of them. Some suggest that we could integrate them or that it is helpful to be eclectic and choose the elements that fit the needs of each situation. Others suggest that the integrative and eclectic positions risk ignoring significant theoretical and philosophical differences. And others again suggest that the development of theory in music therapy has just begun, so that the future of the discipline might see quite different perspectives from those that dominate today. The latter claim is quite possibly true but in any case we argue that responsible and responsive practitioners will seek deep understanding of one or a few perspectives yet also be open to the kind of theoretical flexibility relative to situation that Bruscia, McFerran and others have advocated. We will continue to touch upon such issues.

---

92 Many such theoretical ideas will be discussed in relation to the examples from practice in Chapters 4–7.

3 Sound, music and music therapy

Introduction

A music therapist is sitting with a group of pre-school children. The therapist, who is a violinist, slowly and quietly takes the instrument out of its case, checks the tuning, tightens the bow and plays a single low sound, one beautiful tone. The sound emerges imperceptibly out of the relative silence, is held constant, rises to a peak of loudness and dies away back into the silence. The children look to the source of the sound, attend to it as if drawn along and sharing in this brief sound journey. No words are spoken, yet the atmosphere in the room changes completely and some form of non-verbal communication has taken place.

This is a simple example of an opening gesture in sound but it contains some of the essential tools of a music therapist's trade. We are assuming that the reactions of the children and the changes in atmosphere are related to the interactions of the elements inherent in the sound: the unique quality of the sound produced by the violin; the duration of the sound as it emerged from and returned to silence; the growing and fading of the level of loudness; the pitch of the sound. We are also assuming that it is a social situation which in itself is productive. It is not only what is played that matters but also who perceives it and where, when and how participants interact.

In this chapter we will explore the elements of sound and music and try to understand how they may be used in music therapy practice. From the acoustic and perceptual qualities of the basic sound elements, namely timbre, pitch, loudness and duration, we will examine how humans – through active play with sounds and silence – can form the elements of rhythm, melody and harmony, which constitute music as we know it today. We acknowledge that to present elements separately is a reduction of what music is for people, but it is a convenience that enables us to write.[1] Usually it is the interplay of elements that

---

1 We are also following a tradition within music therapy. Alvin, for example, based some of her teaching on a common-sense study of these basic elements of sound, observing that in any collection of sounds there was usually one element in a dominant position (1975: 61). And see Nordoff and Robbins' writings, for example on the use of rhythm (1971: 63–7).

fascinates us. We also acknowledge that what we think of and act upon as music varies with time and place. There are many 'musics',[2] and what might be an exquisite experience for one person could be trite or overwhelming for another. We will therefore begin with a brief excursion into the notion of music itself.

Music as resource for action

Music has a physical reality. Usually some object or body is set in vibration, producing sound waves through the air that reach our ears and bodies. The effects are at times amazing. We hear beautiful melodies that lift us and feel 'grooves' that move us. It is helpful to think of these experiences as more than reactions to music, since musical perception is inextricably linked to action and personal agency. In other words, music has properties that are physical as well as subjective, social and cultural. It can be a spiritual experience, for some people, on some occasions.

The music anthropologist Kenneth Gourlay has considered the 'non-universality of music' as well as the 'universality of non-music'.[3] The former term indicates that we all live individual histories in which we develop unique relationships to the world. The term also relates to the 'musics' we mentioned above, the many different musical traditions. Some of these, such as Western classical music, use rhythm, melody and harmony as central elements.[4] But not all musics employ rhythms based in a pulse or single regular beat; some musics pay little attention to pitch; and if there is engagement with pitch, there is not necessarily a focus on melody and harmony, for example in traditions of monotone chanting.

Awareness of the 'universality of non-music' is also relevant for music therapists. There is a growing amount of knowledge and research relating to this term. In humans there seems to be a species-specific, and therefore universal, biopsychological capacity for music. Owing to processes of selection in the evolution of the human species, we are all born with a 'proto-musical' capacity through which we engage with sounds and movements interactively.[5] In the beginning this interaction in sound and movement is perhaps not music as perceived culturally, but the process invites a child to begin a process of enculturation. Gradually children learn to integrate elements of sound and music according to characteristics of each particular context and culture.

This concept of universal 'proto-musicality' makes individual and cultural differences no less significant, but it does suggest that a field such as music therapy might develop practices that are relevant for a broad range of people, not just those

---

2 This term is used in analogy with terms such as culture and language (which are used in the singular and the plural). People do not speak language in general; they speak a specific language, say English or Chinese. Similarly, in music there are many radically different traditions, as ethnomusicologist Elizabeth May (1983) made clear in her classic book.
3 Gourlay (1984).
4 See, for example, Martineau (2008).
5 An influential text on this issue was Wallin *et al.* (2000); for a more recent summary, see Cross and Morley (2009).

who are especially talented or interested in music, according to given cultural standards. We know that music as embodied expressive movement is capable of entrainment (a response synchronising with the stimulus) and engaging people in shared expressive activity.[6]

In Chapter 1 we briefly outlined the prehistory and early history of music therapy. Ruud has argued that most of this prehistory and several theories and practices of early modern music therapy were characterised by a more mechanistic use of music. How people react to music as an external stimulus, rather than how they act and interact through music, was the main focus.[7] In Chapter 2 we examined a range of theoretical perspectives that have influenced the profession and discipline. Psychodynamic, humanistic and transpersonal perspectives have contributed to a less mechanistic understanding of music in that personal expression, and interpersonal and transpersonal relationships have gained prominence. What might still be lacking is a clearer understanding of the mutual reciprocity between individuals and their environments. It is here that the various culture-centred or socio-cultural theories have contributed new tools for the understanding of music in music therapy.

In the specific context of a music therapy session we observe how the shapes and forms of music influence people, noting how 'people do things to music and music can do things to people'.[8] In order to communicate that 'people do things to' and through music, the term *musicking* is sometimes used, indicating that music is not just an object or a thing, but also a situated activity.[9] If we observe how the different ingredients of sound and music are used by people participating in music therapy, then we can begin to assess reactions, actions, interactions and transactions, and explore the evolving therapeutic and health-promoting relationships.

Tia DeNora is a music sociologist who has explored musical 'affordances' (the resources provided by music, such as moods, inherent structures and energy levels) and how these are used by individuals as 'appropriations' in unique ways to feel, think and act in the world.[10] As Ansdell notes, the central theme of DeNora's thesis is the relationship between what is offered by music and its uses, for example how we can use slow music to calm ourselves or lively music to excite.[11]

These notions of musical affordances and appropriations will help to provide some theoretical underpinning to the examples for each of the elements discussed in this chapter. We will now explore four elements of sound, namely timbre, pitch, loudness and duration. A study of these basic elements can inform how we physi-

---

6 Bispham (2009).
7 Ruud (1987/1990).
8 Blacking (1987: 30).
9 Small (1998). The spellings 'musicing' and 'musicking' are both used in the music therapy literature. The latter spelling was the one that Small introduced, and his concept of 'musicking' as situated activity and performance of relationships has been most influential in the discipline, even though some music therapy authors choose to use the alternative spelling 'musicing'.
10 DeNora (2000). For an updated elaboration of this perspective in music therapy theory, see Ansdell (2013).
11 Ansdell (2004). For further discussion of the concept of affordance, see Stige (2002: 96–8).

cally sense and then perceive sounds, although it cannot help in our understanding of the relationship between elements. Alvin preferred to call this an 'awareness of an order in relationship' within a 'sequence of sounds'.[12]

Via an awareness of these complex relationships between sounds and silence, we are brought closer to the phenomenon we tend to call music. Our violinist in the opening example begins to explore sounds by organising them into rhythmic patterns and sequences of tones. More than one sound is played at the same time. We add into our melting-pot the more complex ingredients of rhythm, melody and harmony. In what follows, we cannot overlook the fact that each element, even if regarded as a self-sufficient phenomenon, is bound additionally by context, learning, behavioural state and cultural patterning. The individual personality and unique musicianship of the violinist in our example are also major factors in the communication process.

Timbre

The 'colour' of a sound can sometimes be a catalyst for a significant change in music therapy. Alvin recorded the striking response of a 9-year-old autistic boy, Brian, to a small instrument imitating the sound of a nightingale. Brian tended to remain immobile and inactive, not reacting to environmental sounds or to any musical sound. After many weeks of trying to interest him, Alvin then played the nightingale 'instrument':

> The effect on the boy was immediate and surprising. He suddenly came to life, his eyes brightened, his face lit up. Even his posture changed. He straightened up his neck and emitted rapid bird-like shrill sounds in response to the nightingale, then stopped[,] waiting for a reply. At the same time he made bird-like movements of his neck and head. He also made ritualistic movements of his finger-tips, tapping rapidly on the table. The same response happened several times before he left the hospital. He held real dialogues with the bird.[13]

We can see how the 'affordances' provided by the specific tone colour or timbre of this instrument were 'appropriated' by both child and adult.

So what is timbre? If we listen to one deep bass note on the piano, we can hear other sounds vibrating simultaneously with this one note. We are hearing the sound of the whole string vibrating (the fundamental tone) and the other vibrating parts of the string (the overtones), as well as resonating sounds from other strings set into motion. Any particular timbre results from the combination of the individual

---

12 From Alvin's lecture notes written for the 1979–80 training course at the Guildhall School of Music and Drama in London and given to Bunt for use in his future teachings. Some of the ideas from these notes are developed in the early sections of this chapter.
13 Alvin (1975: 16–17).

patterns of overtones and their relationship to the fundamental tone. Each instrument will have its own pattern of emphasis given to the different overtones.[14] Differences in timbre enable us to distinguish between, for example, a clarinet and a flute playing at the same pitch and level of loudness.

Timbre is not just about the relationship of overtones to one fundamental tone, however. Other factors include:

- the mental preparation for the sound;
- the beginning attack resulting from the physical 'gesture' made to start the sound;[15]
- alterations to the sound during its steady stable period (for example, slight changes in pitch due to vibrato);[16]
- the ending fading of the sound;
- overlap, grouping and the 'segregation' of different 'streams' of sounds.[17]

Our experience of timbre is also affected by the nature of materials (wood, metal, skin, etc.), the resonating capacity of instruments, the location of the instrument within the space and the entire space where the music is being made. Timbre merges with the other elements when, for example, an increase in loudness opens up more overtones and changes the timbre. We also must not overlook how each musician colours the sound, a sense of personal style.

As babies, we quickly learn to discriminate between the sound of a human voice and other significant sounds. On an everyday level, an understanding of timbre enables us to give meaning to sounds and to attach labels to significant events. We hear a door slam and recognise the sound, without even needing to see the particular door. The timbre of a friend's voice on the telephone can tell us something about our friend's emotional state. Differences in tone colour seem to be among the first that are apparent to the musically 'untrained ear'.[18]

Timbre has long been associated with making an immediate and sensuous impression on the listener, adding meaning to sounds, rather in the way that a painter will add different shades of colour to a canvas. The term 'tone colour' is often substituted for 'timbre', reinforcing this link to the other senses. This has resulted in the use of timbre for creating atmosphere and mood and for emphasising musical ideas and lines. Personal preferences are involved; after any musical performance we often hear comments that relate both to personal taste and to differences in timbre: 'I liked the sound of the flute more than the clarinet'; 'I didn't like that particular tenor's voice'.

---

14 See Levitin (2006: 40–5) for further explanation of the relationship between the fundamental frequency and the overtones that differentiates timbres between instruments.
15 Ibid.: 51.
16 The changes introduced by vibrato and other perceptual attributes are summarised by McAdams and Giordano (2009).
17 Ibid.: 76
18 Copland (1952: 24).

Timbre can be used to excite interest and curiosity. Adults seem to share with children a fascination with the shape, colour and size of instruments, even if it takes rather longer for adult inhibitions to be put aside and for instruments to be explored with the spontaneity of a 4-year-old. 'How is the sound made?' 'What is the instrument made of?' 'Can I play it?' These are the kinds of question that are often raised when one introduces a new group of adults to a wide range of tuned and untuned percussion instruments. The group's members may then need support and time to give themselves permission to explore and play the instruments, to access the carefree child part within. If provided with a comprehensive range of instruments to explore, people of all ages will often develop a certain personal preference for a particular timbre or group of timbres, continuing to return to these instruments. Such a discovery of this kind of identity in sound is often a point of entry for the music therapist and the beginnings of contact and some shared activity. It may take weeks or months to discover or it may happen in the first session.

A specific timbre that is unique and special to each of us is our voice. We do not choose our 'voice-print'; it is to a large degree something that we are born with. What we can do is to try to be aware of our voice and use it confidently as a means of self-expression. Sometimes the voice may be hampered by a particular physiological problem, but most people can sing, and before we begin to sing we can cry, laugh, hum and vocalise a whole range of pre-verbal sounds. Our voices change in different emotional and aesthetic contexts, and voicework has always been significant within music therapy.[19] We may require help to explore or re-explore these processes before we can feel free enough to use our voices in singing or chanting. Singing can be an exposing and risky business. Memories of school music-making, not being invited to sing, still tend to plague a lot of adult groups.[20] Comparisons are often made with recordings of favourite singers, and doubts about musical competence and talent need sensitive handling by the music therapist.

Timbre seems to have a direct associative potential. We do not know why people are drawn to various sound sources. There may be biological links, connections with the natural world or specific life events. What this element does teach us is that people of all ages are often 'disturbed by an imposed choice'.[21] People have a right to explore a range of musical sounds and experiences for themselves. As music therapists we are in a privileged position to observe people's choices, the specific appropriations, and to begin to explore a channel of musical communication. Offering people a range of choices so that preferences can be observed does take time, often a great deal of time, and patience.

19 Baker and Uhlig (2011). See also Austin (2008).
20 See Chapter 6 regarding the current rise in community singing.
21 A further telling phrase from Alvin's notes.

Pitch

Pitch is another basic sound element. Our perception of it depends on the frequency of the sound waves we hear. Pitch has a direct connection to the 'musical' elements of melody (a series of pitches occurring horizontally on a musical score) and harmony (vertical patterning). There appear to be biological influences and cultural associations; sudden high-pitched or low-pitched sounds sometimes cause distress. It appears that we usually prefer the middle pitch of three sounds, whether the sounds themselves are in high or low registers, something we shall observe in our preferences for the safe middle range of loudness.[22]

Strong physical responses to pitch, particularly to the extremes, can be observed in music therapy. Some people seem to be stimulated by particular areas of pitch. High cluster sounds, for example, might not cause distress but stimulate and excite (as we noted in John's session in Chapter 2). Conversely, while a sudden low and loud sound might cause physical discomfort, low sounds may be perceived in very different ways, even, when sustained, as a means of calming. Individual responses can occur in all parts of the body.

A child with profound physical disabilities and learning difficulties was referred to Alvin for an assessment. Could sound and music make an impression when it was difficult to motivate this child or encourage movement? There was a great deal of scepticism as to whether any sound would have any effect. Alvin played some sounds on her cello and, with her typical emphasis on detailed observations, watched for even the slightest physical movement or possible reaction to the sounds and the specific pitches that she played. At the end of the session the doctor accompanying the child apparently reported that the initial scepticism had been confirmed and there had been no observable reaction to the sounds. Alvin apparently directed the doctor's attention to the child's foot, as she had been working with responses there, in particular the connections between low sounds on the cello and movements of the foot. The particular opportunities connecting pitch and movement were played with in this unique way by the child.[23]

This example reminds us of the unpredictability of responses to sounds and how vigilant music therapists need to be in observing the minutest of actions. Pitch is

22 Such preferences were characterised by Daniel Berlyne (e.g. 1971) in the form of Wundt's inverted 'U' curve as part of his 'experimental aesthetics' and work on information theory, whereby connections are drawn between the level of arousal and complexity.
23 Bunt remembers Alvin providing this example during one of her classes at the Guildhall School of Music and Drama in London in 1976.

also a feature of sound and verbal memory systems. Specific pitch work has potential for music therapists in helping sort out prosody, intonation and general comprehension of language and speech. Differentiation of pitches can contribute to a developing sense of sound discrimination, so vital for language development.[24]

We use pitch to help us determine the relative position of a sound in some form of scale, be it the Western chromatic range of twelve notes (semitones) or more complex Indian systems (where quarter-tones are found). There is a clear link between the physical aspect of frequency – the number of cycles of the sound wave's vibration per second – and our subjective impression of the sound. Slow vibrations produced by the thickest and longest string of a double bass, for example, excite the surrounding air molecules to vibrate at a similar slow rate. Conversely, the thinnest string on a violin produces faster vibrations. In turn these vibrations are translated into the same rate of vibration within our eardrums, creating the information that passes through the inner ear, where it is transformed into the electrical impulses en route to analytical processing in the brain.[25] Vibrations also reach other parts of the body, as reported, for example, by people with hearing impairments.

Our experience of pitch is influenced by timbre, loudness, the harmonic context and the effects of vibrato. Usually we interpret the pitch of any sound in relation to the fundamental frequency. When this fundamental is missing from the other overtones, we might still hear the pitch as the fundamental.[26] We can normally hear from around 20 to 15,000 cycles per second (alternatively labelled as hertz – Hz): that is, from the lowest sounds of an organ to the highest overtones of a piccolo. Cultural conventions have changed pitch standard over the centuries, and today orchestral musicians typically tune to an A of 440 or 442 cycles per second. Tuning systems also change; the concert grand of today sounds very different from a keyboard before the time of Bach. Sensitivity to the upper and lower end of pitch discrimination does relate to the person's age and there are many individual variables, for example among people with hearing impairments. The thresholds are not the same for animals, as in the classic example of the dog whistle which we cannot hear but dogs can.

Pitch involves an association between tension and relaxation: the law of gravity implies an effort in going up and relaxation in coming down. Singers and string, wind and brass players are only too aware of the physical relationships between levels of tension, relaxation and pitch. A simple practical exercise can demonstrate this link of pitch with our bodies:

Try to be as relaxed as possible, sitting comfortably in a chair with your feet firmly on the floor. Make sure you are in a vertical position with

---

24 For the connections between pitch, timbre and language, see Patel (2008: chapter 2).
25 Levitin (2006: 18–19); Wigram *et al.* (2002: 48–52); Stainsby and Cross (2009).
26 Stainsby and Cross (2009: 51).

your spine nice and straight. Now, if this feels OK, close your eyes and relax your breathing with slow, deep breaths, being aware of the gentle movement of your diaphragm. Try to clear your head of extraneous thoughts and hum a sound on an out breath, again taking care that this is comfortable for you. Play around with this sound, explore the vowel sounds and experiment with different consonants. Try making the sounds go up and down in pitch. By now you should be aware that different parts of your body are resonating with the various pitches you are sounding. What happens if you make the sounds go up or go down? Are you aware of where any tension might be occurring? Is your throat becoming tighter as the sounds become higher in pitch?

There is nothing startlingly novel about this exercise: such exploration with sound has been practised for centuries in the East, where there is much written on the connections between pitch, different parts of the body and physiological states, including the system of chakras.[27]

Pitch is the most salient element in 'vibroacoustic therapy', where there is a specific use of low-frequency sound. The first attempts, using a kind of 'low-frequency sound massage', were devised by Olav Skille in Norway in 1980.[28] In vibroacoustic therapy the patient lies on a bed or sits in a chair and sound is directly transferred through the mattress or cushions. Special selections of music have been made, with the extra ingredient of a pulsed low-frequency tone. The researchers create this tone by placing two pitches in close proximity, for example 40 and 40.5 cycles per second. A topical review has summarised the work across thirty years.[29] The authors point out that there are many indications of the potential therapeutic impact of vibroacoustic therapy but that more research is needed. They also note that although this therapy is related closely to the effect of low-frequency sound, other contributing therapeutic factors include the integrated music and interactive relationship with the therapist.

Loudness

Loudness is a third basic element of sound. Physically, it is related directly to the energy of the source of the sound, which in turn affects the power and intensity of the sound, and finally our subjective impression of the loudness. To explore a wide range of loudness can be crucial in music therapy processes.

27 McClellan (1991); Hamel (1978: particularly chapter 5).
28 Skille and Wigram (1995: 25).
29 Punkanen and Ala-Ruona (2012).

Mike was 10 years old when he started music therapy. He had mild learning difficulties but the main reason for his referral was his occasional outbursts of aggressive behaviour. Mike wanted to play the drums, and at the start of the therapy his music was very loud. The therapist had the impression that Mike was surprised when these loud outbursts were supported by even louder playing on the piano. His playing was not going to be stopped. The loud sounds were contained in the improvised music, which contributed to a growing trust. Mike began to be interested in sounds at the opposite end of the spectrum, coming to the piano and asking for quiet sounds, what he called his 'sleep music'. He would often pretend to sleep as the soft sounds enveloped him. He began to find within the music what he was looking for. We could begin to interpret this behaviour from different therapeutic perspectives. From a music-centred point of view the therapist was interested in his creative use of loud and soft sounds, how he uniquely made use of them. Once Mike had explored the extremes of very loud and very soft sounds he became increasingly interested in the middle range of loudness. We could also assume that being provided the freedom to explore within this wide range of loudness gave Mike opportunities to make inner connections, integrating and balancing difficult areas of his life.

With this element there is a continuum from the very soft to the very loud. Scientists have devised the unit of the decibel to measure different levels of loudness, using a logarithmic scale, so that if the intensity of the sound is doubled there is an increase of 3 decibels. The threshold of hearing is towards the lower end of the scale (0 decibels), while the threshold of pain is around 130 decibels.

In modern societies, in our highly mechanised city sound landscapes we are only too aware of the threshold of pain, exposing ourselves to high levels of loudness in busy cities, airports, on roads and in clubs, with the risk of premature hearing problems, in spite of our ears having in-built protective features that compress sounds when they are too loud.[30] If invaded for extended periods by high levels of loud sounds, our ears need time to recover, for example from the ringing in the ears and dulled sense of hearing after an evening out at a club. If we surround ourselves with high levels of loudness too soon, perhaps by a return visit to the club on the following night, then we may not be allowing our ears sufficient recovery time. At the other end of the scale we need to pay attention to how loud a sound needs to be before it reaches a sufficient level to be heard. As with preference for timbre, people appear to have a preferred level of loudness. For one person some music may be too loud, whereas for another the opposite is true.

30 Levitin (2006: 68).

In the Western classical tradition, musicians use vague and imprecise terms, from *pianissimo* to *fortissimo*, in describing loudness. It depends greatly on the nature of the music being made and the shape, furnishings and size of the room. When we experience degrees of loudness in whatever musical situation, many factors are involved, such as:

- the threshold of masking – that is, the level of sound necessary to cover another and gain significance (very obvious in group work);
- the grouping of sounds of similar loudness to help the segregation of different streams of sounds;[31]
- pitch, particularly at the extremes;
- the resonance and physical properties of instruments and our voices;
- the strength of the movement needed to make an instrument sound, including the physical preparation for the movement;
- the motor control needed to control the level of loudness and the shifts in level;
- contextual aspects such as location and distance.

As in all the sound and musical elements, learning and cultural processes are very significant, although there appear to be certain fundamental features to which we can respond viscerally. We all seem to react to a sudden loud sound in a similar way (a reaction exploited to great effect in horror films), and a simple soft sound tends to create a general calming atmosphere. Changes in the level of loudness can also be used as a means of gaining attention, initiating new perceptual activity.

Is there a human need for loudness? At birth the young infant certainly has no inhibitions about making loud sounds, making an immediate impact on the surrounding environment. In music therapy practice we observe people 'appropriating' the full range of loudness. Loud playing could indicate a release of physical tension or a desire to communicate aggressive and frustrated feelings. It could also indicate confidence, focused attention and internal strength. But too many assumptions can be made about people's feeling states from their loud or soft playing. There are many subtle variations. An autistic child may be using loud drumming as a way of withdrawing from contact with the therapist, the loud sounds being used as a barrier to more direct communication.

Very often a group's first improvisation will indicate a preference for a safe middle ground of loudness.[32] Some people find it difficult to project themselves in loud sounds, even to the extent of stopping a movement so as not to do so. A group of adults who are used to being very sensitive towards each other may need to process permission to make loud sounds. There are occasions during group work when some members find playing loudly a liberating feeling. Finding a balance between loudness tolerance and the needs of other members of the group presents

31 Ibid.: 78–9.
32 For a discussion, see Bruscia (1987: 189–204).

a challenge to the dynamics of the group and the therapist's ability to hold the space.

Duration

On a physical and measurable level, duration is concerned with the length of time a sound lasts. Clearly, repeated sounds of long duration create the experience of a slower tempo than repeated sounds of short duration. But there are so many subjective perceptions of time: the time of the scientist is not that of the poet; the time of a Zen meditator is not that of a chief executive. We can link duration to the movement of time in music: 'The statement of music is made moment by moment; what it expresses comes to life as it moves in time.'[33] This dependence on time contributes to making a sound musical.

In music therapy we try to enable external durations to meet the needs of a person's world, whether in individual or group work. Understanding and matching the speed of a child's movements is the crux of the following example, which reveals how a child can learn to make use of the particular opportunities offered by the durational properties of music. The example also has links to the later discussion of rhythm.

Natalie, a bright 7-year-old, was about to move up into the junior section of her school. This meant moving upstairs. She had mild cerebral palsy and, with this physical difficulty, a related lack of self-esteem. She walked with an irregular pattern and for quite some time the physiotherapists had been trying to work towards helping her achieve a more organised walking pace and pattern. Could music therapy help? The music therapist found that her preferred and spontaneous tempi were slower than the tempo of the physiotherapists' clapping to help organise her walking. From making music with Natalie we discovered the point at which her pulse became steady. Through discovering her comfortable tempo and not imposing an external pulse, it was hoped that this slower tempo would connect internal and external durational patterns. This steady pulse became the basis of a song that Natalie practised with the other members of her family, as she walked down the street, when at school, and at times when she felt anxious about any movements, such as facing the gym apparatus. She came back to her next appointment and walked carefully down the corridor at a slower and more organised pace. She was using the internalised tempo of the song by singing it to herself. This developing self-organisation began to be transferred to

33 Nordoff and Robbins (1971: 7).

finer movements on a horizontal plane. As the short period of sessions progressed, so did her confidence, with a more upright girl leaving the room at the end of each session. The physiotherapist at the school reported later that this musical interlude had provided Natalie with a secure basis for when she found herself losing control or feeling afraid. Her comfortable tempo had been discovered but Natalie herself was making an intelligent use of the musical material as a self-help tool.

How did Natalie perceive time and the different durations of the sounds? Do we have inner biological clocks? We are intimately connected with a whole range of biological tempi: heartbeats, thyroid activity, menstrual and kidney cycles, for example. A baby is quickly exposed to a variety of durational experiences: *in utero* and at the breast; the early beating of the feet, movement of limbs and rocking movements.[34] In *Music and Communication*, Terence McLaughlin suggests that disturbances in these normal inner tempi create tensions in our perception of time.[35] This leads to the question of whether there is a natural tempo point from which all other tempi are judged as faster or slower. If we are accustomed to playing music we will be aware of the difficulties of sustaining a very slow tempo, when we may have to subdivide the main pulse, and also of keeping a fast tempo up to speed. We do seem to overestimate short sounds and underestimate long ones. More accuracy appears to occur in the area of our heartbeat tempo of 75–100 beats per minute.

It is interesting that the durations of our heartbeats and of our 'spontaneous' and 'preferred' tempi seem to fall within a similar range.[36] We meet this spontaneous tempo in music therapy when a new group, improvising together for the first time, will often settle into this comfortable heartbeat and body-based tempo. It usually follows on after a period of random exploration of the available sounds. Perhaps the natural durations of our physiological functioning go some way towards explaining certain primary relationships between us and music, a basic physical response to sound. Our own bodies do appear to have their own unique ways of being rooted in music, and conversely music evokes in us all manner of individual resonances and emotional responses.

In his well-known book *Awakenings*, the neurologist Oliver Sacks gives examples of the effects of different durations on adults with post-encephalitic Parkinsonism. He provides evidence that inner biological pacemakers and regulators are impaired in Parkinsonism. He claims that music's reliance on time is a strong factor in helping to free the patient while the music lasts. Sacks narrates the example of Edith T., a former music teacher:

---

34 Fraisse (1982: 152).
35 McLaughlin (1970: 31–40).
36 Fraisse (1982: 151–4).

She said that she had become 'graceless' with the onset of Parkinsonism, that her movements had become 'wooden, mechanical – like a robot or doll', that she had lost her former 'naturalness' and 'musicalness' of movement, that – in a word – she had been 'unmusicked'. Fortunately, she added, the disease was 'accompanied by its own cure'. I raised an eyebrow: 'Music', she said, 'as I am unmusicked, I must be remusicked.'[37]

The implications of helping people to become 'remusicked' go far beyond the confines of Parkinsonism. There appears to be a strong connection between a person's perception of time and of illness, disease and health in general. Musicians and music therapists are fortunate to be working in a form that provides opportunities for experiences of such a kind to occur. Although music has a relationship to linear, measured, clock time (in Greek, *chronos*), being immersed in the making of or listening to music shifts our perception of time and brings us more into the limitless world of *kairos* (in the Greek, a counterpart to *chronos*), where we reassess time as in 'a state of flux'.[38] In an essay on the theologian and musician Jeremy Begbie's text *Theology, Music and Time*, Ansdell writes, '[M]usic is not simply "in" time (especially not in clock time) but it *creates its time*. Then, to go one stage further, *it creates our time*, when we "become music".'[39] There are resonances here with psychologist Mihaly Csikszentmihalyi's concept of 'flow', as we can experience when being totally absorbed in creating and playing music.[40]

Imagine how a single sound encompasses what has gone before, including even the briefest moment of silence after the previous sound, and yet carries within it the potentiality and expectation of what is to come. Music provides such opportunities to stay utterly focused in the sentient present, the moment now, yet the moment at one and the same time can be contained within and transcend both past and future. Psychologist and psychoanalyst Daniel Stern points out that when sounds join to form a 'short musical phrase' (we are moving towards the building-blocks of melody here), this is perceived as a whole, 'a global unit with boundaries'. He describes it as a 'flowing whole occurring during a now' and says that 'the future is implied at each instant of the phrase's journey through the present moment'.[41] Stern's thesis is of interest in making connections between such present moments in music and moments both in psychotherapy and in everyday life.

While aware of the complexity of the theories of duration, we can make assumptions about correlations between physiological functioning and durations. We can talk about a harmony or disharmony with time, being in phase or out of phase with time. A major responsibility and conundrum for music therapists is attempting to understand the particular and unique time framework of each

---

37 Sacks (1991: 60).
38 Aldridge (1996: 37).
39 Ansdell (2005b: 24). See also Begbie (2005) and Pavlicevic (2001).
40 Csikszentmihalyi (2008).
41 Stern (2004: 26). This text and quote by Stern are also cited by Sutton (2007: 177).

participant in music therapy. A young child may only be able to cope with a small amount of sound information at any one time. There may be the question of over-arousing an already excitable person. The duration of the sounds may be the reason why somebody has stopped attending to the sound. The sounds may be too fast or too slow. The session itself may be too long. We need to set aside both time and space to make contact with each person's unique temporal framework – to go alongside and 'meet the person where he or she is', to make use of an often-quoted therapeutic maxim. This notion is close to what Ansdell and Pavlicevic describe as 'being-together-in-time', and they also refer to Aldridge's discussion of *kairotic*, time when a person sounds not as a 'mechanical' being (more linked to *chronos*) but as a 'symphonic' one.[42]

Silence

Silence is crucial for giving space and significance to a sound, and we could think of music-making as active play with sound and silence, in embodied and socially embedded forms. The songwriter Sting wonders 'as musicians whether the most important thing we do is merely to provide a frame for silence'.[43] If this is true for musicians generally, it is perhaps especially true for music therapists, who also very often use silence as a frame for people's participation in sound. 'We should not forget that music therapy is the therapeutic method most able to treat silence in a creative way,' writes the Japanese composer Yu Wakao.[44]

In a study of how intellectually disabled people participated in a cultural festival, Stige became interested in 'participatory diversifications': when the contribution of individuals or sub-groups introduced something new and different to the situation. These events often emerged as creative contrasts to silence. In the simple greeting song for a group, the music therapist dedicated one verse to each participant, adapting the emotional and musical expression to suit the interaction with each person. Their creative musical contributions were framed by their silence while waiting for their turn:

> John sat patiently, but with visible eagerness, waiting for his turn. When the music therapist came to his verse, the song and the situation was immediately transformed. John grabbed the hands of the music therapist and initiated a rocking movement and an acceleration of the speed of the song. The music therapist attuned her contribution by increasing the volume of her singing and the situation was energized considerably.

> ... [W]e could call John's contribution *adventurous*, but we must also pay attention to how others in the situation attune to the adventure. In this case

---

42 Ansdell and Pavlicevic (2005: 23).
43 Sting (1998: 32–3).
44 Wakao (2002).

the music therapist allowed the adventure, perhaps to some degree anticipated it, and accommodated quite actively. Both were adjusting their participation in relation to each other. And it did not stop with increased speed and volume of the song and rocking movements from where John was sitting on the chair. All of a sudden he stood up and hugged the music therapist warmly and enthusiastically, and for a long time.[45]

Breaking a silence has both a physical and a psychological impact. Silence acts on the memory and can build up pleasurable feelings of expectancy – when is the next sound going to come? For some people it can be frightening. The imagination can be let loose – what will the next sound be like? The Irish philosopher and poet John O'Donohue viewed this gap between sound and silence as a liminal place where the imagination is 'free to create beauty'.[46] He considered the 'nightmare' that would exist for us if such a 'threshold' did not exist, noting that

> [M]usic is the surest voice of silence. From the beginning silence and sounds have been sisters. Music invites silence to its furthest inner depths and outer frontiers. The patience in which silence is eternally refined could only voice itself in music . . . The dream of silence is music.[47]

In a compilation entitled *Silence, Music, Silent Music*, musicologist Jenny Doctor notes that the revised *New Grove Dictionary of Music* does not contain an entry on 'Silence'.[48] But whether as composer, listener, performer or music therapist, we are continually aware that sounds need to emerge from, and return to, silence in order for their true nature to come alive and be communicated. Arvo Pärt is a contemporary composer who gives clear instructions regarding the lengths of the silences. When performing his music, the attention of both performers and audience members needs to be drawn just as much to the gaps as to the sounds themselves. It is interesting that a period of retreat and meditative study of ancient Russian Orthodox music separates Pärt's earlier music, some written within a serial framework, from his later, more contemplative style.[49] John Cage's famous composition 4′ 33″ teaches us that we need to be thinking about silence as relative and whether there can ever be a real silent moment. Even when Cage entered the silent space of an anechoic chamber, he still reported hearing the high sound of his nervous system and the low one of his blood circulation.[50]

Music therapists need to feel comfortable being, holding and staying with all kinds of silence. And as the psychiatrist and psychoanalyst Gilbert Rose notes:

---

45 Stige (2010a: 137).
46 O'Donohue (2003: 60).
47 Ibid.: 64–5.
48 Doctor (2007: 15).
49 For another example of silent contemplation, see Philip Gröning's award-winning film *Into Great Silence*, which documents life inside a Carthusian monastery.
50 Brook (2007).

The therapeutic process may usefully be thought of in terms of music. Music is not about playing notes; music consists of silences that breathe and shape the sound, engendering depths of feelings to be experienced without the necessity for immediate understanding.[51]

Julie Sutton has written extensively on the 'powerfully expressive, yet at times delicate, nature of silence in music therapy'.[52] Sutton positions silence as part of the communicative repertoire between people, differentiating silences from the more produced sound objects. Silent moments allow the therapist to start a session from a place of quiet and during the session to take some breathing space and time for further reflection. She also points out that the therapist needs to open up internal listening attentive spaces, some of them being painful, in order for the full potential of such shared meetings in the therapy space to take place. We need to be aware, however, that such attention to listening to the gaps between the sounds can cause suspense and in some cases anxiety for some patients. Darnley-Smith and Patey give the example of a woman in her seventies with Alzheimer's disease becoming anxious and stopping her playing during any brief moments of pausing or silence in the therapist's music, only feeling able to play again when the therapist provided a continuous musical underpinning.[53] Awareness of context and a sense of balance are key issues here. As with all the elements, great care is needed in observing how individuals respond. An open-ended approach is needed, based on having no expectations or preconceptions, particularly when meeting a patient for the first time. The gap can be a silent place of attending, witnessing and not knowing, a place of deep listening and sharing.

Rhythm

Rhythm involves the punctuation and patterning of sound in time, organised in relation to a pulse. It occupies a crucial place in music therapy and follows on naturally from a discussion of duration and silence, inextricably linked with both of these areas.

When working with people with profound learning difficulties, we often encounter a lack of understanding of pulse or lack of understanding that one sound event can generate the next, a kind of pre-pulse behaviour. An emphasis on rhythmic interactive play can help in such instances to predict and anticipate events and to associate two or more events within the same present.

Anne is 2½ years old and has profound and multiple disabilities (a diagnosis of Rett syndrome). When presented with a skin-top tambour

---

51 Rose (2004: 10).
52 Bunt (2008: 102), referring to Sutton (2002a, 2006, 2007); and see Bunt (2007).
53 Darnley-Smith and Patey (2003: 76–7).

she reaches out and makes an occasional stroking movement. The therapist replies in a similar fashion. There is a long delay before her next sound gesture, which is reflected back to her. Over the weeks of short individual sessions her sound gestures come in quicker succession and after twelve sessions she is beginning to play in short bursts of sounds, playing at times two separate sounds. She starts to vocalise and a connection is observed between a vocal sound and the short rhythmic patterns. For the most part her behaviour can be regarded as essentially pre-pulse activity but with signs of the beginnings of connections between two events within the same present. It may be that she is learning about connections from the interactional dialogue, where each group of sounds (child and therapist) takes place within a short space of time, very much within a two-second interval. She is appropriating in her own way the rhythmic and energising opportunities of the music.

Rhythm carries us from one beat to the next, so to speak. The crucial, arguably defining, feature of musical rhythmic behaviour is that the temporal structuring of actions is built upon a regular pulse which allows individuals, within temporal boundaries of a psychological present, to interact in real time through a process of entrainment.[54] This has long been acknowledged within music therapy: 'Without rhythm there would be no music . . . the unique potential of rhythm to energise and bring order will be seen as the most influential factor of music.'[55] Here the energising and organising aspects of rhythm are stressed, these being central ingredients of both music and music therapy. In *The Origins of Music* the editors argue that many animals have the ability to move in a metric, alternating fashion, when walking and running for instance, but that the human rhythmic capacity is unique in the entrainment of movements to an external timekeeper such as the beat of a drum or the movements of another person.[56] Music psychologist John Bispham has suggested that sustained musical pulse and the capacity for mutual correction of a pulse are human-specific traits and that we can think of musical rhythm as a framework for interactive communication.[57]

Scholars have for a long time acknowledged that understanding and relating to rhythm does not rely solely on auditory pathways and mechanisms.[58] People with hearing impairments often report that rhythm is the ingredient that provides the easiest access to comprehending music. There are many examples of musicians with hearing impairments with sophisticated rhythmic understanding; we think immediately of Beethoven.

54 Bispham (2009).
55 Gaston (1968: 17).
56 Wallin *et al.* (2000: 11–12).
57 Bispham 2009.
58 Gardner (1984: 104–5).

At its simplest level rhythm can be a 'repetition of the same stimulus at a constant frequency' of occurrence, as in clockwork or the repeated pulsing of a metronome.[59] We can observe this in a basic pattern such as walking, when one event predicts the next. We can regard such activities as spontaneous and, as we noted in our discussion on duration, they occur within a given tempo range with slight environmental and individual differences. So when is our walking just metric? When is it also rhythmic? We are aware of the differences when walking down the street with another person. As we get to know the person better we are able to synchronise the walking more easily, lovers demonstrating beautiful synchrony. Gaston considered that these close rhythmic connections to motor function and the organisation of these fundamental body-based patterns contributed greatly to the early acceptance of music therapy.[60]

The development of expectations and anticipation is central to our understanding of the rhythmic process. This development introduces further expressive functions such as the pause between two events in time and the concept of accent.[61] An accent can be created by changes in loudness, duration or even in tonality. Rhythmic details such as different accents define and locate a beat.

Also relevant is each person's individual tempo, witnessed in such characteristics as rhythmic tapping and finger-strumming.[62] Rocking and hand-flapping can be included here, behaviours that are frequently observed when communication with the environment is greatly reduced through impairment or disability. The rhythmic behaviour could be viewed as releasing tension in these contexts. In an initial music therapy session it is possible to observe this sense of individual tempo in the musical play and spontaneous movements presented by the child or adult. A music therapy setting provides an opportunity to support each person's metric tempo, to make an initial contact at that level before moving away from this focal point to explore rhythmic and temporal experiences. We observed this taking place in the example of Natalie's walking song and we shall return to it in Chapter 6 when discussing how music can help adults with gait and movement irregularities.

Music therapists need to be aware of the different emotional responses produced by different rhythms. The hypnotic and calming effect of repetitive and steady rhythms is at the root of lullabies; in the minimalist school of composers, repetition and added complexities of subtle changes and inflection in the rhythm can produce a meditative response. Conversely, we are familiar with the use of rigid rhythmic patterns in martial music throughout history to drum up warlike feelings.

---

59 Fraisse (1982: 151).
60 Gaston (1968: 17–19).
61 See Fraisse (1982: 154–5) for discussion about anticipation and the temporal interval between sounds.
62 Tempo is connected to the speed of a piece of music and usually measured in beats per minute; metre refers to how the various beats are grouped together, for example in groups of two, three or four. See Levitin (2006: 55–61) for further differentiation between rhythm, metre and tempo and Martineau (2008: 12–13, 24–5, 51).

Music-making may take place synchronously or antiphonally. Both contribute to grouping of rhythmic patterns into manageable 'chunks', enabling storage of such events in the short-term memory. We can add other variables in the grouping procedure such as changes in pitch marking off a new rhythmic group and, in the West in particular, larger melodic and harmonic structures.

Melody

'A melody is created by the succession of tones through time. Step by step, note by note, an outline is formed, a path carved.'[63] Melody is concerned with the way pitches shape contours in a sequence, the resultant combination of sounds being organised in phrases and in larger organisational units. A melody is usually perceived as a whole with a beginning, middle and end. Whether any sequence of pitches creates a melody is both culturally significant and highly subjective.

To be able to sing a melody, we need to be able to produce sounds that independently vary in pitch, timbre, loudness and duration. This ability does not come without effort but the capacity to produce such sounds seems to be unique for the human species; the musicianship that is required for such an achievement appears gradually in human infant development.[64] Physically, it is achieved by independent control of a range of muscles involved in vocal production, but the process requires cultural learning, including adjustment to the musical scales most typical in the culture in question.

Some steps in scales seem to have a prime position when placed in melodic sequences. In his discussion on 'musical universals', music psychologist John Sloboda highlights some of these 'privileged' reference points.[65] He notes that a 'drone', for example, is often used to delineate the principal pitch or pitches in much instrumental music of many cultures. In purely vocal melodies, such as plainsong, we note that certain pitches act as similar structural reference points. The octave seems to be one such point and additionally there is a natural doubling of a melody at the octave between female and male voices. The octave is the first interval in the harmonic series with a straightforward doubling of the frequency. The octave can also be used to mark off a new repetition of the sequence of pitches; here we start again from the 'same note' at a different pitch. The octave also supports the notions of scale and tonic.

The development of reference points in music, Sloboda adds, is closely linked to instruments of 'fixed pitch' such as bells and many tuned percussion or stringed instruments where the pitches remain constant during a particular musical activity. These kinds of instruments are used a great deal in active music therapy work. There are other pitches that seem to be 'privileged', namely those that approximate to the perfect fourth or fifth, which when added together make up an octave. There

---

63 Martineau (2008: 18).
64 Wermke and Mende (2009).
65 Sloboda (1985: 253–7).

are close links again here with the natural world of acoustics and mathematical proportion.[66]

When we examine smaller intervals we come across the complexities of human organisation. The falling minor third (G to E, for example) is used in many cultures as a call for gaining attention. Young children might call their mothers with it ('Mum-my') and use it as a ritual in their play. This interval, which frames a short phrase when an interval of a fourth is added at the hub (an A in our example), is so common in children's play in many Western cultures (G, E, A, G, E) that Nordoff and Robbins labelled it 'the children's tune' and used it extensively as a 'calling phrase'.[67]

If the notes C and D are added to the E, G and A in 'the children's tune', a five-note pentatonic scale is formed, as in the black notes on a keyboard. This scale is the basis of much folk music, for example from America, China, Ireland and Scotland. If pitched at a comfortable level, the sounds of the scale are well within the range of children and even the most musically inhibited of adults. The absence of the discordant intervals of the augmented fourth, minor second and major seventh in this scale makes it popular and convenient in much music therapy work. Tuned percussion instruments such as xylophones, metallophones and glockenspiels can be 'set' for a pentatonic scale. All participants can then take part in melodic exploration with satisfying results.

Singing or playing in a pentatonic scale can free people from the confines of the Western diatonic system: the desire to play the 'right note' and to search for a favourite melody. Increased freedom from confining conventions is also often possible when tuned instruments are set in other scale systems, such as those commonly known as the modes. Here, each mode is made up of a particular order of semitones and tones. If you play only on the white keys of a keyboard, you have the opportunity to explore, within our present-day approximations, modes such as the Dorian (D to D), Phrygian (E to E), Lydian (F to F) and Mixolydian (G to G). The following example of a teaching session illustrates how a group can quickly use the freedom from diatonic convention to move from individual exploration to group cohesion.

> During an exploration of the modes, a large group of Italian students began by gently singing the notes of the Dorian mode and setting up call and response sequences in the mode. The students were then asked to set the tuned percussion in the Dorian and one by one they introduced their sounds. To begin with, the members of the group explored the mode for themselves. Gradually connections were made

---

66 See McClellan (1991: 9–20) for an account of the physical world of sound, including the natural harmonic series; and see Martineau (2008) for a concise discussion on intervals and melody.
67 See 'Exploration fourteen' in Robbins and Robbins (1998); and for further use of 'the children's tune', see 'The pentatonic scale' in Nordoff and Robbins (2007: 471–2).

with other melodic fragments; answers were provided to implied musical questions. The music became more focused and locked into a comfortable heartbeat tempo. It was a large hall and gradually the students began to move, getting up and dancing with their instruments and each other. The loudness level increased as everyone began to sing and to play. The music began to subside and by the end of the improvisation the group realised that the Dorian mode had been explored for over forty minutes.

It is not only the pentatonic scale and modes that help us go beyond conventions that may confine. Melodies we have heard and used in our everyday life are part of our identity and may be a resource for expression, communication and reflection in music therapy. Very often patients/participants make use of songs and melodies they already know. Other specific uses of melody in music therapy include melodic intonation therapy in the rehabilitation of aphasia,[68] song creation in improvisational sessions,[69] and various approaches to songwriting[70] and song performance (within sessions and outside sessions).[71]

Harmony

When pitches are sounded together simultaneously, harmony is introduced. Harmony is significant in many forms of music and in a range of different ways. In Western classical music, harmony is central to the complex and evolving 'architectural structures', which are often felt within to build and release tension. In popular music, harmony might be simpler and more predictable, used as part of a stable foundation for creative play with other elements.[72] In music therapy, harmony often plays an important role, although use of it sometimes operates within clear limitations, as here:

'Which chord do you prefer?' The music therapist was warm and friendly but I was not sure I liked the two chords he offered. I tried not to think about which chords he was playing but they were ordinary triadic chords anyway and I felt like something different with a bit more tension. 'Can you give me an alternative?' 'Yes, of course,' said the music therapist. He waited for a few seconds before playing again. I

68 Baker (2011).
69 Aldridge (1996).
70 Baker and Wigram (2005).
71 Turry (2005).
72 Keil (1994) introduces the term 'participatory discrepancies' to describe the creative play with small nuances of especially pitch and rhythm that you find in many types of music.

remember asking myself whether he was trying to give me some space. Being a client in music therapy was new to me. Usually I would be the music therapist. The reason for my self-referral was a need to explore my emotional relationship to my own voice, and the music therapist I contacted was a specialist in voicework. I knew that he would often accompany vocal improvisations with a few simple chords. Why didn't I like the chords he was offering? Were they actually so limiting for me or was I trying to make things difficult? The hands of the therapist moved to the keyboard again. The chords that emerged were only slightly different, perhaps inverted now and with a ninth added or something, but I felt more prepared to join in. I started singing, very carefully in the beginning. As I started to hear my own voice more, there was a change in my body, and something happened with the therapist's music too. He was probably still playing much the same chords, but the attack was shifting and I could feel that our rhythms gradually came together. The simple chords were like open fields now, where my voice and I could play together, like two children. It was strange and surprising. The simple chords were like invitations.

In this example, the music therapist's assessment was that 'less is more' when it comes to harmony; simplicity often affords possibilities for participation. At the same time, the many possibilities of harmonic variation are tools that can be used in therapeutic practice, in interaction with other musical elements.

Harmony is often considered a 'vertical' component of music since simultaneity is a defining characteristic. There are as many overlaps between melody and harmony as there are harmonic implications in melodies, and harmony can itself generate melody. Our perception of harmony depends on the tonal centre (the key) of the music. Harmony and tonal centre together can create a 'game of expectations', offering possibilities such as alternations of chords, unexpected chord sequences, modulations and so on.[73] Often these possibilities interact with melodic developments, but we can also perceive a series of chords as musical events in themselves, without an obvious melody.

The acoustic and physical foundations of harmony can be explained if we go back to what we said about pitch and timbre earlier. When we hear a single tone, we are actually hearing several tones merging together because there is a series of overtones to the fundamental frequency (the frequency we think of as the pitch). We remember that the relative intensity of each one of those overtones is crucial for our experience of timbre. When an instrument or voice channels energy at frequencies that are 'integer multiples' of the fundamental frequency (twice the

---

73 The examples are based in the logic of tonal music, while so-called atonal music also has a place in music therapy if and when it suits the needs and the interests of patients/participants.

fundamental frequency, three times, four times, etc.), we describe the sound as 'harmonic'.[74] This is of course a quality of timbre but the phenomenon of overtones also helps explain the intervals we use when working with harmony.

The series of overtones explored from a simple integer ratio perspective may help us understand the experience of consonance and dissonance in intervals to some degree, although there are problems with this explanation. The simplest integer ratio possible is 2 : 1, and this ratio defines the octave.[75] The octave is almost universally considered consonant. The fifth and the fourth are two other intervals that are commonly accepted as consonant and they also can be explained by simple integer ratios between frequencies. The ratio 3 : 2 defines the perfect fifth, while the ratio 4 : 3 defines the perfect fourth. In ancient Greece, Pythagoras famously discovered these ratios while experimenting with a monochord. As was mentioned in Chapter 1, he was also interested in developing the more metaphysical theory of the 'harmony of the spheres'. But perhaps we should not conclude too quickly that harmony and consonance are natural phenomena. Overtones are natural and our brains are 'hard-wired' to detect them, but learning and culture play an extra and central role in our perception of consonance and dissonance. In Western music since the days of Bach, for example, the equal-tempered chromatic scale has not included 'perfect' fourths and fifths, only slightly adjusted mathematical approximations. Although we still tend to think of these approximations as consonant, assumptions about what constitutes consonance and dissonance develop over time, in the history of both the individual and the culture.

Harmony can be regarded as the most complex element and, as developmental psychologists indicate, is only mastered after melodic understanding is secure; it comes relatively late in a child's musical development. Children's understanding of harmony and tonal hierarchy is usually quite limited until about 7 years of age, and continued refinement of this knowledge is apparent for several years.[76] When we start relating to harmony we find predictability reassuring but are also aroused by the harmonically ambiguous. What seems to make Mozart or Haydn stand out from their contemporaries is at times the unpredictability of their music, the musical events that are different from what we expect. We will be surprised by the music's sudden change of direction from the implied harmonies. It was this sense of the harmonically unexpected that Sloboda found produced physical reactions in his respondents as shivers down the spine or goose-pimples in his respondents.[77] We can relate these moments to the music psychologist Leonard Meyer's notion of our expectations being either 'fulfilled' or 'violated'.[78] The composer provides all the necessary harmonic background and information for the

---

74 Levitin (2006: 40).
75 For instance, if the A above middle C has the frequency of 440Hz – the general tuning standard in many countries – the A one octave above has the frequency of 880Hz. See 'Pitch', pp. 60–62.
76 Trainor and Trehub (1994).
77 Sloboda (1985: 33–46).
78 Meyer (1956: 22–32).

implied expectation; we assume the next harmonic change must be this. On some occasions our expectations are fulfilled, at other times they are violated: the progression did not move as expected.

Some participants in music therapy may be harmonically very sophisticated and fluent. When working with others, for example people with profound learning difficulties, a complex harmonic world may prove to be redundant. Too many changes may be unsettling. Tensions in harmonic progressions and harmonic resolutions will need careful balancing, too much of either being counter-productive. How can a level of interest be maintained? At a very fundamental level, a harmonic basis can be provided by a drone or a small repeating pattern of simple chords, over which melodies can be supported or emerge.

Music therapists develop highly contrasting ways to underpin and support patients' music through harmony, from highly sophisticated keyboard or guitar accompaniment to simple weaving of lines in bass or treble with single-line instruments. Therapists might layer riffs, creating lively bass lines in association with a rhythmic groove, or build a mixture of live and computer-generated improvisations as a framework. A careful study of harmonic implications, with all the interplay of tensions and expectations, can further the music therapist's understanding of these complex processes. In improvisational music therapy, while some pioneers explored possibilities of harmony in tonal music,[79] others opened up perspectives for using atonal music, focusing on elements such as timbre, loudness and rhythm.[80] Lee, writing from a music-centred perspective, has expanded the case for harmony to include both tonal and atonal music.[81] Even though harmony might be too complex and off-putting at times for some patients, it is also one of the elements that creates moods and enhances our aesthetic experiences, so it is clearly an element that can motivate for musical participation.

Concluding points

In our survey of sound and musical elements the implied focus has been on how people use the elements, either receptively or actively, and particularly within the frame of affordances and appropriations. There is an implied emphasis on interaction. 'Through musical interaction, two people create forms that are greater than the sum of their parts, and make for themselves experiences of empathy that would be unlikely to occur in ordinary social intercourse.'[82] Shared activity seems to be one key for understanding the organisational and temporal nature of music. In society such musical activity might occur in a communal festival, as an incitement to work, dance or play, or in a planned musical performance such as a concert. These musical experiences are functionally different but all are shared

---

79 See Robbins and Robbins (1998).
80 Priestley (1975/2012, 1994).
81 Lee (2003).
82 Blacking (1987: 26).

and communal. Perhaps one of our deepest satisfactions from music results from the emotional support gained in such collective action.

With its origins in expressive, interactive movements, music is described by ethnomusicologist John Blacking as 'humanly organized sound',[83] or, as a patient once suggested, 'sculpted sound'. We find personal resonances in these musical sculptures. If we are forming some new musical patterns, be it re-creating a pre-composed piece or on-the-spot 'playing with sounds' in an improvisation, we will be working hard to give form to inner feelings and experiences. Our cognitive and emotional processes are being brought into the music: the cerebral processes involved in motor control, feelings, cultural experiences, social activity, intellectual activity, and so on. All this helps us to differentiate one person's music from another's. The transactions that musical activity offers cut across conventional divisions such as internal and external reality, individual and community experience. If we begin to think of music in these terms, music therapy becomes a radical force and an opportunity for change in people's lives.

The term *health musicking* could be used to summarise how these changes might happen. We want to avoid being restricted to a mechanistic understanding of how music operates as a stimulus and take on the idea that music is a personal expression and, beyond that, to embrace social participation. We need to sensitise ourselves to the ecology of sound, self and social situation. The notion of *health musicking* suggests that participation in music serves a health agenda through careful appropriation of the elements that we have discussed in this chapter, in a social situation where we relate to other people and the negotiated purpose of the activity.[84]

We use music for a range of purposes but what matters in therapy depends on the values and needs in any given setting. Music enables change, but change can be problematic. We all develop and change our relationship to music throughout life and, in parallel, we all experience health challenges and setbacks. Chapters 4–8 will present music therapy practices from a lifespan perspective in the sequential contexts of child health, adolescent health, adult health and senior health.

83 Blacking (1973: 26).
84 See Stige (2002, 2012).

4   Music therapy and child health

The young child: sounds, rhythms and music

Interest in the early perception and use of sounds and music has been emerging from many fields over recent decades, including contributions from psychologists, musicians and musicologists, educationalists, sociologists, neurologists and neuroscientists. Developmental, cognitive, evolutionary and cultural profiles of music have been explored, and together these create a rich foundational resource for music therapists working with both children and adults. Some themes from these different fields are introduced here, with reviews of the literature provided as guides for further exploration.

We begin by noting that our sense of hearing is central in our prenatal experience of the world, with sounds beginning to be processed by the cochlea at 'around 20 weeks'.[1] In 1996 the psychobiologist Jean-Pierre Lecanuet reviewed the rich mix of *in utero* sounds. These include the maternal heartbeat, blood circulation and voice; the foetus's own heartbeats and rhythmic body movements; and external sounds, including music.[2] Musicologist Richard Parncutt echoed Lecanuet a decade later in two reviews, pointing out that these sounds are 'muffled' and that the sound of the mother's voice is primary. The pitch contour and higher pitches of voices seem more 'audible', possibly predicting the young infant's early attention to the mother's voice and sing-song speech. Parncutt notes connections between pre-birth patterns and those in the sound and musical experiences after birth.[3]

It is clear that 'infants do not begin life with a blank musical slate'.[4] Music psychologist Sandra Trehub and colleagues have carried out extensive research on the early responses of very young infants, noting their ability to recognise differences in pitch, intervals and particularly melodic contour, even when a melody is transposed.[5] Trehub reviews 'musical predispositions' for infants who

---

1 Parncutt (2009: 220).
2 Lecanuet (1996: 3–34).
3 Parncutt (2006: 1–31; 2009).
4 Trehub (2003: 13).
5 Trehub (2003, 2006).

'are tuned to consonant patterns, melodic as well as harmonic, and to metric rhythms'.[6] Such research seems to provide evidence for a biological template for music, but how we appreciate the differences between, for example, consonance and dissonance later in life also depends on our personal history and cultural context (enculturation).

When we turn to young infants' spontaneous sound-making, researchers have differentiated short sequences of pitch in their crying and early babbling. Psychiatrist Peter Ostwald and colleagues studied these early cries, observing a rising–falling pattern with maximum loudness at the peak. The loudness, pitch and duration of these early cries are closely influenced by factors such as pain, hunger and distress. Quieter humming and cooing sounds are often associated with feeding or other pleasurable experiences. Ostwald concluded that '[n]ewborn babies produce sounds that have melodic structures and rhythms which seem to be fixed by the neurophysiological and respiratory apparatus of the infant'.[7]

The time of the first smile elicits not only social but also vocal interaction from the caregivers. The baby begins to explore a variety of sounds, beginning with vowel sounds such as 'ah' and 'oo'. Songs and lullabies are natural experiences for young babies at this stage, often calming them, especially when combined with rocking. The baby also becomes increasingly interested in environmental sounds and those made by hands, feet or the baby's entire body. But note that during the first few months the newborn will react to sudden sounds with reflexive muscular contractions, the Moro reflex.

Is there a developmental sequence to a child's musical profile? In the 1970s the German music psychologist Helmut Moog developed a model of the musical experience of the pre-school child.[8] Moog observed children aged from 6 months to 6 years as they responded to pre-recorded tests. He noticed that young babies aged between 5 and 6 months would stop still and turn to the source of sound. Babies aged 6–12 months engage in babbling, and 'musical babbling' especially in response to music. Infants aged around 2 years imitate songs, or parts of songs. Young children of 2–3 can keep to a personal temporal framework, but not so much to music heard, and use snatches of learned melodies in spontaneous song-singing. As children move towards the age of 5 there is gradually more control and accuracy across the various musical elements.

A decade later, British music educationalists Keith Swanwick and June Tillman published *The Spiral of Musical Development*, based on Tillman's research. Tillman analysed compositions by children from age 3 upwards, evolving a sequence of musical development on the figuration of a spiral. This developmental sequence moves from an early focus on mastering the musical elements through sensory manipulation of the 'materials', to processes of imitation and expressive

---

6 Trehub (2003: 13–14).

7 Ostwald (1990: 11–27). See also Wermke and Meade (2009).

8 Moog (1976). Moog's observations are summarised in chapter 6 of John Sloboda's *The Musical Mind* (1985) and in chapters 3 and 4 of David Hargreaves's *The Developmental Psychology of Music* (1986).

imaginative play, to more awareness of musical form and symbolic understanding of the 'value' of a piece of music. This flexible spiral configuration presents a carefully constructed model for beginning to understand the musical gestures presented by children from both individual and social perspectives.[9]

Recent theories of human development tend to have more ecological orientations and to be critical of stage- and age-based theories. Accordingly, Moog's observations and parts of Swanwick and Tillman's model can be seen as rather linear, not placing enough importance on cultural and contextual factors. This view is shared by scholars such as music educationalist Pamela Burnard researching the nature of children's approaches to musical creativity.[10] We can, however, use these older constructs as tools for understanding of musical profiles as developmental. The stage- and age-based theories illuminate how musical profiles usually change over time as the child matures and has experiences typical of most children, at least within the cultural contexts that the authors of these models chose to study. Additionally, differences in access to education and technology might create variations in musical profiles. Some forms of musical engagement are more specific to some sub-groups than others, and there are also experiences that are unique to individuals (such as intense musical stimulation from other family members).

The theories described above mainly originate from traditions within psychology and education. In years to come, we will undoubtedly learn more about children's relationship to music, as new research explores the evolutionary roots of human musicality as well as the socio-cultural practices that nurture musical development. Contemporary approaches now include biological as well as sociological perspectives.[11] Two that have been particularly influential in music therapy are Malloch and Trevarthen's biopsychological study of infant communication and DeNora's sociological research on music in everyday life.[12] Developments in neuroimaging are furthering our understanding of how the perception and processing of the different elements of sound and music can occur across many parts of the brain.[13] And it will be interesting to observe how music therapists respond to the challenge addressed by music psychologist and educationalist Adam Ockelford: is detailed musicological analysis of improvised musical transactions feasible? Ockelford's approach to this is informed by his own 'zygonic theory', focusing on the way the elements of music repeat with some slight variation (*zygon* being Greek for 'yoke').[14]

Diverse as the above theoretical perspectives are, many of them share the focus that children's development of relationships to music are embedded in their

---

9 Swanwick and Tillman (1986).
10 Burnard (2006).
11 See McPherson (2006) for a compilation from various perspectives.
12 See Malloch and Trevarthen (2009) and the discussion later in this chapter; see DeNora (2000) and the discussion on music as a resource for action in Chapter 3 (p. 55).
13 See Peretz and Zatorre (2003) for a compilation of perspectives.
14 Ockelford (2013). For discussions of musical analysis within music therapy, see Lee (2000, 2003) and Wosch and Wigram (2007).

attempts to build relationships to the world. We now turn to a case example where some of these early patterns in a child's relationship to music can be observed, noting how a young child and her family members, specifically the primary caregiver, appropriate some of the early features of musical communication for use outside the music therapy setting.

Music therapy with a baby and her family: the story of Alex

During Alex's time *in utero* there was a history of maternal alcohol abuse, with the potential diagnostic label of 'foetal alcohol abuse syndrome' surrounding her birth.[15] During her first few weeks of life she became distressed on handling, making it difficult for her foster parents to form any close bond with her. She was referred at six weeks to the child development multidisciplinary team at the local hospital for a full assessment. The physiotherapist found that Alex had a high degree of muscle tension, particularly in her shoulders and upper arms, when she was handled. She continued to cry when being handled. The team began to be concerned that the alcohol abuse might have caused some brain damage affecting both physical and mental development, manifested in the early problems she had in moving her limbs freely. A series of physiotherapy exercises was introduced to help the foster-parents in their handling of Alex. She was referred to music therapy to see whether sounds could attract her interest and distract her from any discomfort caused by the movements.

Her foster-mother brought Alex to a combined music therapy and physiotherapy session when she was nearly 5 months old. A pair of beautiful Indian bells seemed to fascinate her. Something about these bells – the colour, shape, size or a sound that was different from the surrounding environment – clearly attracted her. She would turn to the source of the sound and stop crying. During the first few sessions the therapists began to use very simple combined techniques that were developmentally age-appropriate, such as:

- a simple vocal phrase to reflect movements from lying to supported sitting, a rising 'time to sit up', and falling 'time to lie down';
- instruments played across her field of vision, providing a focal point for her developing attention;
- a drum-based pulse to support specific movement patterns;
- the introduction to instruments, such as shakers, to reach out for and grasp;

15 For information, see www.fasaware.co.uk.

- the encouragement of 'listening' to short melodies played on a little pipe while being supported in a sitting position.

Sessions lasting up to twenty minutes occurred twice a week in these first few weeks of intervention. Her foster-mother would often bring her other children to the sessions. Increasingly, all members of the family were able to observe Alex's growing interest in, and curiosity about, the sounds. When she was aged 5 months it was clear that Alex attended to the bells and the sound of the music therapist's voice, and was able to accept direct handling by the physiotherapist, who commented that the music also helped her to relax, enabling her to work more effectively. The family began to take the simple musical ideas home to play together as part of family life.

In a video filmed when Alex was aged 6 months we see her turning to the bells on alternate sides when two pairs are played in sequence, one to her left and one to her right. She reaches out to touch the bells with both hands together in the mid-line position. She takes the bells and other instruments to her mouth to explore. She holds a pair of bright yellow shakers and moves them for a few seconds before releasing them from her grasp. She is curious about a skin-topped tambour (drum), exploring the instrument in all manner of ways, including scraping and then spontaneously tapping. Alex is particularly curious about another drum in the form of a wooden box, a 'tongue drum'. Various slits in the top of this hollowed-out box enable sounds of different but rather indiscriminate pitches to be played. What seems to attract her attention is waiting for this sound. The therapist lifts up the stick with the bright orange head and stops halfway down, whereupon Alex vocalises as if to indicate that she enjoys anticipating the sound. She giggles or vocalises again when the drum is played, but sometimes, if it is too sudden, will react with a Moro reflex. She vocalises much more during the rest of the session, particularly in response to short melodies played on the pipe. She vocalises in the gaps between the short phrases, as if to add her contribution to the music. A turn-taking dialogue is set up: pipe–Alex–pipe–Alex, and so on. The therapist plays a livelier phrase, which elicits movements from Alex: side to side, bouncing up and down, bottom shuffles and backward movements. The therapist then ends the session with a longer, quieter and slower melody, to which Alex appears to give full attention, with much eye contact and fewer movements.

The intervention continued with this intensity for a few more months, eventually reducing to one weekly session. Alex began to move quickly through developmental milestones; the initial concerns about possible brain damage were gradually discarded. She began to demonstrate age-appropriate behaviour in the sessions. Her range of movements and vocal sounds developed and she became increasingly exploratory and relaxed in the sessions as her trust in the therapy team developed. This emerging spontaneity in vocalising, moving and interacting was fundamentally influenced by the secure and loving environment provided by her now adoptive parents and family. By the time of her first birthday it was appropriate to withdraw the physiotherapy/music therapy input, seeing that she was developing so well. The team at the clinic suggested monitoring the situation at longer intervals, as is the case in any normal development. Future contact with the family indicated that Alex was functioning very well and the team learned later that at school Alex was developing into a sociable and popular young person.

Synchrony, communication, attachment and participation

On the development of 'communicative musicality'

The story of Alex, in spite of her early difficulties, is an example of a young baby using the patterned nature of sounds and music to seek out active ways to communicate with adults in the outside world. She demonstrated an innate biological predisposition to understand the world and to be understood, well before the first spoken word. Since the 1970s, enormous strides have been made by developmental psychologists and researchers from related disciplines in understanding the young infant's capacity to take an active part in these kinds of pre-verbal communication systems. The manner in which Alex moved and interacted rhythmically evolved into vocal turn-taking dialogues labelled by the anthropologist Mary Bateson as 'protoconversations'.[16] Psychologist William Condon and psychiatrist Lois Sander demonstrated evidence for the young infant's capacity not only for an inbuilt self-synchronisation of movements but also for an interactional synchrony with the patterns in an adult's movements, facial expressions and vocalisations.[17] As Alex's sessions progressed, it became possible to observe her own emerging self-synchrony and also how the music therapist was able to 'tune in' to the timing and patterns of Alex's movements, thereby encouraging more interactional synchrony.

Child psychiatrist Margaret Bullowa is one of several researchers who in the 1970s began to use musical terminology to describe the early interactional play between parent and child: 'Movement, sound and rhythm make up much of the common experience infant and parent bring to their meeting – patterns of synchrony

---

16 Bateson (1979: 65).
17 Condon and Sander (1974).

and potential patterns of counterpoint and syncopation.'[18] Synchronising patterns of movement within a musical frame with Alex seemed to help reduce her muscular tension, to encourage more movement and to be a motivating springboard for vocalisations to develop.

Two researchers who have had a significant impact on our understanding of the musical patterning and intersubjective exchanges central to the activities in Alex's story are psychobiologist Colwyn Trevarthen and musicologist Stephen Malloch. After listening to some of Trevarthen's recordings of young babies communicating with their mothers, Malloch developed the term 'communicative musicality' to label what he was hearing. He noted that this 'consists of the elements pulse, quality and narrative – those attributes of human communication, which are particularly exploited in music, that allow co-ordinated companionship to arise'.[19] In this context, 'pulse' defines how 'regular succession' of movements and vocal sounds move 'through time'; 'quality' relates to 'the modulated contours of expression moving through time'. When combined, 'pulse' and 'quality' form expressive 'narratives' over time, enabling the partners in the interaction 'to share a sense of sympathy and situated meaning'.[20] As observed in Alex's story, the interaction is very much two-way, both participants influencing each other so as to maintain contact through the subtle patterns within the ongoing relationship.

'Communicative musicality' stresses inborn and biological roots to communication. Trevarthen proposes that connections are made within the brain by the generation of an 'intrinsic motive pulse', our brains coming equipped both to detect and to reproduce patterns.[21] It is not surprising that music therapists have appropriated 'communicative musicality' as one theoretical underpinning for their work, as possibly observed with Alex and her emerging sense of self. It can also help in providing music therapists with a rationale to work developmentally, the patterned-based nature of the musical interactions providing platforms for future speech and language, and physical, cognitive and social development. As Malloch and Trevarthen point out, 'Music is much more than just "non-verbal" or "pre-verbal", and its use in therapy is based in the life-long human trait of creating companionship with another by structuring expressive time together.'[22]

Ansdell and Pavlicevic have considered the notion of 'musical repair' within 'communicative musicality' when the flow of the communication is impaired in some way. As they point out, music therapists can address this in two ways: 'The first involves "reading" human behaviour "as" music, and the second is to "translate" such a hearing into responsive musical improvisation'.[23] In a later chapter they indicate that 'communicative musicality' could be expanded to

---

18 Bullowa (1979: 71).
19 Malloch (1999–2000: 32). For details of the development of 'communicative musicality', see, for example, Malloch and Trevarthen (2009: 1–11).
20 Malloch and Trevarthen (2009: 4).
21 Trevarthen (1999).
22 Trevarthen and Malloch (2000: 14).
23 Ansdell and Pavlicevic (2005: 201).

incorporate wider social and cultural contexts, proposed as 'collaborative musicing'.[24] Perhaps we were observing both 'musical repair' and moves in a direction of 'collaborative musicing' in Alex's story, particularly given the extension into the family relationship beyond that between the child and music therapist.

On attachment theory and a brief note on holding and containing

John Bowlby was a psychiatrist, psychoanalyst and psychologist who in the 1950s started developing a body of work that has had considerable impact on the current understanding of human development of attachment from birth. The biological roots to attachment theory seem to echo 'communicative musicality' in the way the young infant seeks to sustain close proximity with the caregiver(s). According to this perspective, developing early healthy attachments is crucial for providing an internal template for evolving and assessing all future relationships in life. The child develops an 'internal working model' of what is hopefully a secure and safe attachment, enabling this internal point of reference to stay throughout life.[25] The developmental psychologist Mary Ainsworth collaborated with Bowlby and identified different kinds of attachments and styles of communication between the players in the interactions. Psychologist Inge Bretherton, reviewing the significant contributions of Bowlby and Ainsworth to the development of attachment theory, writes:

> If the attachment figure has acknowledged the infant's needs for comfort and protection while simultaneously respecting the infant's need for independent exploration of the environment, the child is likely to develop an internal working model of self as valued and reliable. Conversely, if the parent has frequently rejected the infant's bids for comfort or for exploration, the child is likely to construct an internal working model of self as unworthy or incompetent.[26]

We observed in Alex's story how the patterns within the musical interactions were used as building-blocks to establish over time a sense of security and trust within the developing therapeutic relationships. In this way the joint physiotherapy/music therapy experience could have provided a 'secure base', a notion drawn from attachment theory.[27] Without a sense of trust it is difficult for any therapeutic work to begin. Significantly in this example, these emergent processes were witnessed by Alex's foster-mother and members of her family. What was being developed in the music therapy transactions could then be translated into the growing

---

24 Pavlicevic and Ansdell (2009: 357–76).
25 Bowlby (1988). See Wallin (2007) for a comprehensive overview of attachment theory and how it can be applied in psychotherapy.
26 Bretherton (1992: 762).
27 Bowlby (1988).

attachment between mother and child. Music therapy was being used to facilitate the development of these bonds and of supporting healthy attachments. Clearly, Alex was appropriating the basic elements of sound and using them as part of her everyday life and interactions with her key caregivers.[28]

Edwards provides practical, theoretical and research-based underpinning for music therapists wanting to work with families, both in fostering healthy attachments and in repairing any breaks or disruptions in the relationships between parents and infants. Edwards notes that '[b]y providing a musical container, or skin, in which both the parent and infant can be held, music therapy can offer the dyad a chance to safely encounter and explore one another anew'.[29] Here Edwards introduces 'holding' and 'containing', common terms that have entered the music therapy lexicon but have their origins within the psychodynamic literature, as noted in Chapter 2 and, for example, in the writings of psychoanalysts Donald Winnicott and Wilfred Bion. The shapes and patterns of music can be analogous to a parent's supportive holding of the infant. In Alex's story there appeared to be something consistently reassuring and comforting in the way the various sounds and improvised music surrounded her, a kind of musical cocoon.[30]

The ecology of human participation

As the story of Alex reveals, the child's development takes place not only within the microsystem of the music therapy session but also within other systems, such as the family, school, local community. In Chapter 2 we discussed Bronfenbrenner's contribution to our understanding of the various contexts and systems that influence human development and can note how the approach to Alex's sessions bridged elements of what Bronfenbrenner refers to as both 'microsystems' and 'mesosystems'. The therapists worked within a developmental framework with Alex but it is interesting to note how some elements of a more social, transactional and ecological approach to practice were adopted almost intuitively. We also discussed in Chapter 2 the development of community music therapy as a broad movement within music therapy where ecological approaches take place.[31] We can see elements of working within these frameworks in Alex's story.

Music therapy contexts and related research: part one

Music therapy and very early intervention in hospital contexts

We noted at the start of the chapter the primacy of the sense of hearing before birth and the rich uterine sound environment. The young baby retains a memory of these

---

28 Note the inclusion of attachment not only to the mother but also to significant others.
29 Edwards (2011b: 16).
30 For further discussion, see Bunt and Hoskyns (2002: 39–41).
31 See, for example, Pavlicevic and Ansdell (2004), Stige *et al.* (2010), Stige and Aarø (2012) and Chapter 2.

experiences, particularly the sound of the mother's voice. Given the increased understanding of pre-birth experiences, coupled with growing awareness of the musical underpinning of the patterns in early parent–infant interactions, it is not surprising that there has been a growing specialism in music therapy within the intensive hospital environments taking care of premature and very young babies.

For example, in 2004 Monika Nöcker-Ribaupierre produced a collection of theoretical, clinical and research perspectives on music therapy for premature and newborn infants.[32] In one review chapter, Fred J. Schwartz cites, from a medical perspective, research evidence for the use of recorded music, particularly lullabies, to increase the baby's weight and reduce length of hospital stay and levels of stress.[33] In her own chapter, Nöcker-Ribaupierre describes how the relational processes in her music therapy approach extend the use of the mother's voice as a 'bridge' to foster closer engagement and the bonding and attachment between mother and her premature infant.[34] In another chapter, Helen Shoemark describes how she makes use of the full range of the elements of music in singing and being alongside the young baby, also considering the needs of the whole family.[35] She situates this approach within, among others, the frame of 'communicative musicality'.

Interestingly, Shoemark and Malloch have collaborated to examine links between 'communicative musicality' and Shoemark's hospital practice. The results of this study are promising, as the infants ('full-term and late pre-term') who had the music therapy intervention 'were better able to maintain self-regulation during social interaction with an adult, were less irritable and cried less, and were more positive in the response to adult handling, when compared with infants who did not receive the intervention'.[36]

Early intervention and working with carers or parents in community-based contexts

The context of the work with Alex during her early months, while working with the family, was still medically based, a multidisciplinary assessment unit. An example of a highly successful early intervention within a community-based context is the international Sing and Grow programme, which originated in Australia, where music therapists work to foster relationships between young children and their caregivers, while encouraging the children's development. Jan Nicholson and her colleagues have collaborated with Vicky Abad and Kate Williams, key leaders of this programme, in carrying out an extensive study

---

32 Nöcker-Ribaupierre (2004) and her case study in 2011.
33 Schwartz (2004).
34 Nöcker-Ribaupierre (2004). See also Robb (2003) for further discussion of music therapy in medical and hospital-based contexts.
35 Shoemark (2004). Musical elements were also the focus of a Spanish study in which binary rhythms were found to be particularly effective in producing 'respiratory synchronisation' for babies between 0 and 6 months in an intensive care unit; see Del Olmo *et al.* (2010).
36 Malloch *et al.* (2012: 386).

involving 358 parents and young children in the programme's ten-week cycles of group music therapy.[37] The children and adults taking part included children with disabilities, and families from areas of social disadvantage. 'Significant improvements were found for therapist-observed parent and child behaviors, and parent-reported irritable parenting, educational activities in the home, parent mental health and child communication and social play skills.'[38]

Alex was a vulnerable young baby who later was adopted by her foster-parents. Music therapy with vulnerable children and their parents, including those fostering or planning to adopt, is on the increase. This work is taking place in a range of community-based contexts, sometimes funded by charities. The literature describing this work is also growing; for example, see the chapters by Tiffany Drake and Colette E. Salkeld in Amelia Oldfield and Claire Flower's compilation of music therapy work with families. Drake's chapter focuses on working with vulnerable children in a charity-funded 'drop-in centre' and Salkeld's on how a family approach to music therapy can develop securer attachments with children who are adopted.[39]

Music therapy with a pre-school child: the story of M

Sometimes a music therapist is able to work with a young child during the formative pre-school years and in charting progress during an extended period. Such is the case of M, who attended music therapy between his third and fifth birthdays.

Referral and background

M was referred for music therapy by his speech and language therapist for problems with his expressive speech, fleeting interaction both with other children and adults, and a developing social isolation. His comprehension was within his age-range (he was 3), with a passive vocabulary well ahead of this. It had been difficult to test for his actual level of expressive speech.

M's mother's doubts about his hearing were confirmed by the diagnosis at 24 months of some hearing loss, resulting in grommets being inserted. M was then able to hear more clearly but his mother observed that there were no dramatic improvements in his communication or general behaviour. When M spoke, his speech was quiet, rapid and indistinct. He became upset and frustrated when he was not understood, which also caused him to withdraw more and isolate

---

37 Nicholson *et al.* (2008).
38 Ibid.: abstract.
39 Drake (2008); Salkeld (2008).

himself. By 3 he was reading and writing. His play was rather solitary and he appeared fascinated by mechanical objects. M was not socially very aware, apparently often quite shut off from events and people around him.

Music therapy assessment and first sessions

The setting for the music therapy sessions was a pleasant, airy room with a one-way observation mirror. Instruments included a piano, a free-stranding drum and cymbal, and other tuned and untuned percussion instruments stored on shelves.

The picture of M, as reported by his mother and from the referral, clearly presented itself in the first sessions. M made only fleeting contact with the instruments, seeming to be more interested in the way they were made than in their sound-producing potential. He would appear to be content to stay for an entire session exploring one instrument, for example taking the metal bars off a glockenspiel and putting them back on again, often also idiosyncratically naming the letters of the notes. He did not appear very aware of his mother or the therapist's presence in the room, walking directly past the adult with little eye contact. There were some fleeting moments of engagement and short bursts of joint instrumental activity, usually when M was initiating an idea. Occasionally he would imitate one of the therapist's musical gestures but he tended to cut himself off and withdraw more if there was too much encouragement to sustain joint musical play.

During one of M's moments of solitary play on a glockenspiel, the therapist spontaneously improvised some music to accompany and support his play. He hoped that the music would articulate and contain some of the feelings in the room: M's apparent need to withdraw from any sustained contact, the therapist's own feelings of not being able to provide the kind of musical stimulation to interest M, and his mother's feelings (aired after a previous session) that M was avoiding contact with the therapist. The resulting steady music, based in E minor, felt poignant, yet the upward phrases of the melody seemed expectant of future contact. The therapist sang M's name after a pause in the music and M turned from what he was doing and looked back towards him. M seemed aware of what was happening but perhaps was not ready yet to trust the therapist enough to share in any joint music-making. What then was called M's music, transcribed from the recording of the session, became a rich resource of ideas for variation and exploration in future sessions – a kind of musical calling-card or leitmotif for M.

It was clear that M needed a great deal of space, both physically and musically, with as little overt pressure from the therapist to play as possible. M began to feel more comfortable towards the end of the initial period of work and there were the first signs that musical interaction could become an area where much could be explored. Two examples illustrate this. The first was when his interest in mechanical objects was transferred into a musical activity. During one session M became fascinated by the clips on the piano's music-stand. The therapist took up his idea by playing the notes directly under each clip. M became very animated, repeated the two-note pattern on each note and bounced up and down in his chair. M had initiated this idea and seemed excited that the therapist had incorporated it into the joint activity. The second example was a floor-based activity using two tambours, one each for M and the therapist. An alternating musical game evolved: playing on the therapist's drum, playing on M's drum. Once this simple pattern had been established, the therapist paused before naming his drum, providing M with an opportunity to indicate the next turn. He indicated this by nodding, looking at the therapist and smiling – one of M's most direct communications to date.

Development of the relationship and early work

It was considered that regular music therapy might enable M to develop a relationship with an adult over a period of time and to begin to explore non-verbally some of his difficulties in communication. The first stage of this process involved building up various secure and predictable activities. M's apparent excitement in anticipating musical patterns and sequences led into structures using a variety of instruments: for example, alternating gestures on drum and cymbal; and imitative and turn-taking sequences on drum, cymbal and xylophone. He began to explore the musical parameters of fast/slow and soft/loud with increasing control, and confidence. M was able to sustain his attention for ever-longer bursts of activity. His sensitivity to changes in mood became more apparent, and active music-making would alternate with moments of reflective listening. It is hard to be sure whether a child is listening, but over a period of weeks it becomes possible to observe subtle changes in posture or mood as possible indications. For example, M would sometimes rest his sticks on the drum, look towards the therapist or play in a softer and more lyrical vein.

Three months of weekly sessions had occurred and a sense of trust was developing. The therapist incorporated M's musical ideas into their joint music-making and M began to take up some of the therapist's ideas. In effect M was beginning to tolerate more turn-taking and more playful exchanges of musical ideas. Some of these exchanges appeared to carry over from one week to the next. At the end of one session the therapist said 'Goodbye', whereupon M returned to the drum and produced a two-beat musical version of 'Goodbye'. A rhythmic exchange of short phrases began, sometimes soft, sometimes loud. The next week M went straight to the drum and began the session with a two-beat pattern that the therapist transformed into 'Hello', before engaging again in a similar rhythmic exchange as the week before. The music seemed to have provided a link from one session to the next.

M was becoming more engaged in the music and was demonstrating a highly imaginative use of the instruments. As the work moved into the fourth and fifth months he began to resist some of this contact, however. He would play for by far the greater part of the session before taking 'time out' by opting to sit in a chair in the corner of the room. The therapist would continue playing to him. This need to sit in his chair began to occur at earlier points during the next few sessions, moving closer to the start of the session. One week he entered the room crying, 'No music today', repeating 'No'. He needed much calming before any contact could be established, and during this session only tolerated some gentle singing. M appeared to still find it difficult to become too involved, in spite of a growing sense of confidence and trust in the music and therapist.

After these rather difficult sessions there was a return to less demanding musical activities, with more side-by-side playing on tuned percussion instruments. This appeared to reduce some of the upset and felt like a period of consolidation. M was about to start attending a local nursery and five joint sessions were arranged with another child and her music therapist to support this transition. The aim was to see whether M could tolerate more sharing and to develop social awareness by extending some of the turn-taking already achieved in the adult–child context. At first M seemed only to tolerate activities on his terms and of his choice. Gradually he began to respect some of the needs of the other child and respond to the more directive approach deliberately adopted by the adults. At times M would vocalise while playing, and often sing the melodic rhythm.

The middle stage of the work

After a three-month summer break M returned to a further period of individual work; it was now ten months after the initial referral. The main aim now was to consolidate reciprocal sharing in the activities. There was a balance between improvised music and more clearly structured activities. A song incorporating a part for M on a reed horn extended his interest in counting, with much enjoyment as different numbers of sounds were exchanged on the horn and piano. The music-making became more extended, with long piano dialogues and instrumental exchanges. There were moments of synchronous musical play and interactive antiphonal exchanges when M seemed to delight in setting up musical question-and-answer routines. Nowhere was this more clearly demonstrated than in one lengthy exchange at the keyboard where there was rich mutual interplay of musical ideas demonstrating flexibility and awareness of the rhythmic and melodic structures. Such an interaction was free of the tension and sense of isolation that had influenced the earlier music-making.

At around the time of his fourth birthday M brought along some of his soft-toy cats to a session, sharing their names. A song was created jointly over several weeks. M's words for each new verse would invite the cats on various excursions which the therapist would incorporate into a new verse for the next session. M would choose different instruments to represent the different cats and activities. This song not only helped him to imbue the instruments with a more representative and symbolic meaning but also provided opportunities for the development of musical memory and spontaneous talk. M had known the therapist for over a year and would now often enter the room talking. He could string together quite complex sentences, although his speech was still unclear at times and still tended to be rapid and quiet. M was also able to tell his mother what had happened during each session, since during this stage she would wait outside for him.

The final period

As he approached his fifth birthday M was preparing to start primary school. The music therapy continued with this balance of song-based and improvised music. Flexibility and resourcefulness were fundamental since some days M clearly wanted to improvise for the whole session. An example from near the end of the work demonstrates this flexible approach. The therapist had written a song about M's imminent move to the new school and as a preparation for the end of the music therapy. M did not want to play or hear this new song. Instead he asked for two cymbals and the drum, playing with loud sounds to a 'Goodbye' song, using the drum for the therapist's name and the cymbals for his own. During the ensuing weeks he used the same structure, once choosing to play a quiet ending and with apparent difficulty in leaving the room. He seemed to be working through his own way of bringing the work and therapeutic relationship to a natural ending.

Postscript

When M began school, the educational psychologist assessed his reading age at over 8, although there were still some communication difficulties and problems in socialising. It is clear that music therapy had been a medium in which M was able to find some positive self-achievement. He was able to learn several non-verbal coping strategies that he could use outside the sessions. For example, his nursery nurse provided an anecdotal account of M showing other children how to play the piano with one or two fingers rather than random banging of the keys.

His speech had developed over the period of intervention, and although there are the obvious maturational factors and outside influences such as the nursery school, it does seem possible that increased organisation and clarity in his music-making could have contributed to this development.

We are still left with a picture of a child with a complex range of needs, but music therapy had enabled M to find some outlet for expressing his feelings and exploring several areas of development. He was able to play for extended periods of time; there were fewer moments of isolated play, the music therapy being able both to support such moments and to extend them into more reciprocal and interactive activity.

Later, at his secondary school, M flourished academically but there were still some difficulties with socialising. His mother reported that he continued to be interested in music but had not taken part in any formal group music-making at his junior school. His early curiosity, observed so clearly in his music, translated into an interest in writing highly original stories. His mother provided an example of this early creativity, a poem M composed during the middle period of his music therapy:

> Today's over,
> The night climbed down from step to step.
> Oh Sunlight, talk to me.
> I am cold in the moon,
> I am cold and pale,
> Dim under evening star,
> Cold am I.
>
> Sadly the sun went down
> Till night dropped stars around.

This poem has provided much inspiration during music therapy trainings when students have taken it as a basis for an improvisation or original song. In this way M continues to inspire, his words being kept alive in these unique compositions.

Attunement and play

Within M's story there are many examples of music therapy methods for working with people throughout the lifespan, such as improvisation, songwriting, listening and verbal reflection. In this section we will focus on improvisation and explore how it can be understood as an exchange of feelings and as play when working with children.

Tuning in to the child

The establishment of non-verbal codes via, for example imitation, initiation and turn-taking, can help us understand some of the transactions within an interactive music therapy session. The sequence of musical gestures becomes part of the evolving history between the child and adult. The gestures are observed, listened to and attended to by the therapist. They potentially take on significant meaning that is shared and understood by both. This interactive history has an impact on each session, on every shared present moment of transaction within each session, and enables the participants in the music to influence and shape the immediate future.

If we look back on what happened during some of M's early sessions, it is clear that moments of any sustained interaction usually occurred if M initiated an idea and the therapist followed or imitated. There were only fleeting moments when M imitated any of the therapist's musical gestures. This parallels an early developmental process as a means of establishing contact, with the adult imitating the young infant prior to the infant imitating the adult.[40] There were also early instances when M's playing seemed rather isolated and the therapist played some sustained accompanying music to hold and reflect what was occurring.[41] But only rarely did the therapist mirror exactly or made a direct imitation of M's music. There was a choice of what and how to imitate: when M was improvising on the drum, the therapist would often support him on the piano by tuning in to the overall tempo. If M made changes to the loudness or tempo and this was quickly picked up by the therapist, then M could begin to realise that he was being heard and could influence the therapist's music. This all happened without recourse to verbal exchange. This is a kind of musical matching, a theme that has been developed by several music therapy writers, for example Wigram: 'To achieve a "match" in

---

40 Pawlby (1977: 203–24).
41 See chapter 4 in Wigram (2004) on improvisation that defines such methods as 'accompanying', 'holding' and 'reflecting'. Wigram also refers to Bruscia's (1987: 535–7) 'Sixty-four clinical techniques in improvisational music therapy'.

musical terms means that the therapist's music is not identical to the client's but is the same in style and quality.'[42]

But how can a therapist be sure that what lies behind a musical gesture is understood, getting behind the external sounds to make contact with the child's internal world of feelings? Here we can turn to Stern's notion of 'affect attunement'. In order for there to be a satisfactory 'intersubjective exchange' (a mutual exchange of feeling states) between child and adult, Stern considers that the adult needs to find some way of 'reading' the child's 'feeling state' from the external behaviour.[43] The adult then demonstrates some understanding of the child's behaviour by providing something that is more than an imitation of that behaviour yet bears some similarity to it, as in the therapist's matched piano-playing. (Note that there does not need to be a sharing of the same mode of activity.) The child then needs to 'read' this 'corresponding' adult behaviour as being connected to the child's original behaviour. This is a real attempt to connect with the child's feelings. In the example with M, this is a kind of 'musically based affect attunement', as Stern has noted when referring to Wigram's description of moments of 'matching' when improvising in music therapy.[44]

But to what kinds of feelings does the adult respond? Here Stern differentiates between 'categorical affects' and 'vitality affects'.[45] Categorical affects are the discrete human emotions, for example anger or joy. Pavlicevic explains vitality affects as 'the amodal dynamic, kinetic quality of our experiences . . . it is these which permit us to experience a perceptually unified world'.[46] Vitality affects ensure our experience of continuity through change, and, as Stern explains, they can be connected to qualities and processes such as 'surging', 'fading away,' 'fleeting', 'explosive', 'crescendo', 'decrescendo', 'bursting', 'drawn out', and so on.[47] Henk Smeijsters has proposed that there are deep analogous connections between Stern's internal 'vitality affects' and what is played out externally in musical improvisations.[48]

In his most recent (2010) text, Stern used the phrase 'dynamic forms of vitality' to encompass 'movement, time, force, space, and intention/directionality', which 'together give rise to the experience of vitality'.[49] In M's story it was clear how the therapist responded to M's shifting emotions by changing an approach, and yet also during sustained periods of musical engagement how the experience of vitality was lived, shared and played back to M through the process of attunement within musical forms.

---

42 Wigram (2004: 84).
43 Stern (1985/1998: 139).
44 Stern (2010: 139). It is interesting to note that in the introduction to the paperback edition of *The Interpersonal World of the Infant*, Stern comments on his 'pleasant surprise' that this original 1985 text provided 'a language useful to many psychotherapies that rely on the nonverbal' (1998: xv), and he included music therapy as part of the list.
45 Stern (1985/1998).
46 Pavlicevic (1997: 106–7).
47 Stern (1985/1998: 54). Note the use of musical terminology in this list of examples.
48 Smeijsters (2005).
49 Stern (2010: 4 and note 1:17).

The music therapy playground

In *Homo Ludens*, Johan Huizinga notes how 'music never leaves the play-sphere'.[50] Play in music can also be a means of exploring a whole range of feelings. In many ways a musical instrument can be regarded as taking on, to use Winnicott's terminology, the properties of a 'transitional object', bridging the gap between the inner and outer worlds of the child and between the child and another.[51] Alvin notes that instruments can be regarded as prolongations of the body through contact, for example, with hands or mouth, through which feelings of both protection and projection can be explored.[52] A child can look at, touch and even smell an instrument. The object/instrument can be charged with all manner of private feelings by the player yet also used as a means of communication with another person. The child can hear the sounds being immediately reflected back and also experience the play of the adult. The child can begin to explore all the boundaries between 'me' and 'not me', and 'self' and 'other'. Alvin used to comment how instruments resist action, however slight, and in so doing provide the player with a sense of mastery and control.

An instrument will not retaliate, music cannot be hurt; the child soon learns that music can sustain a vast range of feelings, even those destructive feelings too frightening to verbalise. Instruments are also consistent objects, which is an important factor when one is working with insecure children who may need that sense of sameness in their surroundings. Instruments can be invested with special qualities. They can take on specific characteristics or even become imaginary figures. And we can view not just the instruments as 'transitional objects' but music itself as one of Winnicott's 'transitional phenomena'.

In *Mirroring and Attunement*, psychoanalyst Kenneth Wright explores the ideas of Winnicott and Stern, in particular early processes in the mother's mirroring and reflecting back to the child (Winnicott) which emerge into 'her attuned enactments' that are analogous to her child's 'vitality affects'(Stern).[53] Like Stern, Wright uses language with musical connotations to develop his ideas. He chooses 'resonance' as a thread throughout his book, weaving connections between the many forms of non-verbal communication and the manner in which 'like resonates with like' in the way that people communicate intuitively with one another.[54] Wright views attunement as 'key' in 'understanding creativity', as, for example, 'it enlarges our conception of what it means to get something back in a transformed and enlivening way' and 'reveals the structure of such an interaction'.[55]

Play is a central term in music therapy theory. Kenny writes about the 'field of play' and Karette Stensæth relates play to 'musical answerability' and a theory

50 Huizinga (1955: 158).
51 Winnicott (1971: 1–30).
52 Alvin (1977: 7–13); and see chapter 11, 'Playing with Winnicott's reality', in Pavlicevic (1997).
53 Wright (2009: 137).
54 Ibid.: 7.
55 Ibid.: 68. Wright also refers to Bion's writings on how the mother 'contains' the projected feelings of her child and gives them back in more manageable form; see, for example, Bion (1962).

of action.[56] Stige argues that play should be understood not only as a vehicle for expression and exploration of inner processes but also as exploration of the world. Play could then be understood as a context in which children investigate the practices that they observe around them, again not through strict imitation but as improvised participation in aspects of cultural 'scripts'.[57] The playground is open for creative exploration of how the microsystem at the heart of a musical transaction within music therapy bridges and nests in the surrounding social and cultural patterns (macrosystem), a biopsychosocial investigation integrating both nature and nurture. What are the connections, for example, between the work of Bronfenbrenner and that of Stern? There are further challenges when seeing how such biopsychosocial perspectives overlap with current work in neuroscience, for example in the exploration of mirror neurons.[58]

Music therapy contexts and related research: part two

In this section we will continue the description of various areas of practice, including related research studies. We will start with music therapy in pre-school and school settings for children with special needs and continue with the development of research in more differentiated areas.

Music therapy in pre-school and school settings for children with special needs

Bunt's early research focused on contexts in which music therapy had a history of effective practice: pre-school and school-aged children with a range of physical and learning disabilities.[59] Two observational studies used video analysis to compare pre- and post-scores for children (up to the age of 12) moving through equal-length periods of music therapy and no music therapy (a cross-over design). In both projects time and frequency measures were used to record changes in the frequency, mean length and time spent in five areas: making the instrument sound (a measure of playing time); vocalising; looking at the instrument; looking at the adult; and looking away.[60]

In the first study, eighteen pre-school children were divided into two groups, individually matched for chronological and developmental age, gender and condition. All children took part in twelve-week blocks of individual music therapy and no music therapy. Significant differences were found across all the

---

56 Kenny (1989, 2006); Stensæth (2008).
57 Stige (2002: 32–3).
58 Overy and Molnar-Szakacs (2009) explore the implications of mirror neurons for music therapy within their model 'Shared Affective Motor Experience' (SAME).
59 This research was funded by the Music Therapy Charity.
60 See Bunt (1985; 1994: chapter 5). Note that references from ethology (the direct observation and description of behaviour in naturalistic settings) were used to underpin the methodology.

five measures when the children's play using five small percussion instruments was analysed. The vocalisation measure produced the most significant changes across all the instruments. There was a longer engagement with the instruments at the end of the music therapy period. Music therapy appeared able to reduce the amount of looking away and increase the amount of looking at the instrument and the therapist. The tentative conclusion was that a period of music therapy (even as short as twelve weeks) created changes within these measures that were not so apparent in a period without music therapy.[61]

In the second study, filmed individual play sessions with the child's teacher or teaching assistant were used as a further control. Here a different eighteen children from three different departments of one school were allocated randomly to two groups (average age 7½, with none of the children having any recognisable speech). In this study each block of sessions lasted for half the school year. There was a replication of the increase in vocalisations in this longer study, with very significant differences in the amount of vocal activity between music therapy, play and no music therapy. The music therapy effected changes. This second study introduced a more qualitative analysis, where there were significant differences in the amount of adult support and direction when the two settings (music therapy and play) were compared. A main result was a very significant level of turn-taking occurring in the music therapy. There were further increases within music therapy in the 'child's imitative skills and ability to initiate an activity', and looking in the direction of the adult.[62]

Music therapy and children with communication difficulties and developmental delay

Analysis of turn-taking was also part of Ulla Holck's doctoral study, which placed this kind of interplay in music therapy for children with communication difficulties within the theoretical frameworks both of parent–infant interaction and of conversation analysis.[63] In addition to analysing how turns were negotiated in antiphonal musical play, Holck noted similar features such as pausing and 'turn-yielding' when the child and therapist engaged in simultaneous or synchronous play. Thinking of the case examples, such moments of simultaneous engagement and more antiphonal interchange were beginning to take place in Alex's sessions. Negotiating a balance between moments of shared play and more interactive activity was also a feature of the sessions with M, where therapist and child worked towards developing an equal partnership in the sharing of leadership roles in the music, taking turns both to initiate and to imitate musical ideas.

61 Ibid.
62 Bunt (2003: 187).
63 Holck (2004: 45–54).

Children on the autistic spectrum

In 2006 Oldfield published two interlinked texts that included case studies, discussion about her approach to the work, the results of a research study on the impact of music therapy for children on the autistic spectrum, and a chapter relating to the evolution of a music therapy development assessment tool.[64] Her research focused on the progress of a small sample of ten children on the autistic spectrum referred for music therapy and who attended with their parents. A research assistant analysed the video films for initiation, playing an instrument, vocalising and for connections to each child's aims for therapy. Oldfield also interviewed the parents and reviewed her music therapy reports. Overall, Oldfield concluded that the findings were positive, particularly regarding the way the parents responded to the intervention.

In the same year as Oldfield's publications, Christian Gold and his colleagues published the meta-analysis 'Music therapy for autistic spectrum disorder' for the Cochrane Collaboration, very much regarded as the 'gold standard' for indicating evidence of effective practice.[65] This kind of meta-analysis combines results from existing studies to identify patterns among study results, such as the size of the effect, more precisely than can be derived within a single study.[66] In a Cochrane review the studies analysed are all randomised controlled trials (RCTs), which seek to overcome problems of generalisation by studying a large number of participants who are allocated randomly to either an intervention arm or a control arm. Systematic differences in outcome, as indicated by pre-selected measures, are then examined statistically.

This particular review highlighted three studies with children where a week of daily music therapy sessions indicated that this 'was superior to "placebo" therapy with respect to verbal and gestural communicative skills, but it was uncertain whether there was an effect on behavioural outcomes'.[67] More research was recommended, as was the use of larger samples so that the results could be beneficial for practice.

Jinah Kim conducted a small-scale randomised control trial (ten children with autism) which was not completed at the time of the Cochrane Review. She found 'significant evidence supporting the value of music therapy in promoting social, emotional and motivational development in children with autism', three areas in which these children are prone to difficulty.[68] Kim's research adds to this growing

---

64 See Oldfield (2006a: chapter 7) for a description of her research study and (2006b: chapter 7) for information about her Music Therapy Diagnostic Assessment Tool. Karin Schumacher and Claudine Calvet-Kruppa (1999) have produced an analytical system to evaluate the quality of the music therapy relationship in music therapy that can be used for children on the autistic spectrum. The scale ranges from no contact with the instruments, through some fleeting moments of connection to the instrument and then the therapist, to joint activity. Wigram and Gold (2006) have also published on issues relating to the assessment of children on the autistic spectrum.
65 Gold *et al.* (2006).
66 The notion of 'effect size' is explained by Gold (2004).
67 Ibid.: summary.
68 Kim *et al.* (2009: 389). See also Whipple's (2012) meta-analysis and Simpson and Keen's (2011) narrative review.

body of descriptive and evidence-based research but larger collaborative studies are still needed. At the time of writing, Gold is leading a large, international randomised controlled trial on music therapy and autism called TIME-A, with many children, therapists and different sites across different countries.[69]

Music therapists can increasingly point to a range of social, psychological and neurological perspectives to underpin practice with children on the autistic spectrum.[70] Istvan Molnar-Szakacs and Pamela Heaton reported on research which indicates that children on the autistic spectrum not only appear to privilege attention to music but also have the ability to categorise a range of emotions perceived in both music and expressive speech.[71] Given such predilection for music, how then can musical exploration and indirect communication via the instruments lead to more direct social interactions, particularly given the autistic child's apparent difficulty in holding another person's perspective in mind?[72] More is also being understood on the role of the limbic system, particularly the amygdala, in regulating our emotional responses to music and how this correlates with growing research into neural mechanisms within the brains of autistic children and adults.[73] Finally, given that the sensitive autistic child can be prone to sensory over-arousal, it seems appropriate for music therapists to be exploring how music can act as a means of sensory regulation and integration, the approach adopted by, for example, Dorita Berger.[74]

Concluding points

In this first of four practice-based chapters we have used two case narratives as the basis for some theoretical and research-based reflections from within both music therapy and related disciplines. Alex's story led us to explore early innate responses to the interactive potential of music as a template for future development, particularly using the concept of 'communicative musicality'. Her story did not just focus on sessions in the clinic but was contextualised in using music to develop attachments to her primary caregivers. We noted these processes at work in some of the further reviews of practice when working with young babies in hospital and community-based contexts.

M's story demonstrated how the range of music therapy approaches over an extended period of time can enable a young child, once trust has been established, to explore different ways to communicate and thereby gain some more confidence and sense of self during these crucial pre-school years. As well as being M's journey it was a joint process. The accompanying music therapist was required to

---

69 See the website of TIME-A for information on project, team, events, publications and so on: http://helse.uni.no/default.aspx?site=48&lg=2.
70 See Kern (2012) and Dimitriadis and Smeijsters (2011).
71 Molnar-Szakacs and Heaton (2012).
72 See Baron-Cohen *et al.* (1993) for information on 'theory of mind'.
73 See, for example, Hill and Frith (2003) and Koelsch *et al.* (2006).
74 Berger (2002).

tune in and adapt to meet M's needs at various stages of the therapy – very much a negotiated series of transactions developed over time.

Our selection of areas of practice has been limited by lack of space. We note the important growth of work in children's hospices and mainstream schools, with refugees and in areas of conflict and sexual abuse, for example.[75] Growth in these areas necessitates a great deal of flexibility on the part of the music therapist, working in different settings and with different approaches. Here the focus might be on such perspectives as inclusion and health promotion. Some of these issues will be discussed in the following chapter on music therapy for the adolescent.

75 See, for example, Bunt (2003), Carr and Wigram (2009), Pavlicevic (2005), Strehlow (2009) and Sutton (2002b).

5   Music therapy and adolescent health

Young, wild and free? Adolescents and music

Adults often remember their adolescence quite vividly as a time of discovery and adventure, sometimes coupled with despair and dejection. Many would argue that adolescence, more than anything else, is an energetic and troublesome search for identity. Thinking it over, perhaps what we remember is the intensity. Music most probably was a part of it. It is not uncommon to claim that music is especially important in adolescence and that there is a unique passion that characterises young people's relationship to music, as listeners and often also as songwriters and performers.

The word 'adolescence' originates from the present participle of the Latin verb *adolescere*: to grow up. Interestingly, the word 'adult' has the same root; it originates from the past participle of this verb. It is surprising for many to realise that the idea of adolescence as a specific period between childhood and adulthood is a relatively new one. The alternative view that after childhood comes adulthood still prevails in some cultures.[1] Demos and Demos, a historian and a psychologist, examined a broad range of texts written between 1800 and 1875 and found almost no usage of the word and only a limited degree of concern with young age as a specific life period with particular behaviours.[2] However, G. Stanley Hall, one of the pioneers of American psychology, made adolescence the focus of a new branch of study. In 1904 he published a tome with the telling title *Adolescence: Its Psychology and Relations to Physiology, Anthropology, Sociology, Sex, Crime, Religion and Education*. It was an enormous work in two volumes, broad in scope and rich in ideas, including a few reflections on music. Hall was obviously sensitive to the significance of music to human development and argued that 'music plays on the whole gamut of our emotional life'.[3] He also highlighted the

---

1 It is not easy to define adolescence in a precise way. Some relate it to puberty, others to the division created by the teenage years, yet others to the social role in between protected childhood and responsible adulthood. However, both the 'biomarker' of puberty and the social roles of young people differ across time and cultures; see Hendry and Kloep (2012). We therefore use 'adolescence' as a sensitising notion, not as an exact concept.
2 Demos and Demos (1969).
3 Hall (1904: 185).

idea that adolescence is a period in life when people are especially sensitive to music:

> Music, which may have been cultivated much before, now comes to mean unutterable things and acquires a new interest. Very often discords too become painful to an unwonted degree, and if war, love, and religion be the three factors that have cadenced the soul to the rhythm out of which music was born, this is what we should expect at this age, when the instincts which underlie all three are so greatly reenforced. Most of these new manifestations are transient in those who do not develop great musical power, but even in these they are often well unfolded for a time.[4]

Hall's work on adolescence evoked a broad popular response, obviously resonating in its time. The 'discovery of adolescence' can be related to broad changes in American life in the early twentieth century, especially changes in the structure of the family related to the new urban and industrial order.[5] Hall generalised on the basis of the changes he saw around him and claimed that adolescence is characterised by 'storm and stress' (note the similarity with the proto-Romantic notion of *Sturm und Drang*). Young people are not only much more moody than other people, but also wilder and more reckless, he argued. This idea has so permeated popular culture that many of us take it for granted. But is it accurate?

Most researchers argue today that Hall's idea of adolescence as a time of 'storm and stress' for the majority is somewhat distorted and biased. In a review of contemporary research, psychologists Hendry and Kloep found that adolescence-specific antisocial behaviour is not particularly common. Many people never develop such behaviours, while those who do might maintain them throughout the life-course. In the United Kingdom today, only 20–25 per cent are law-breakers as adolescents and they then become law-abiding adults. These researchers also note that the statistics relating to crimes are flawed: small offences not so uncommon among adolescents are in the statistics, while environmental destruction and ethnic cleansing – much more likely to be performed by adults – are not.[6]

Young people have substantial developmental challenges to deal with, but adolescence is no more filled with conflicts, depressions or risk-taking than later phases of life. Certainly mental health issues increase in adolescence compared to childhood but they do not decrease again in adulthood.[7] Most people handle the challenges of development in adolescence. As in any other phase of life, problems typically emerge if we have to handle too many issues at the same time. An overload of concurrent developmental challenges can convert them to risks.[8]

4 Ibid: 23.
5 Demos and Demos (1969).
6 Hendry and Kloep (2012: 36–57).
7 Ibid.: 47.
8 Hendry and Kloep (2012).

One reason why we should care about all of this is that myths about adolescence might lead to negative stereotyping of young people. If we expect young people to be reckless, we might contribute to conditions that increase the possibility for irresponsible behaviours. This is especially important in some contexts of practice. As Viggo Krüger has noted, young people under the care of child welfare[9] often feel that they are stigmatised because they are in care.[10] If the stigma of being 'young, wild and reckless' is added, it hardly helps. As Krüger's work illustrates, there is a risk, then, that adolescents will be 'demonised' and the social mechanisms that contribute to their situation 'minimised'.

While Hall exaggerated how young people are different from other people, perhaps he was right in suggesting that adolescence is a period in life when people are sensitised to music in a new way? If so, how could young people use music as a resource? On the basis of previous research in music psychology, sociology, media research and music therapy, music psychologist Suvi Laiho (now Saarikallio) has developed a theoretical categorisation of how music supports adolescents' psychosocial development. She suggests that adolescents use music in the four developmental areas of interpersonal relationships, identity, agency and emotions:

> The categories are considered from the perspective of the developmental tasks of adolescence. They represent different areas of psychological goals or functions that are central to adolescent development and mental health and can be supported by musical activity. The first category, interpersonal relationships, includes experiences of belonging and privacy. The category of identity deals with the possibilities of music to promote the reformulation and strengthening of identity and conception of self. Agency is related to control, competency, achievement, and self-esteem. The last category, emotional field, considers the diverse mood- and emotion-related functions of music. The psychological functioning of an individual is a highly complex phenomenon in which several processes are interlinked. The four psychological functions presented in the model are most likely to be interconnected. Indeed, the structure of the model is a triangle in which all the functions could be linked with each other. The emotional functions are situated in the center because they have been shown in several studies to be the most important reasons for engaging in musical activities.[11]

In an article on the use and functions of music in a lifespan perspective, Saarikallio suggests that similar strategies are employed from adolescence through to adulthood, including older adulthood, but perhaps especially intensively during adolescence and then again in a new way among older adults.[12] Several other

---

9 In some countries, terms such as 'child protection' or 'child protective services' are used.
10 Krüger (2012).
11 Laiho (2004: 51–2).
12 Saarikallio (2011).

researchers have added to our understanding of how important music is for many adolescents.[13]

Increased amounts of leisure time and access to advanced technology have contributed to music's significance as a resource for young people. Mostly, positive outcomes have been described in the literature. In summarising the literature, McFerran has introduced the metaphors of 'mirror' and 'stage' to suggest two of the functions music can have for adolescents: reflective functions and performative functions. These functions are intertwined in multiple ways and they could both be said to relate to identity development.[14]

The area of 'problem music' also deserves attention. There are many popular songs that deal with crime, sex and drugs in ways that make adults worry about the effects on young people.[15] But is 'problem music' a helpful term? Whether we are young or old, we are never passive recipients of the effects of music. Problematic use of music in a specific context rather than the idea of problematic music might be what we need to explore. Research suggests that some young people at risk also risk using music destructively, in ways that do not help them cope with their emotional and relational challenges.[16] Should we, then, turn to censorship of the music used in this way? Tsvia Horesh explains that in some rehabilitation centres for young people with drug addictions, censorship of music linked to rituals of drug abuse is common. She argues that not enough attention is paid to how integral music may be to the identity of the person. After drug rehabilitation young people often return to their own music and risk triggering drug abuse again.[17] In contemporary music therapy the idea of censorship has been challenged. Instead, reflective awareness and creative appropriation of young people's music are encouraged.[18]

The practice of music therapy with adolescents

The most comprehensive discussion of music therapy with adolescents is developed by McFerran in her book *Adolescents, Music and Music Therapy*. On the basis of a review of the existing literature (in English) on music therapy with young people, she gives an overview of the practice of music therapy with adolescents. We shall briefly summarise and comment here upon some of her findings.[19]

Teenagers spend much of their time in educational contexts but McFerran's analysis of the literature reveals that only 21 per cent of the published articles

---

13 Behne (1997); Bossius and Lilliestam (2011); Miranda and Claes (2009); North *et al.* (2000); Saarikallio and Erkkilä (2007).
14 McFerran (2012).
15 North and Hargreaves (2009).
16 McFerran and Saarikallio (in press).
17 Horesh (2010).
18 Hadley and Yancy (2012).
19 A total of 140 texts published between 1970 and 2010 (almost 50 per cent of them after 2000) were reviewed. For further details, see McFerran (2010: 25–47).

discuss music therapy in school settings. The majority of music therapy work still takes place with young people who are institutionalised in hospitals, inpatient mental health institutions, residential settings or hospices (51 per cent). When examining the theoretical orientations of the music therapists, McFerran finds that a psychodynamic orientation is most common (37 per cent of the 140 texts reviewed). Behavioural approaches are not as strongly represented (9 per cent), while humanistic and developmental approaches together are represented in 31 per cent of the texts.[20] For a substantial number of texts (23 per cent) McFerran argues that the theoretical orientation is unclear.

When it comes to how music is used in sessions, the review identifies four main groups of methods: musical games; use of live songs (choosing, playing and writing); improvisation (with instruments or with voice); and use of pre-recorded music (listening, discussing and relaxing).[21] Most music therapists use more than one method. Combinations of songs and improvisation are most common. McFerran underlines, however, that classification of methods is extremely complex because authors focus on different aspects of an activity. Definitions also vary with orientation:

> For those identifying with a psychodynamic approach, improvisation provides material for interpretation and projection of unconscious drives. From a humanistic perspective, it provides opportunities for success because it is not possible to play a 'wrong' note and therefore complete acceptance is guaranteed. The use of improvisation by a behaviouralist is based on opportunities to play freely that have been earned through other achievements. It is clear that the definition of improvisation used by each of these practitioners would vary.[22]

McFerran explains that musical groups are not described very frequently in the material; the literature reflects an emphasis on individual work. She regards this as surprising, given the importance of peer relationships to young people. As she suggests, this tendency might reflect the fact that a majority of the texts describe practice with institutionalised adolescents.

McFerran also examines the different conditions that challenge the adolescents in the literature reviewed. She found that it was possible to discern five main categories: young people with physical illness,[23] mental illness, disability, emotional and behavioural problems, and teenagers 'at risk'. As with the other categorisations in the review, there were challenges related to differences in the use of language:

---

20 These were the three categories used in McFerran's text. Music-centred approaches, for instance, were subsumed under humanistic approaches.
21 In Chapter 1 we discussed different types of 'activity' in music therapy. Here we employ the term 'method', which is used by McFerran and several other music therapists in the Australian and American traditions.
22 McFerran (2010: 36).
23 McFerran uses the term 'illness' here as a general term for ill health, disease or disorder but the term is sometimes used to refer to the subjective experience of ill health (see Chapter 7).

Different groups of professionals also perceive more or less value in the use of labels such as diagnosis – for some they are a useful tool in providing access to the most helpful services, for others they reduce the individual to a code and fail to account for the unique variations experiences by that person, not to mention his or her family, cultural and historical context.[24]

When reviewing the purpose of the music therapy, McFerran finds that few of the texts focus on a plan using specific assessment, treatment and evaluation strategies.[25] Case studies with descriptive outcome are more typical. McFerran examined the goals, outcomes and intentions described in the articles and found that many music therapists of all orientations focus on goals related to self-understanding and relationships with others:

> Further cementing the centrality of social and identity driven goals is the fact that this was evenly spread across the different client groups – being the first and second most common goal across each categorization of the conditions challenging teenagers, except those with disability, where physical and cognitive goals were described as equally important.[26]

In concluding her review, McFerran makes a number of comments. As an example, she notes that 'enhancing resilience' is only occasionally referred to as a goal in the music therapy literature. In the broader literature on adolescent development, music has consistently been identified as a resource for coping, so McFerran suggests that this aspect might be more significant than music therapists have considered so far. She also notes that the literature presents a very conventional model of practice.

Like McFerran, we think that there is considerable room for development of contemporary music therapy practices with young people, given the current interdisciplinary literature which stresses resilience and resources, inclusion and community participation. We also agree with McFerran's assertion that there is much value in the conventional practices described when helping young people deal with their emotional and relational challenges. In addition, conventional approaches to music therapy can be extended to include work with social resources and community connections. We will elaborate on this theme by visiting in some detail the music therapy process of Gregorio, who came to music therapy after being referred to an institution for young people affected by serious mental health issues.

---

24 McFerran (2010: 38–9).
25 McFerran is here referring to the music therapy treatment plan as outlined in standards of clinical practice in some countries (see Chapter 8).
26 McFerran (2010: 41).

Gregorio's process in music therapy: the first phase[27]

The setting for the initial stages of this narrative is a semi-residential centre in Italy which addresses the needs of adolescents affected by serious psychopathological disorders. The multidisciplinary team, including psychiatrists, educators[28] and a music therapist, aims to improve the adolescents' clinical conditions and promote individual abilities and autonomy. Gregorio was 17 when he first came to the centre. He was diagnosed as having a schizoid personality disorder with the risk of early-onset schizophrenia.[29]

A year earlier, Gregorio had started to have difficulties at school, gradually isolating himself. Difficulties in studying and concentrating increased to the point where he stopped attending school. He started to spend most of his time at home, playing the guitar. He was self-taught on the instrument and played alone, often until his fingers bled. Moments of delusion began to surface when Gregorio announced that he was the 'prophet' and that some of his schoolfellows were his 'disciples'. He had been referred to the centre because he was reluctant to accept any kind of therapy, medication or psychological testing.

The team aimed to help Gregorio to establish relationships with people of his own age and adults through therapeutic, educational and social activities. When the team members first met Gregorio they were struck by both his intelligence and his composure. His choice of words was very correct and precise. He spoke in a torrent of words expressing complicated lines of reasoning that appeared rather disconnected from the language used commonly by his peer group. For example, he said at the time, 'I always live in the present; I do not know the future, I no longer have the past; the first bothers me because in it everything is possible, the second because in it nothing is real.'

The first phase of music therapy lasted about six months, with 'music as a rescue' and 'I am only my music' as central themes, as described by his music therapist. At the first meetings with the therapist, some months after Gregorio came to the centre, he talked about his musical tastes. Some were very specific and surprising, such as Schoenberg's dodecaphony, even though Gregorio never listened to

---

27 We are grateful to Italian music therapy colleague Barbara Zanchi and to 'Gregorio' for permission to use this case study, which was first presented at the Tenth World Congress of Music Therapy, held in Oxford in 2002. A fuller version of the case study with theoretical underpinnings is published in the conference proceedings; see Zanchi (2002).

28 In Italy these professionals work in health and social care settings with a psycho-educational approach.

29 The diagnosis was based on definitions from DSM–IV.

any of his music. Gregorio spoke using complex language about the dissolution of tonality and form and of the relationship between consonance and dissonance.

Like most teenagers, Gregorio listened to a lot of music, generally rock songs with English lyrics. For a short time he had set up a band with two other boys. He played guitar and, with another friend, wrote the music and the lyrics, again all in English, which he wrote and spoke to a high standard. He was fascinated by Kurt Cobain, the leader of the rock band Nirvana, whose suicide Gregorio felt was the inevitable and coherent conclusion of an existential and creative process. Cobain seemed to represent for him something more than an adolescent myth. His character and music were a stylistic expression of Gregorio's difficult search for identity: 'Is living', he seemed to ask, 'going beyond the limit, dissolving all that has been before?' At the beginning of his music therapy journey, this was less of a question than a statement, repeated in many ways. It was frightening for all the people who met him, and probably also for himself.

He had been at the centre for about a year when, during a difficult time for his family, he told the team he wanted to stop attending. His words had 'run out' and nobody could do anything for him. He hoped that his sister could escape from their family by his parents divorcing, whereas he could only do the same by dying. During this difficult moment, music seemed to come to Gregorio's rescue. This was music not spoken about, but listened to with other people, a shared experience. The music was Beethoven's Piano Sonata no. 32, Op. 111. Gregorio had previously spoken of this music as described in Thomas Mann's *Doctor Faustus*, a book he had suggested his educator read. Gregorio was invited to meet his educator once more to listen to the Beethoven sonata together and then to decide whether he wanted to continue attending or not. Gregorio accepted this invitation. When asked whether he wanted to listen to the music, he answered that he had come for that very reason. Gregorio and his educator listened to the Beethoven sonata in a kind of reverent silence. Gregorio found the experience quite difficult but agreed to meet again to listen to the same music, this time with the music therapist, who helped him to follow the score. The music therapist and the educator agreed to collaborate in working with Gregorio.

The next session was the first of a series of listening sessions by Gregorio, the music therapist and the educator. This was the first time Gregorio brought some of his own CDs. The first track he proposed was 'Tourette's' by Nirvana, a very fast and short piece made up of almost incomprehensible cries and seemingly senseless words. He emphasised that it was the only track of the CD that had no (traditional) lyrics and said it communicated something between pain, anger and desperation.

The second track was 'Paranoid Android' by Radiohead, listened to with great intensity for its six minutes' duration. Listening to it again and again, Gregorio said it was a very difficult song, divided into two parts: 'The first one is harder; the second one is more inner and melodic.' His remarks were centred on musical form and he asked for specific technical information, which the music therapist tried to give. On listening again to this track and others by Radiohead, Gregorio described some melodies emerging from a series of descending progressions as 'sad'. The conversation had moved on to the emotions that music can evoke. The music and the discussion reminded the music therapist of some modal progressions, which she demonstrated on a keyboard while the music continued in the background. Gregorio then seemed compelled to play a series of notes on the keyboard, trying to reproduce the piece in the background. The experience left him speechless, resulting in a long silence and some sustained eye contact.

Gregorio continued to speak about modal music, saying that it dimly reminded him of music for children. The therapist empathised by playing some modal-based songs for children. A feeling of ease ensued, with Gregorio's speech becoming less rapid and jerky. At the end of this session he suggested a further meeting so as to listen to the other pieces he had brought. He also mentioned to the educator that nursery rhymes were often suitable even for adults. He added that he would like to write so simply; he would no longer try to correct his stories.

In the next two sessions Gregorio listened to more Nirvana: 'Love Buzz' and 'All Apologies'. He now felt that Kurt Cobain's character seemed less marvellous and his suicide less mythical. Gregorio spoke of the value of life versus death and of 'company' versus 'tedious loneliness'. He spoke of people's expectations and the difficulty of change: 'The others always expect you to do the same things, so, when you change, they don't accept it, even though it is a change for the better.' He mentioned that his band had won the chance to use a recording studio for three days. They planned to make a demo, which Gregorio offered to bring to the session after the summer break. After listening to some more songs by the Beatles and Radiohead, Gregorio concluded with a question: 'Is it possible for me to create something intelligent and deep, but also cheerful and less sad than the music I have listened to up to now?'

Gregorio's process in music therapy: the second phase

The second phase of Gregorio's music therapy process lasted about a year, with 'the presence of the other', 'dialogue' and 'the search for different ways of being in the music' as central themes described by his therapist. As promised, Gregorio returned after the summer break with a demo of pieces composed by him and his band. For the next two months the educator continued to be present in the music therapy sessions. which were centred on shared listening to his songs.

This sub-phase contained a series of core themes emerging from pairs of opposites. The first pair was words versus music, highlighted by the songs created by Gregorio and his band. In the English lyrics Gregorio appeared to intend to break the rules of the narrative flow of speech, which he scrupulously respected in Italian, and to follow an ono-matopoeic and evocative 'stream of consciousness'. He insisted on reading the lyrics, such as 'Mr Prophet':

'Hey Mr Prophet, wozzup? Get up! Was wondering if you have seen a little rabbit crunchin' a carrot near the sea?'
'I don't know! I've brought my beard right there! Was sleeping when an apple fell from a tree over me . . .'
'Dear, what a pity! That remembers me . . . Yesterday at school we were talking about Shakespeare and I said . . .
2B, or HB . . . That is the pencil . . .
2B, or HB . . . That is the pencil . . .
Oh Oh I can't read, I can't write . . .
Oh . . . Oh I'm so worried tonight . . .'

In contrast, the music was conforming to established harmonic rules and rhythmic-melodic progressions, drawing from pop music. Gregorio was very pleased with what he had achieved. The music therapist pointed out that the recording had involved hard work and hours of intense concentration, and that his care and passion had led to results.

It took many sessions to listen to all of his recordings. In addition to sharing the satisfaction resulting from his achievement, the music therapist tried to help Gregorio to have a more conscious appreciation of all the creative processes involved, including working and dialoguing with the others in the band. When they had listened to all the songs, Gregorio presented the music therapist with a copy of the CD. She felt this was an important moment and marked a phase of the work she defined as 'meeting and collecting'. She had tried to meet and contain his experiences. The gift of the CD appeared to symbolise a request to keep all of this.

At this point the music therapist suggested Gregorio could explore some of the instruments in the room. For the first time he looked interested. After some sessions, and not without difficulty, Gregorio took up the guitar and made a series of chords for one of his songs. It took him a long time to tune the instrument; he seemed never to be satisfied or ready to pass from preparation to performance. He filled up the time with remarks, speaking very quickly, and his words made the music therapist realise how intense this experience was for him. She felt that it was important to wait patiently for him and she paid attention to non-verbal elements such as his posture, breathing and the rhythm of his speech, which were all very quick and contracted. When Gregorio finally began to play, the music therapist supported him rhythmically on the piano. At the beginning she followed Gregorio's disjointed rhythmical progressions, but gradually the music became structured around a shared pulse, over which Gregorio proposed some harmonic variations. This was the first joint playing experience and produced an intense emotional feeling and, subsequently, a loosening of Gregorio's muscular tension and a slowing down of his speech.

From then on, the music therapist always tried to listen to Gregorio's language from a more musical point of view by sympathetically tuning in to the non-verbal parameters. This produced in Gregorio a slowing down of the rhythm of his speech and the beginning of a dialogue in which it was possible to communicate lived experiences and emotions within his customary verbal virtuosity.

His approach to the instruments, especially to the guitar, started to become more direct and immediate, and his curiosity for exploring possible variations increased. At the same time, he did not feel the need to be listened to in the same way as before. There were opportunities for more mutual exploration of musical ideas. It was during this period that Gregorio wrote, at the music therapist's suggestion, an article for a youth magazine, in which he said:

> Sometimes you are on your own, other times you're with someone, but whichever, listening to music is as if we received a message from somebody unknown, often saying exactly what we would like to hear, or what nobody tells us. If this happens, it seems like a kind of magic, as people, through this important instrument which is music, have since ancient times spoken about their lives, expressing their anger, hope, happiness or discomfort. That's why, in time, music has become a universal language, which almost makes us think that there really is something which unites and that perhaps we are not so far from one another.

In addition to 'words versus music', two further pairs of opposites were 'modality versus tonality' and 'monophony versus polyphony'. In his early improvisations Gregorio used harmonic progressions he knew, and would talk at length about tonal organisation in music, appearing to be interested in the rules in order to question them. He returned to the earlier theme of twelve-note music and the evolution of the concept of tonality towards atonality. Gregorio elaborated with the music therapist on the metaphorical connections between the structure of the inner world and relational dynamics.

At this stage the music therapist reintroduced the flexible notion of modality. Gregorio was curious to improvise with the music therapist, using the different modes and listening to the effects produced by the different harmonies. He also felt comfortable exploring the modes on the piano, previously an instrument he had found difficult. This flexibility resulted in an easier way of expression and reduced his need to intellectualise.

'Monophony versus polyphony' emerged during a musical improvisation on the theme of a Christmas song. Gregorio found it difficult to sing the main melody of a song. Melody was not the most natural musical element for him and in his band he would often sing the counter-melody. He described this personal attitude metaphorically: if, in order to reach a place, it was possible to choose between a main road and a path in a wood, he would take the second one, which was far more interesting for him.

The music therapist played Gregorio some pieces to demonstrate how different voices can be perceived monophonically or polyphonically. Gregorio became interested and the music therapist suggested listening to different interpretations, sometimes following the score, of some fugues from Bach's *Well-Tempered Clavier*. He was able to recognise and follow the progression of the different voices. It was then that Gregorio defined himself, with a sense of gratitude and release, his therapist felt, as a 'polyphonic personality' – a metaphor that involved both risk and potential.

Gregorio's process in music therapy: the third phase

The third phase of Gregorio's music therapy process lasted about a year and a half. Music as a resource for 'being in the world' was the central theme, as described by his therapist. During this last phase of the work, Gregorio, now 20, was discharged from the centre but agreed to continue with music therapy within a community-based music therapy context. This setting perhaps contributed to Gregorio's being able to express and face some of the polarities typical of late adolescence, for example individual versus group, internal versus external action, ego versus the world. He gradually renewed his contact with various external situations, commenting that 'there had been a long break'. He also said he felt 'on the move again', even though not yet at his preferred speed. He started to speak of what he felt he had gone through during the years of disconnection and of the fear which had always accompanied him and which was still 'the main emotion . . . the one you mostly and always feel'.

During this phase there was more focus on conversations exploring moods. His music therapist continued to listen musically and it was now possible for Gregorio to tolerate long moments of silence. He explored in detail his many wishes and fears, as well as the possibility of renewing contact with various aspects of his life that were important for him, such as school and studying. Gregorio started to attend a private school and after a three-year gap passed an examination that recovered two years of schooling in one.

Exploring relationships was still demanding. Gregorio chose a stable group of friends with whom he regularly socialised, even though he sometimes found it difficult to accept the tastes and ways of communicating with some of the group. His taste in clothes changed, as did his general appearance. Gregorio still regarded music as a great friend but now in a different way. His band had split because of his friends' various commitments. This was a hard blow for him, and not just because he missed the music. His peers were now taking on new responsibilities in life, something that was still very difficult for him.

Music became more present in his everyday life in the form of listening. He enjoyed preparing compilations that reflected the periods he was going through. He was still oriented towards rock in the British and American traditions, although he would now also listen to Italian music, which he defined as 'lighter'. He brought the song 'Thank you' by Dido to one session and said that the song, as well as the singer, reminded him of a simple way to face life and to be grateful for it.

In one complex session centred on the themes of appreciation and contempt, Gregorio accepted the music therapist's suggestion that they should play together. For the first time he chose a non-conventional instrument, the rainstick. While they were playing, the music therapist had the strong impression that Gregorio was saying, first of all to himself, that, just as with the rainstick, something had started flowing through him, even though it still often needed to be controlled and restrained.

During one reflection about his relationship with music, he said that of the different ways to deal with music, his favourite one at that moment was of being an 'amateur'. Gregorio seemed to have moved from a relationship of dependence on music to considering it as company and a resource for his life. This change had been possible by using music as an instrument of discovery and self-knowledge within a therapeutic relationship contextualised by interaction with other significant persons. For Gregorio, music was no longer what made his body bleed; it had become a sound resource to 'meet' his emotions, share his passions, and enjoy himself with his friends in the bar.

Music became the relational bridge from isolation to Gregorio's own and unique way of 'being-in-the-world'. Towards the end of the therapy process Gregorio produced some lines on the subject of listening, which, better than prose, express the meaning of this story:

> Living is choosing,
> But there is no living together without harmony.
> And in every harmony there is dialogue,
> Which is possible only if we listen to each other.
> Living is choosing to listen.

Researching experiences and effects

In an interview that took place six years after the end of the therapy process, Gregorio was asked about this experience of music therapy.[30] Here are some of his words (translated from the Italian) and some comments from the music therapist (presented in italics). The interview sheds light on the case example and exemplifies how music therapists sometimes study the processes of music therapy using qualitative approaches to research. Gregorio spoke about how specific musical choices mattered to him but also about the risks involved.

> It's not music in general; it's a different thing. You can use music in many situations, as background or to combat boredom. I don't use it like this; I like the music I want to listen to. I also like silence very much. When I was listening to Kurt Cobain and I was playing, that was the music that reverberated in me . . . to reach my inner world, not to entertain or for doing things . . .

> Music is not always the same. I gave the example of Schoenberg; OK, it was unlistenable, but it was interesting to know that a person made such music . . . It was beautiful to know that you could search for something different than everything that came before . . . why do you have to search? Because the soul also needs this, to search for something that is different . . .

30 Parts of this interview have been published previously in Italian; see Zanchi 2011.

You cannot use music as a refuge. It's not possible, at least I believe not. But there is a risk that you can use music as a refuge but then you lose yourself.

Gregorio's search took place within the context of a therapeutic relationship. In the interview he introduced the image of a 'bookmark', which could be understood to symbolise the role of the therapist. The 'book' could be read as symbolising the shared musical work:

It's like having a bookmark that was not in all the pages but in some . . . without preventing reading all the other pages. Its function is not to lose the thread but to help to make sense. But not too much, because being given sense from another is the opposite of freedom . . . I was told that I was free to choose to play or not to play. 'Doing' was my decision . . . there was the possibility to explore together . . . The meaning was a shared thing.

In the early part of the music therapy process Gregorio found it difficult to differentiate what was happening internally for him from his relationship with the 'objects' in his external world. The music mirrored and contained some of this confusion, and gradually, by making connections with different kinds of music, for example the transformational moment of listening to the Beethoven sonata, he found ways of creating more separation and differentiation.

The synthesis occurred by listening . . . but not only of the soul . . . the problem was in the real world and the listening must focus on everything else: hunger, boredom, desire . . . difficulty, anger, even shame.

First of all there was confusion; perhaps the different thing is that now I can listen to myself in the real world, recognising when I am hungry, when I desire something, if I want to eat sweet or savoury things . . .

It was evident . . . that in my case the interior world was the one closer to undifferentiation than differentiation.

Resonance was what made it possible to differentiate, listen, to see . . . to give a name to things . . . otherwise you are unable to see in the confusion.

During the interview Gregorio was able to look back across the period of music therapy. He realised how unwell and low in mood he had been at the start of the process. He also talked with insight on how he was now able to recognise low points and deal with them more effectively.

The passage from that moment until today was to pass from confusion to listening when you can differentiate those things which you can understand a little better, you can put things in order . . . yes, to feel bad or not feel bad, but feeling or not feeling bad is not enough: you need to give a name to everything . . . it's also to know from where the need arises . . . it's not the same thing as being angry or hungry or sleepy.

The main purpose of this interview was to gain a deeper understanding of how a patient/participant perceives and interprets the music therapy process from a distance of years. Gregorio's words were grouped by the music therapist into themes that emerged from the interview and were considered to relate to the music therapy process: music and identity, the symbolic 'other' in the therapeutic relationship, other 'objects' in Gregorio's life, and personal change in a therapeutic process. Gregorio's music therapist worked according to a psychodynamic framework and interpreted his statements using this approach. When the therapist uses the term 'objects' in her reflections, for instance, it refers to the psychodynamic theory of object relations, which proposes that early childhood experiences of relationships with caregivers influence our subsequent relationships to other people, activities, artefacts and situations.[31]

For music therapy as a discipline, it might be productive to look at the same empirical material from several theoretical perspectives. Given the importance of music in everyday life, of friends and of other social resources in Gregorio's case, we could for instance examine the material through the lens of an ecological perspective on how music helps. In a qualitative study, McFerran and Saarikallio found that most adolescents have strong beliefs about the power of music to help them during challenging times. The researchers suggest that those beliefs are grounded in an adolescent culture in which music is highly esteemed. It appears that in the majority of cases young people are successful in using music to improve their mood, express their identity, cope with challenging situations and manage their relationships. However, the researchers also found that vulnerable adolescents with mental health challenges have the least success in their use of music and might use it in ways that worsen their mood or isolate themselves from others. Music therapists, these researchers suggest, can offer help in focusing on young people's relationships to music and, with sustainability in mind, connect with caring friends, family members and professionals who also could offer help in relation to the young person's efforts in building 'musical resilience' in everyday life.[32] Such perspectives could throw light on Gregorio's process in the involvement of the other professionals in the team and with the increasing involvement of his friends. Our understanding could also be developed further through theory on relationships between social resources (such as social support) and mental health.[33]

Qualitative studies are particularly apt when we want to explore experiences and participant perspectives. As we have seen, qualitative research might also sensitise us to different ways of understanding therapeutic processes theoretically.

31 Gomez (1997).
32 McFerran and Saarikallio (in press).
33 Stige and Aarø (2012: 87–114).

However, when we want to examine the effects of music therapy, quantitative studies are often the preferred choice. In a case such as Gregorio's we have very good reasons to assume that music therapy is helpful but without controlled research we do not know how unique the effects are or how much of the change is due to music therapy and how much to other helpful factors. As was explained in Chapter 4, quantitative studies such as RCTs attempt to overcome these problems by studying a large number of participants who are allocated randomly to either an intervention arm or a control arm. Systematic differences in outcome, as indicated by pre-selected measures, are then examined statistically.

Christian Gold, Tony Wigram and Martin Veracek performed the first comprehensive meta-analysis of quantitative studies on the effects of music therapy for children and adolescents with psychopathology.[34] The review showed that music therapy has a highly significant medium to large effect on clinically relevant outcomes. The results also suggest that eclectic practice, in which techniques from different models or theories are mixed, is particularly effective. One important interpretation of this finding, according to the authors, is that it is helpful if therapists are flexible and open when working with young people.

In reviewing the current research literature, Gold, Saarikallio and McFerran show that there is a growing body of research supporting music therapy as an evidence-based intervention for adolescents, especially in relation to mental health-related issues.[35] Research evidence supports particularly the application of music therapy for adolescents with depression, schizophrenia and autism. The research results to date are promising, the authors suggest, but many of the existing studies are small and methodologically weak. More adequately powered randomised trials focusing specifically on music therapy with adolescents are needed.

Reflections on emotional aspects of music therapy

Gregorio's story might also illuminate themes that are theoretically interesting across practices in music therapy, one such theme being the emotional aspects. As Gregorio pointed out in his article for the youth magazine, 'people, through this important instrument which is music, have since ancient times spoken about their lives, expressing their anger, hope, happiness or discomfort'. We can explore the different connections between music and emotions in Gregorio's story and how his emotional awareness grew during the music therapy process. Recent interest in music and the emotions has brought together researchers from different disciplines, for example musicology, philosophy, psychology, sociology and music therapy, as presented in two compilations by music psychologists Patrik Juslin and John Sloboda.[36] In this section some of these different perspectives will underpin aspects of Gregorio's story.

34 Gold *et al.* (2004).
35 Gold *et al.* (2011). See also discussion on research with adults with schizophrenia or schizophrenia-like disorders in Chapter 6, given Gregorio's possible schizophrenic-like tendencies.
36 Juslin and Sloboda (2001a, 2010). See also Gabrielsson's compendium *Strong Experiences with Music* (2011).

When Gregorio first met the music therapist, he began to talk about his connections to music and the value he placed on it, intellectualising about the ideas behind Schoenberg's dodecaphonic style, for instance. A shift seemed to occur when he began to listen in the presence of 'the other'. There was the breakthrough experience of listening to the Beethoven piano sonata in a kind of reverent awe. This was followed by more physiological responses to the angry and desperate feelings that the music of Nirvana communicated to him. Gregorio began to move from talking about music in intellectualised ways to allowing and recognising body-based resonances to emotions being evoked by the music.[37] He also began to name specific emotions connected to the music, for example melodies emerging from a series of descending progressions as 'sad'.[38]

A softening seemed to occur as Gregorio began to play the piano and make associations, a further source of emotional connection reviewed by Juslin and Sloboda. When the therapist introduced Gregorio to the concept of modal harmonies, he made associations to the music of childhood and a simpler approach to writing and, potentially, living. He expressed his intention to write music that was more cheerful than the sad songs he was accustomed to listening to. This important emotional shift helped him see the value of life as well as death.

When Gregorio began to explore the instruments, his awareness of the range and intensity of emotions grew. He was now able to explore the emotional effects of playing in the different modes, combining his interest in listening to music with active playing, and also creating more relaxation and lessening of tension. Although, even in the final phase of the music therapy, fear was still very much a central emotion for Gregorio, he was beginning to explore 'lighter' music. There was evidence that he was starting to use music more as a resource for his own emotions and external social relationships. He began to take more emotional risks as the process developed, depending less on the music itself and using it instead as a resource to meet his different needs.[39]

The whole music therapy process could be summarised as a gradual shift from a somewhat defended position, when Gregorio would use complex words and ideas to discuss music on an intellectual level, to a gradual allowing and acceptance of the powerful emotions being evoked by the music he listened to and played, first through physiological resonance and then by naming the emotions. A less complex approach to listening and playing was mirrored in the music of his everyday life and in his emerging social relationships with his peers. The emphasis on emotions was central to how the music therapy process worked for Gregorio and there seemed to be strong links to relating and socialising.[40] Many music

---

37 Scherer and Zentner (2001).
38 See Juslin and Sloboda (2001b), who discuss both intrinsic and extrinsic connections between music and emotions, and see Bunt and Pavlicevic (2001) in relation to music therapy.
39 See the section 'Music as resource for action' in Chapter 3 (pp. 55–57).
40 For a specific discussion of perspectives on emotions from music sociology, see DeNora (2010).

therapists would argue that emotional aspects are central to how music therapy usually works.[41]

Closely related to emotional aspects and music therapy is motivation, and one area where this is particularly important is in addiction. This seems to be a growing area of music therapy practice and research, relevant not least in relation to young people.[42]

Working with human rights and social resources

We have already seen in McFerran's review of the existing literature that there is room for development of contemporary music therapy practices, with more focus on strengths and resources, human rights and community participation.

When Gregorio came to the centre he was diagnosed as having a schizoid personality disorder with the risk of early-onset schizophrenia. Diagnoses are based on the medical model (see Chapters 2 and 8) and they might help us develop specific practices tailored to the needs of each individual. Increasingly, music therapists have also argued that practices based on the medical model have their limitations, not least with regard to mental health and related fields, as there is a tendency here to focus on individual pathology and underestimate social problems and possibilities.[43]

Some music therapists include a focus on human rights which complements music therapy's more traditional focus on human needs. Community music therapy exemplifies this approach and is informed by appraisal of possibilities for human connectedness rather than by assessment of individual pathology.[44] This does not suggest that there is never any pathology to consider but rather that the separation of therapy and socio-cultural participation is often artificial and not helpful. Elements of an ecological understanding of music therapy could coexist in more conventional approaches, as Gregorio's case has exemplified.

We suggest that human needs can be fruitfully examined in the light of human rights.[45] People in need often experience challenges to their dignity, as when a sick person finds that his freedom is restricted by the regime of an institution or a poor person finds that her access to resources in society is hindered. Many social and cultural rights, such as the right to education, adequate health care and cultural participation in society, cannot be achieved by laws and regulations alone. They must be actively sought. It is therefore important that we as professionals see our obligations not only in relation to the needs of individuals but also in relation to human rights in broader contexts.[46]

---

41 See Pellitteri (2009) and also Thaut and Wheeler (2010) for two quite different general arguments for the significance of emotions in music therapy. For a discussion on emotions and music therapy with young people, see Trondalen (2003). See also the discussion of vitality affects in Chapter 4.
42 See Aldridge and Fachner (2010) and Silverman (2003, 2011).
43 For a critique of the medical model in the field of mental health, see, for instance, Rolvsjord (2010).
44 Pavlicevic and Ansdell (2004); Stige *et al.* (2010); Stige (2003/2012).
45 See Stige and Aarø (2012).
46 Centre for Human Rights (1994).

Requests for involvement from a music therapist often reflect situations where human rights are violated or not realised. Music therapists will actively relate to this at the intersection of where threats to human rights meet social-musical possibilities. The challenge is to address the relationships between individuals and communities, instead of localising them as individual pathology. Krüger's work in child welfare exemplifies this. He chooses to ground his work in the United Nations' Convention on the Rights of the Child (CRC)[47] and in culture-centred theory perspectives, and has explored how music therapists can take action and contribute to rights-based practice. His argument is that the situation of young people in child welfare is clearly at odds with human rights, as specified in the CRC. The articles of this convention call for provision of the resources necessary to protect children from neglect, exploitation and abuse, and to promote children's participation. The latter is crucial in fostering young people's resilience. Krüger argues that music can enhance young people's possibilities for participation and he focuses on music as a resource for individual agency as well as for communal and democratic participation. Specifically, he works with songwriting and performance in order to help young people articulate and reflect on their experiences, collaborate and support each other, and communicate their perspectives and concerns to a broader audience, including the decision-makers in the child welfare system.[48]

A range of music therapy projects for young people, explicitly or implicitly embracing a human rights perspective, has been developed lately.[49] In Cape Town a group of music therapists has formed a non-profit organisation called the Music Therapy Community Clinic, which provides music therapy to disadvantaged people from poorer communities within the area. Music therapists Sunelle Fouché and Kerryn Torrance describe work in one neighbourhood in the Cape Flats, which were established as a result of the apartheid government's forced removals of black and 'coloured' people from the city in the 1960s. In the city, extended families used to live in the same house, often close to other relatives. In the new settlements the social and emotional support previously provided by family and neighbours was lost. In a situation of poverty, lack of work opportunities and lack of social support and control, gang culture started to flourish, with increasing problems in the community related to drug-dealing and other criminal activities. Many of the young people saw these gangs as their only way of being part of a group that had a purpose. The music therapists working in this context decided that instead of focusing on the personal problems of each adolescent, they wanted to build music therapy services that could operate as alternatives to the local gang culture and contribute to the development of the local community.[50]

47 United Nations (2009).
48 Krüger and Stige (in press -b).
49 Taking young people's cultural resources into consideration might be one essential dimension of this. See Hadley and Yancy (2012) for a discussion of therapeutic uses of rap and hip hop.
50 Fouché and Torrance (2005).

Concluding points

Young people have to deal with substantial developmental challenges but to a degree it is a myth that adolescence is more filled with conflicts, depressions or risk-taking than other phases of life. Most young people handle the challenges of development. As is the case for all of us, problems might emerge if there are too many issues to handle at the same time. For a young person there might be concurrent experiences of puberty, conflicts in the family, poverty and contact with gang culture. In this chapter we have therefore argued that conventional music therapy practices focusing on individual needs should be complemented by practices which realise human rights in relation to participation and community development.

Several studies have demonstrated that music can be a powerful resource for young people in their everyday life, such as in improving mood, expressing identity, coping with challenging situations and managing interpersonal relationships. Recent research also suggests that some adolescents in vulnerable situations do risk using music in ways that are less than helpful for them. This is one of the reasons why music therapists might take the ecology of human development into consideration and explore community partnerships when working with young people. How useful music is going to be for each adolescent is dependent not only on the characteristics of that person but also on broader social processes determining access and distribution of resources.

At the same time, music therapists will continue to cultivate their skills in providing individually tailored therapy experiences for young people like Gregorio. As we will discuss in more detail in Chapters 8 and 9, music therapy is currently in an intriguing phase of development, where practices are being developed in both more rigorous and more flexible ways than before and where theoretical frameworks are being refined and redefined.

6 Music therapy and adult health

The adult musical profile

Music plays an important part in most adults' lives. In the Introduction we noted the diversity of music available today and the interest in taking part in various musical activities. We provided brief overviews in the two previous chapters of how children and adolescents respond to and make use of music. In relation to the lifespan theme of this book we continue with a brief overview of the adult's musical profile. What are the connections between an adult's personal, social and cultural history, musical preferences and musical identity? How can such connections be respected and integrated in music therapy practice?

We begin to answer these questions by observing that most of us are able to recall a favourite tune and sing at least snatches of it or tap out its rhythm, particularly if the tune has an emotional significance. People can remember the shapes and patterns of music. We are all exposed, to a greater or lesser extent, to our surrounding musical culture with its wide range of subcultures and musical genres.[1] Music listening, therefore, is an important aspect of many people's relationship to music. With the development of technology during the twentieth and twenty-first centuries, this aspect has become increasingly prevalent, as many adults now use portable MP3 players actively, for example to accompany exercise routines or to influence mood. Individual differences in listening habits and tastes are vast in any case, and cultural patterns tend to multiply and be less standardised in contemporary societies.[2]

When it comes to playing an instrument or singing, we often observe a lack of confidence among people who consider themselves musically untrained or untalented. Although the maxim 'it's never too late to learn' can apply to learning an instrument, we acknowledge that it involves a degree of physical dexterity and cognitive skill. But in parallel with the growing accessibility of music to listen to from all parts of the world, we are witnessing an exploration of different approaches to learning how to play instruments, often bypassing a reliance on

---

1 See 'Music as resource for action' in Chapter 3 (pp. 55–77) and Cook (1998: 5) on how music can take 'as many forms as there are cultural or subcultural identities'.
2 Hendry and Kloep (2012).

musical notation by focusing on aural and proprioceptive body-based memory systems. Individual and group practical musical instruction is gaining in popularity, including drumming circles using instruments such as African djembes.[3] And as regards singing, we are observing a similar rise in popularity, in the United Kingdom for example, of community-based choirs for people of all levels of musical ability, again with a creative blend of learning by rote alongside the use of musical notation.[4]

In their summary of research on adult amateur participation in music in Western cultures, music education researchers Dmitria Kokoktsaki and Susan Hallam suggest that the motivations of participants are personal, musical and social. They also note a spiritual dimension. Personal motivations include self-expression and self-improvement; musical motivations include love of music and wish to learn more about music; social motivations include the desire to meet new people, be with friends and have a sense of belonging. Spiritual motivations include the longing for transcendence and experience of meaning.[5] And whatever the motivation and musical experience, we can all share in fundamental emotional responses to music. Lacking the capacity to verbalise does not detract from emotional reactions.

The relationship of musical training and personal history to musical exploration presents a challenge to music therapists when supporting adults as they discover or rediscover their potential for making and relating to music. It also has implications for the appropriateness of different musical approaches within different contexts, for example listening to music of different genres (recorded or played live by the music therapist), improvising, performing, songwriting or singing favourite songs.

Music therapy and the many pathways of adult life

As we shall discover in the following examples, adults referred for either individual or group music therapy will have had quite different personal musical histories. At the start of a music therapy group or workshop we are often met with comments such as 'I'm not musical', 'I was never good at music at school' or 'I can't sing'. As adults, we often have to find ways of rediscovering a young child's more open spontaneity to free ourselves from the fears, doubts and competitive attitudes that beset us while singing or making music – and this can happen at all levels of music-making. It can often be the case that before people feel relaxed enough to touch the instruments in a music therapy session, the therapist needs to reassure participants that there is no right or wrong way to explore them. One of the key responsibilities of a music therapist, therefore, is to value everyone's contribution to a musical experience and to communicate this sense of valuing, be it one small gesture on a cymbal or a complex rhythmic drumming pattern or melody on a tuned instrument.

---

3 The advent of new computer technologies has now made it possible to explore such traditional instruments in completely new ways.
4 See Clift *et al.* (2010) for the influence of choral singing on health and well-being.
5 Kokoktsaki and Hallam (2011: 150).

In spite of providing encouragement and reassurance, there are risk factors involved in inviting adults to take part in any kind of musical activity. As the examples will indicate, making or listening to music can evoke a wide range of emotions, some of which might be difficult. Music therapists work with some of the most vulnerable people in society. They need to be aware that while the very tools of their trade have the potential to be life-enhancing and contribute to positive experiences, they can also accentuate different kinds of loss, or what might have been, opening up potential areas of difficulty that need very sensitive and careful support.

Vulnerability is a characteristic that is relative to our life history and may take unexpected and sudden turns. Take this example from the context of rehabilitation after traumatic brain injury:[6]

George was a 48-year-old man who lost the ability to use one side of his body (hemiparesis) following a traumatic brain injury when he was involved in a road traffic incident as a cyclist. Although it was clear that George would require therapy related to his reduced physical and verbal ability, a different challenge became real as he came to the therapy room accompanied by his wife and their 5-year-old son. After seeing the drums and cymbals, his son jumped over the footrest of the wheelchair down from his father's lap, grabbing the sticks to keep one and give the other into his father's active hand. Joining the speed and vivaciousness of the son's beating, the music therapist set to work improvising a song about drumming together. In the background of the boy's playing, the patient and his wife looked startled and stared at the therapist with questioning expressions on their faces. The therapist nodded for them to join in somehow, Dad on the cymbal and Mum on a conga drum standing beside the wheelchair. The boy turned, banged with all his might on the conga and cymbal before climbing back up onto his father's lap to drum for a few minutes together. Though the scenario was joyful, at the same time there was a raw and painful knowledge of loss in the room brought out by the excited play of the little boy.

This example shows how music therapy may reveal how the intricacies of human emotion can collide, misfit, coexist and blend. The example also indicates how

6 We are grateful to Simon Gilbertson for providing examples from music therapy practice within rehabilitation and material for the accompanying text (presented in italics), here and later in this chapter. Although related to actual events based on Gilbertson's experience in German hospitals, the examples have been fictionalised to protect the identity of any real individuals. Gilbertson also provides a narrative of a working day for a music therapist working in neurorehabilitation, included in Chapter 8. See also Gilbertson (2013 and in press).

necessary it is to consider the individual, his or her family and the social setting in which he or she lives. For the little boy, his father's situation is related directly to his childhood development, his relationships with both parents and his entire lifespan ahead of him. One of the beneficial aspects of music is the fact that musical structures can be stored in memory. Music once heard becomes material for the memory, for recognising tomorrow the music of yesterday. Music therapy sessions may then work towards a future recognition of remembered events in music.

Music therapists do not only work with individual patients. Often they work in systemic or ecological ways where the transactions of a broader range of participants need to be taken into consideration. Consequently, music therapists sometimes work directly with people who need therapy while at other times they work more indirectly, for instance collaborating with adults who are relatives of patients in therapy. They may also support adults to use music as a resource in their everyday lives or supervise adults who use music as a resource in their work.[7]

Different approaches to music therapy can be adapted and used in specific contexts where adults are offered music therapy individually or in groups. We will begin with two areas that have become well established: music therapy and the adult with learning disabilities, and music therapy and adult mental health. We will then continue with more examples from the context of music therapy and neurorehabilitation, and end the chapter with discussion of a fourth area, namely music therapy and adult cancer care, including palliative care. There are of course other important areas of practice.

Music therapy and the adult with learning disabilities

In many countries, institutions for people with learning disabilities were among the first places where the pioneers of music therapy started to work. This next case example demonstrates the fundamental human connections that are possible through musical interactions, as well as the delicacy, sensitivity and potential risks involved when inviting an adult for the first time to cross the threshold and take part in a musical encounter.

Sally, a 27-year-old woman with profound learning disabilities, would sit curled up in a foetal position in her chair. She appeared to be completely withdrawn into herself. She was referred to music therapy to see whether some form of communication system could be established; Sally had no use of any words to communicate, or of any signing system. The music therapist had very mixed feelings about starting work with Sally and was anxious about the first session. Was an uninvited intrusion appropriate into a world that Sally had created for

7 See Chapter 8.

herself, possibly as a means of protection from the aural invasions of ward noises, including both the television and the radio? The therapist sat beside Sally and began to play some long, quiet and low sounds on a small pipe. The therapist sang Sally's name gently and slowly. Very gradually over the weeks, at each visit Sally began to express some curiosity about these sounds. She began to uncurl herself and turn sideways towards the source of the sounds. A few weeks later she began to reach out and touch some of the small tuned and untuned percussion instruments that the therapist had started bringing. This led to Sally's facing the therapist, who began to sit opposite her. All this took place within an extremely slow time framework; any sudden or loud intrusion would set her back into herself. Sally eventually began to vocalise, making long sounds and sighs. These sounds were framed in a musical relationship, particularly when the therapist supported and matched Sally's improvised sounds. After a period of nine months of weekly sessions Sally would come into the small room off the main ward, sit facing the therapist, sing and reach out for the instruments. Towards the final and transitional stages of the work, Sally would get out of her chair as soon as the therapist entered the ward and move to the quiet room, singing en route. The speech therapist observed and notated a range of sounds that Sally produced in her singing, sounds that could perhaps become the basis for some kind of communication system. Sally began to attend for regular speech and language therapy.

Thirty years ago, around the time of Sally's music therapy sessions, adults with such profound learning disabilities would still be living in this kind of ward-based environment in large institutions in the United Kingdom. The vignette, abridged from the first edition, is a rather shocking indicator of how necessary it was to change health and social policy in order to listen more to the needs of adults living with these kinds of difficulties.

What do we learn about Sally from this vignette? First, that in order to cope in such an environment she had apparently withdrawn into herself. Her isolation had made it difficult for staff working with her to understand her needs, however well-intended such attempts might have been.[8] Second, that she did have a voice and that with an approach adapting to her pace and time-frame, she might find the inner motivation and be willing to open up a little, communicate in her own way and make some initial steps to build relationships. Third, that this process was delicate and risky, as an invitation to Sally to make contact would need to be sustained over

---

8 This possible coping mechanism in the light of living for many years with such difficulties and in such an environment could be a form of 'secondary handicap' as outlined by Valerie Sinason (1992).

time and sensed by her to be potentially worthwhile. The question for Sally's therapists was: what types and levels of communication could be beneficial for her?

While music therapy has a historical record of meeting, through non-verbal means, some of the needs of adults with such profound learning disabilities, the music therapist in this example had some ethical concerns about the sustainability of the process. In addition, the referral had come from a fellow professional acting as Sally's advocate; it was not Sally who had asked to see the music therapist. However, changes in national policy in the 1990s, particularly relating to inclusion and development of more community-based residential settings, have led to the adult with a learning disability being empowered to take a more active part in the decision-making process pertaining to any course of therapy.[9]

The vignette demonstrates how a music therapist is able to work holistically, making contact with the person behind any presenting disability or problem and forming an emotional connection through the musical transactions. The music therapist played to Sally quietly and intermittently at the start, patiently providing as much space and time as Sally needed before she felt able to become more actively engaged in the musical interactions. As we observed in Chapter 3, responses to sound and musical elements do not necessarily rely on complex cognitive processing for comprehension. Bypassing some of the functions necessary for decoding speech, for example, music can make an impact on people for whom a verbally saturated environment may possibly add to confusion and further isolation, as we might assume was the case for Sally. Developmental or physical delay does not prevent a person feeling with the full range of intensity in the same way as somebody with more developed mental and physical faculties.

It is not an easy task to make this kind of musical and emotional contact. The term 'learning disability'[10] encompasses a range of difficulties from the mild to most profound and there are often further confounding problems for the person to live with, including epilepsy, autism, visual or auditory impairments and overlapping mental health issues such as depression or anxiety, often referred to as 'dual diagnosis'. Some people may appear withdrawn and passive, some hyperactive with the additional challenge of self-injurious behaviour.[11]

Cathy Warner's chapter in Tessa Watson's text presents group work with five men who had recently moved to a community residential setting after living together on the same ward for fourteen years. This chapter and the research from which it is drawn can be used to illustrate some of the changes that have occurred since Sally's period of music therapy and the continuing challenges. Warner writes:

---

9 Watson (2007) is a resource for this context, with many examples of both individual and group work. See two of Tessa Watson's own chapters, chapter 1 ('Valuing people: a new framework') for background to the changes in UK-based governmental policy and chapter 2 ('Music therapy for adults with learning disabilities: sharing stories'), for a discussion of issues of referral and consent.

10 There are international differences with this term, for example 'intellectual disabilities', 'learning difficulties' or 'developmental disability.'

11 Richards (2007); Saville (2007); Warner (2007).

The music therapy group, although closed and confidential, formed the focus of a detailed piece of participatory action research involving the residents, care workers, the music therapist and the home managers as co-researchers . . .

The music therapy process enabled the men to move from suspicion and avoidance of relationships towards creation of a sense of community and relatedness. In a parallel process to the therapy, the music therapist and I worked with carers to challenge the perceptions of the residents, and identify and confront where we were tending to ignore.[12]

As Warner indicates in her chapter, more research is needed within this area of practice, including research on how community, relatedness and inclusion can be evaluated in various contexts.

At about the time Sally met her music therapist, in 1983, a group of six adults with learning disabilities in Norway were invited to become members of the local community music school as part of a project focusing on the cultural rights of people with disabilities. Stige writes about how the vision of the members of this group contributed to a shift in his understanding of music therapy. They requested not therapy at an individual level, but help to become active participants in the musical life of the broader community.

The group members entered a music room that looked like any music therapy room, except it was part of the community music school of the town.

The same room was also being used by local choirs as well as by the local marching band, of which there were several pictures on one of the walls. As the group members entered the room, they did not head for the chairs that the music therapists had put out for them in a nice semicircle. Instead, they went right over to the wall in order to be able to study the pictures more closely. A great enthusiasm spread among the group members: 'The band!' 'Look at that! The drum! The uniforms!' When we finally gathered around the semicircle of chairs that had been arranged, Knut, one of the group members, asked: 'May we too play in the marching band?'[13]

Knut's question challenged a range of common assumptions, for instance that music therapy requires music-making and listening in the context of a therapeutic relationship framed by defined boundaries of time and space. Knut's question was a request for support in the service of community participation. At the time it was a radical request.

Today, many music therapists have taken up similar challenges in a range of contexts. For instance, Sandra Curtis and Chesley S. Mercado developed a community music therapy practice for adult citizens with developmental disabilities.

12 Warner (2007: 52).
13 Stige (2003/2012: 20).

They suggest that music therapy practices focused on community participation will also focus on the development of friendships, learning experiences and possibilities for collaborative actions.[14]

Approaches to music therapy and adult mental health

As with music therapy and learning disabilities, music therapy in adult mental health started as a practice in large institutions. More recently the landscape has changed to one of community mental health. So what are the music therapy approaches in this field? In the United States there is a strong tradition of neuro-psychiatric and behavioural approaches.[15] We will concentrate here on two contrasting European contributions, namely Priestley's Analytical Music Therapy and Rolvsjord's Resource-Oriented Music Therapy.[16] The presentation of these approaches, which mainly focus on work with individuals, will be supplemented with some reflections on group work.

In Priestley's approach the patient is encouraged to talk through the issues being brought to the session, as in a classic analytical session, before exploring the issues dynamically in a musical improvisation. If, for example, as seen in a televised role play of her work, the patient presented difficulties in expressing anger, during the first section of the improvisation Priestley might invite the patient to play out some angry feelings on the instruments while she would represent the more controlling side of the patient's personality, supporting very often on the piano. The ways of playing could be reversed in the second section. In order for the two split parts to be heard and integrated, Priestley would play back a recording of the impro-visation. The patient would then hear all the sections of the music and be helped to recognise the component parts of the whole improvisation. The final discussion would become an opportunity for some of these musical insights to be processed verbally with the intention of integrating these contrasting elements within the psyche. We read in Priestley's descriptions of her work that much of what takes place in the musical interaction can be regarded as a reflection or analogue of various internal processes.[17]

The other approach to music therapy in adult mental health just mentioned is Resource-Oriented Music Therapy, as developed by Rolvsjord. It contrasts with Priestley's in many ways. While Priestley's approach is informed by psycho-analytical theory and focuses on the dynamics of transference and counter-transference,[18] Rolvsjord's is informed by the philosophy of empowerment, by a contextual model of psychotherapy and by positive psychology.[19] She focuses on

---

14 Curtis and Mercado (2004).

15 Unkefer and Thaut (2005).

16 For further contributions, see, for example, the work of Jos De Backer (Wigram and De Backer 1999), Johannes Eschen (2002), Inge Nygaard Pedersen (Wigram *et al.* 2002) and case studies in Bruscia (1991) and Meadows (2011).

17 Priestley (1975/2012). See also British Broadcasting Corporation (1983).

18 See Chapter 2 and Bruscia (1998b) for discussion of these concepts.

19 See Rolvsjord (2010: part 1), where she discusses these frames of reference in quite some detail.

how health-promoting processes are nurtured by positive emotional experiences and the mobilisation of personal and social resources. This does not imply that working with problems is avoided, but it highlights the relevance of focusing on the client's strengths and potential and of recognising the client's competence related to the therapeutic process.[20] In practical terms, this means that improvisations and verbal discussions could be, but do not need to be, part of resource-oriented music therapy sessions. In Rolvsjord's approach there is much flexibility when it comes to choice of musical activities, which could include writing and performance of songs related very much to the participants' specific contexts. The intrapersonal and interpersonal focus inherent in many approaches to music therapy is supplemented by more contextual considerations. Current perspectives in mental health provision focus on the possibilities of living a meaningful life, and Rolvsjord argues that access to music in everyday life can be seen as an agenda for music therapy practice.[21]

In addition to individual work, music therapy in mental health services is often offered in a group format. Many music therapists working with groups have found existential psychotherapist Irvin Yalom's description of 'curative factors' specific to group work helpful. Space precludes a discussion of all eleven, but a brief description of the first four and reference to the others, as they could be related to music therapy, will serve to illustrate this way of thinking about group practice:

1   'Installation of hope': At the start of any group process, installing a sense of hope is a prerequisite for both the group members and the therapist. We all hope that the experience of making music together will be beneficial. In music therapy the understanding that there is no right or wrong way to play may increase a sense of playful curiosity and interest, often contagiously within the group.

2   'Universality': The group setting provides opportunities for sharing fears and preoccupations, but also joy and pleasure. Playing and singing unites people in the task of exploring how to make music, as any difficulties are overcome together by all taking part.

3   'Imparting of information': There may be the need, for example, to impart information about how a particular instrument can be played.

4   'Altruism': Group work provides many opportunities for group members to support each other. In music therapy a developing sensitivity to the needs of others can be observed in musical dialogues among group members. People often comment that the music and the group work can take the focus away from immediate problems, helping them to see the situation from a different perspective and in the light of other people's experiences.

---

20 For the therapeutic principles of 'Resource-Oriented Music Therapy' (which are published online), see Rolvsjord *et al.* (2005).
21 Rolvsjord and Stige (2013). See also the section on the (non-medical) recovery approach in Chapter 8.

Yalom's other factors are:

5   'the corrective recapitulation of the primary family group';
6   'development of socialising techniques';
7   'imitative behaviour';
8   'interpersonal learning';
9   'group cohesiveness';
10 'catharsis';
11 'existential factors'.[22]

The interactional and fundamentally non-verbal nature of music-making can contribute factors to the transactional processes within 6–10. It is possible to try out different ways of playing music and it might be easier for some people to take more risks in a musical than in a verbal medium, potentially re-creating and helping to reassess earlier family dynamics (5). And, as in other kinds of therapy groups, Yalom's 'existential factors', such as taking responsibility for our own lives and recognising our own mortality (11), can also be explored in music therapy.

Other group theories have influenced music therapy practice. For example, the group analyst S.H. Foulkes used a musical analogy to describe the evolving processes in group therapy, drawing connections between a group therapist and how a conductor helps to facilitate the various instrumental voices in an orchestra. Somehow the music emerges into life as the conductor helps to balance the different foreground and background musical ideas and textures. When discussing Foulkes, Heidi Ahonen-Eerikäinen writes:

> The therapist is the conductor and individual clients sound different, yet together they make music. Each instrument is needed to make the sections of the whole. The therapist/conductor facilitates the movement of the piece to allow a harmonious therapeutic atmosphere.[23]

As with individual music therapy, there are highly contrasting perspectives on how to work with groups in adult mental health. Ansdell, for instance, describes a community music therapy process with a group called Musical Minds, which meets weekly in an area of East London. Here there is less focus on intrapersonal and interpersonal dynamics in the group as a distinct unit and more on playing music and singing as ways of finding meaning and a sense of belonging. Ansdell uses perspectives such as Wenger's theory on communities of practice in order to explore the process of Musical Minds. He particularly emphasises how relationships of belonging emerge from shared practice, negotiation of shared meaning and the creation of community and identity.[24]

---

22 Yalom and Leszcz (2005: 1–2).
23 Ahonen-Eerikäinen (2007: 46).
24 Ansdell (2010b: 47–51). See also Wenger (1998).

Research on music therapy and adult mental health

In previous chapters we have referred to systematic literature reviews published by the Cochrane Collaboration as representing an internationally recognised 'gold standard'. We begin this section by highlighting two such reviews pertaining to adult mental health: one by Anna Maratos and colleagues on music therapy and depression, and the other by Karin Mössler and colleagues on music therapy and schizophrenia.[25]

The findings from the Maratos review of 'individual randomised trials suggest that music therapy is accepted by people with depression and is associated with improvements in mood'. But the paucity of studies and a relatively low methodological quality make it impossible to make a more substantial claim about music therapy's effectiveness.[26] Of the five studies that met the inclusion criteria for this review, three were with older people and one was with adolescents. Music therapy took place for periods between six and ten weeks and all five studies included follow-up reviews.

The work by Maratos and her colleagues took place before a larger study created international interest when it was published in the *British Journal of Psychiatry*. This RCT, led by music therapist Jaakko Erkkilä, recruited seventy-nine participants of 'working age' and for a longer period of intervention: twenty sessions, twice a week. There were positive outcomes, namely improved 'depression symptoms', 'anxiety symptoms' and 'general functioning', when the follow-up took place three months after the intervention.[27]

There has been perhaps an even larger impact from the Cochrane review for people with schizophrenia, carried out in 2005 and updated in 2011. The authors concluded:

> Music therapy as an addition to standard care helps people with schizophrenia to improve their global state, mental state (including negative symptoms) and social functioning if a sufficient number of music therapy sessions are provided by qualified music therapists. Further research should especially address the long-term effects of music therapy, dose–response relationships, as well as the relevance of outcomes measures in relation to music therapy.[28]

In England and Wales the National Institute for Health and Care Excellence (NICE) Guidelines for core interventions in the treatment and management of schizophrenia invite healthcare practitioners to 'consider offering arts therapies to assist in promoting recovery, particularly in people with negative symptoms'.[29] The recommendation came before this latest updated Cochrane review, which has

---

25 Maratos *et al.* (2008); Mössler *et al.* (2011).
26 Maratos *et al.* (2008: 'Authors' conclusions').
27 See Erkkilä *et al.* (2011, 2012) for two case examples from this study embedded within the chapter.
28 Mössler *et al.* (2011: 'Authors' conclusions').
29 NICE (2009: 23).

influenced the more recent treatment guidelines in countries such as Norway, where music therapy is strongly recommended.[30]

In Chapter 6 of this book's first edition much of the discussion of music therapy and adult mental health focused on the presentation of two evaluation and feasibility studies, the first having been based in one of the older large institutions and the second in a smaller psychiatric unit in a general hospital. These studies are examples of the pragmatic, evaluative projects that could be developed by music therapists working with a limited range of human and financial resources. They are also practically based examples of a research approach that includes some quantitative and some qualitative elements.

The first project explored potential benefits for patients diagnosed with schizophrenia and described as difficult to engage.[31] A simple time-sample observation procedure carried out by a visiting music therapy student checked for attendance, on-/off-task behaviour (for example, playing an instrument/reading a newspaper) and eye direction. The quantitative (numerical) analysis of high rates of attendance (over 79 per cent) provided evidence for a part-time post to be set up at this hospital.

The second project described in 1994 involved groups of day patients with severe depression and anxiety, and some with a previous history of psychosis or schizophrenia. This was a collaborative project involving a psychiatric unit's head occupational therapist, who kept an attendance register and collated the weekly observations of how the group members responded to the music therapy sessions, and a psychologist who devised a straightforward satisfaction questionnaire. The attendance rate was high enough (73 per cent, with the 92 per cent positive questionnaire answers outweighing any negative ones) for a second phase of this project to be funded and set up. In this phase the intention was to compile more qualitative data to discover more about music therapy's contribution to mood, particularly any short-term changes in state of relaxation, feelings of 'happiness' and sense of self-worth within sessions. There were statistically significant subjective shifts to the positive in all three dimensions over the course of the sessions.[32]

Some comments from a patient who took part in the project at the general hospital offer a more subjective and qualitative balance to a section that began with a short survey of RCTs and systematic literature reviews.

> For me, Music Therapy has provided an alternative avenue to the areas of my personality and social interaction closed off, mainly through fear of disapproval. The first cracks in my outworn protective shell occurred before coming into the unit. In the unit, a 'safe place' was provided for the old shell to be shed, and by talking to doctors, nurses and other patients the absence of

30 Helsedirektoratet (2013).
31 The project was funded by the Emperor Fine Arts Trust. See Bunt (1994: chapter 6) for detailed results.
32 Bunt *et al.* (1987).

need for a new shell was slowly established. Group therapy, art therapy and music therapy have each provided contributions to re-establish a true self-image. The unique contributions of Music Therapy are: 1) Co-operation within a group. All efforts of equal value. 2) Contributions towards a unique creation. 3) Other members of the group, staff as well as other patients, having equal problems mastering instrumental technique. 4) Sense of achievement proportional to one's involvement. 5) Aural access to closed-off, 'unsafe' areas of inspiration. 6) Ability to get used to doing something for fun and enjoyment initially and with less unsettling analysis (cf. art therapy). 7) 'Safe' interaction with a group.[33]

The relevance of qualitative research for the study of music therapy and adult mental health has been picked up by researchers such as Ansdell and Rolvsjord, who both have a strong focus on how music can foster relationships, mobilise resources and lead to empowerment.[34] In a qualitative study on client experiences of music therapy, Ansdell and Meehan used the term 'music–health–illness narratives' to describe the clients' experiences of relationships between their everyday lives and music therapy. According to this interview study, music therapy connects with previous and ongoing engagement with music, and can contribute to a reconnection with music in situations where health problems have caused disruptions. Consequently, this study suggests that one of the functions of music therapy is to mobilise music as a health-promoting resource in everyday life.[35]

Music therapy in the everyday world of rehabilitation[36]

Following neurological trauma or illness, the world of rehabilitation is not reliably predictable, constant or stable. Life-threatening injuries to the brain and body cause trauma to the individual's physical and social ecology that often leads to isolation and idiosyncratic behaviours.

Tim was a 24-year-old man who was the sole survivor of a severe road traffic incident in which four of his closest friends lost their lives. On the way home from a party the driver lost control of the car, which collided with a large oak tree at the side of the road. As a result of the incident Tim had suffered a moderate traumatic brain injury that required neurosurgical consultation, and minor cuts and bruises to all of his

33 Ibid.: 25–6.
34 Ansdell and Meehan (2010); Rolvsjord (2010).
35 Ansdell and Meehan (2010). See also Rolvsjord and Stige (2013).
36 As was explained earlier in the chapter, the examples from neurorehabilitation and the reflections in italics have been provided by Simon Gilbertson.

extremities. In view of the severity of the incident it was a wonder that he had survived. The music therapist had met with Tim three times previously during the past ten days in the music therapy room. He was able to walk slowly, stiff from immobility during the past days and weeks, and talked as they walked from the ward to the music therapy room, mumbling something under his breath. Tim was agitated, not sitting but wandering around the room at angles from unconventional parts of the room to another. He smiled and nodded as the therapist offered to play some music at the piano. The therapist began improvising gently, within an octave on a Mixolydian scale[37] with a calm and reliable rhythmicity. While playing, he heard over the soft music Tim's words, 'you were there . . . it was you who was there . . .' He looked diagonally down towards the furthest corner of the room, his eyes flicking around, and asked, 'Aren't you one of the firemen?' While he spoke, the therapist remained in the same music, holding the situation. Tim held onto his theme, convinced of his 'discovery'. To stay with him in this moment was the only choice. Though it is important to provide orientation to the real situation, it was also important not to be destructive of his attempts towards orientation in this early phase of rehabilitation.

Misrecognising people is a common experience for individuals who have experienced damage to the temporal areas of their brains responsible for aspects of facial recognition and memory. The situation can create an enormous potential for anxiety and disorientation for the patient and therapist. In the room with Tim on that day, it was important for the music therapist to improvise clear, calm and serious music to reflect the mood of the shared situation. There was a need to hold the level and quality of contact as it was in the room and to acknowledge the situation Tim was experiencing.

Tim had been involved in a road traffic accident. Gilbertson's essay for the online music therapy journal *Voices* provides an overview of the kinds of techniques used by music therapists to meet the individual needs of people recovering from such traumatic brain injuries.[38] The overview additionally incorporates some of the issues that music therapy can address and the growing body of research evidence. For example, by improvising calm music for Tim the music therapist aimed not only to validate the shared moment in the room but also to help Tim to reduce some of his agitation and anxiety, two emotional states that music therapy can address (with growing supportive evidence).[39]

37 On a piano the white notes from G to G are a version of this scale.
38 Gilbertson (2008).
39 Hitchen *et al.* (2010); Baker and Tamplin (2006).

As we saw earlier in the chapter, the devastating effects that traumatic brain injuries can have are not always limited to the patient. Family members, friends, colleagues and all involved from the moment of the accident through all future stages in the rehabilitation process, usually an entire lifetime, are affected. We can see in the next example how family members and other hospital staff can be engaged in a music therapy group.

The afternoon group was a very special group. Led by two music therapists, the group was for patients restricted to their beds, not yet able to be mobilised in a wheelchair, and their families. Thanks to the clinic's well-planned architecture all of the four music therapy rooms had doors wide enough for the hospital beds to pass through easily. This meant that it was possible to create a group for patients not yet able to come together conventionally with others. We decided that the group should be open to the patients' families, and often other colleagues working with the patients would also come along and join in. In the therapy room there was an unusual collection of objects: six hospital beds, a grand piano, guitars, small and large percussion instruments, a set of orchestral gongs and a video camera. The group session was organised within a regular structure with sections that were flexible depending on the needs and health situation of the patients. In this group, improvisation was used and also songs would be sung, composed and recorded, while families would join, therapists would support and facilitate movements and gestures. No one lay or sat alone in isolation. The group had one single core goal: participation and thus the reduction of isolation.

Commonly, patients who have experienced severe injury or disease remain in their bedrooms for long periods, sometimes only leaving that space for diagnostic procedures, including brain scans and the measurement of brain activity. At the same time, it is common for the staff to experience isolation from their conventional patterns of communicating, and directly experience isolation themselves. Seldom is it possible to confront the extreme level of isolation created not only by the type of injury or illness but also by the architectural and treatment concept of the 'medical patient'. But what the music can contribute is the ability to adapt and respond to the needs of the patient following neurological trauma and illness.

Alice was a 68-year-old woman who had experienced a stroke that led to a paralysis of the right side of her body and the loss of vocal and verbal ability. On that day, though she was mute and created no vocal sounds at all, Alice was able to imitate the mouth movements and breathing patterns of the music therapist when made within a turn-taking song structure. This simple interaction was visibly enjoyable for Alice and led to an increase in confidence in attempting to make vocal sounds. The musical breathing interaction was useful in extending Alice's depth of breathing and diaphragm support, and developing the basis for vocal capacity. This step is highly significant in the very early stages following stroke. It is important to order the different therapies effectively, and the music therapy session was scheduled directly before Alice would go to the speech and language therapist's room just a few doors down the corridor.

For Alice the importance of early intervention is highlighted in the way that the music therapy sessions assisted with the regulation of her breathing patterns and aided her confidence in exploring vocal sounds.[40] The example also demonstrates the close working relationships needed with other members of the multidisciplinary team.

Interdisciplinary research on music and rehabilitation

Listening to preferred music on a regular basis for people in the first period of recovery from a stroke has proved to enhance mood and have a positive effect on cognitive recovery. In 2008 international attention was aroused when positive results from an RCT carried out by psychologist Teppo Särkämö and colleagues (including music therapists Laitinen, Forsblom and Erkkilä) were published in the influential journal *Brain*.

> Fifty-four patients completed the study. Results showed that recovery in the domains of verbal memory and focused attention improved significantly more in the music group than in the language and control groups. The music group also experienced less depressed and confused mood than the control group. These findings demonstrate for the first time that music listening during the early post-stroke stage can enhance cognitive recovery and prevent negative mood.[41]

A further review by Särkämö and David Sotto in the *Annals of the New York Academy of Sciences* explored the potential neural mechanisms that might account for this positive influence of music, including the release of pleasure-evoking dopamine; reduction in stress-inducing cortisol; and the neuroplasticity of the

---

40 For further exploration of vocal work with stroke patients, see Baker and Tamplin (2011).
41 Särkämö *et al.* (2008: 866).

whole system, given music's propensity to induce such wide-ranging brain activity. This review was part of an issue entitled 'Neurosciences and Music' that included a contribution on different music therapy techniques from Connie Tomaino, who set up the Institute of Music and Neurologic Function at Beth Abraham Hospital in New York, where she has worked closely with Oliver Sacks.[42] Her work and their collaboration were featured in Sacks's book *Musicophilia*.[43] Although we have noted that listening privately to preferred music can have a positive effect on recovery from stroke, Sacks reinforces the importance of the relationship between the patient and music therapist and, as we saw with Alice, this can involve processes of imitation not only of vocal shapes but also of breathing and movement patterns. Sacks is encouraging about the way in which music can assist in the recovery process, concluding his chapter on aphasia and music therapy by commenting that 'the right hemisphere, which in normal circumstances has only the most rudimentary linguistic capacities, can be turned into a reasonably efficient linguistic organ with less than three months of training – and that music is the key to this transformation'.[44] Yet this comment is balanced with Sacks's caution that, while a music therapist may be able to assist a patient to sing and reacquire the use of short spoken phrases, there may be a limit on whether further fluency can be restored.

Music therapy can also focus on providing a motivating rhythmic grid for the reacquisition of movements, as in this next example and reflections.

Jean was a 38-year-old woman who was recovering from a dramatic disorder called Guillain–Barré syndrome. In the progression of this disorder, also known as acute neuropathy, patients lose the functionality of their peripheral nervous system, which controls all movements of the body. This loss of function begins at the feet and gradually rises in a short space of time upwards through the body. If left untreated, the person becomes no longer able to breathe without external mechanical assistance. Jean was fortunate enough to have been diagnosed successfully before the progression had become life-threatening and had received the necessary medication. However, the gradual loss of the ability to control the movement of all muscles up to her waist had made it necessary for her to receive artificial respiration to keep her alive.

In Jean's case the medication had successfully led to a step-by-step reversal of the neuropathy. She had become able to breathe again without artificial assistance and had regained some movement in her arms. In music therapy she was determined to play a snare drum with a

42 Särkämö and Sotto (2012); Tomaino (2012).
43 Sacks (2007).
44 Ibid.: 223.

stick in each hand. By improvising music that matched the changing loudness and speed of her drumming, the music therapist could provide a pulse and time pattern that was flexible enough to adapt to her temporally instable movements, and join her in the rhythm of her movements and movement dynamic. This interpersonal micro-relating in time is a fundamental of coordinated interpersonal experience in human life. Jean used drumming in improvisation to both train her body to move again and to create an audible statement of her determined nature and identity in the light of regaining agency over her movements and ability to participate in creative activities with those around her.

This example highlights an approach, as Gilbertson points out, which locates the rehabilitative therapeutic process 'in the social-neural and behavioural interaction' between patient and therapist. A consistent holding pulse was provided for Jean, yet the therapist introduced sufficient flexibility relating to the speed of Jean's drumming and to her changes in loudness. The music therapist could adapt to some of Jean's instability in a subtle 'interpersonal micro-relating in time', as he described it. Such attention and joint musical activity were observed to have contributed to Jean's evolving control of her movements and her sense of agency and creative identity.[45]

This social-neural interactive approach as used in Jean's case (and indicated as an appropriate intervention for patients with this syndrome) differs from approaches in which more external pulse and rhythmic frameworks are provided in order to influence irregularities in gait patterns, as used for other patient groups. For example, rhythmic auditory stimulation (RAS) has been pioneered over many years by Thaut and his colleagues. RAS, as a form of 'gait therapy', is described as involving

> the use of rhythmic sensory cuing of the motor system. RAS is based on entrainment models in which rhythm auditory cues synchronize motor responses into stable time relationships . . . Rhythm serves as an anticipatory and continuous time reference on which movements are mapped within a stable temporal template.[46]

The RAS procedure involves the use of a metronome as well as specially prepared music that incorporates flexibility in relation to the needs of the patients. Thaut's research has focused on stroke patients and a range of other neurological problems such as Parkinson's disease.[47]

45 See also Magee (2002).
46 Thaut *et al.* (2007: 455).
47 Thaut (2005).

Although encouraging results have been reported for the use of music therapy in different areas of rehabilitation, more research is still needed. Joke Bradt and her colleagues were able to include only seven studies that met the inclusion criteria for their Cochrane Review, 'Music therapy for acquired brain injury'.[48] Of these seven, the research team concluded from two studies, with a sufficiently low level of bias, that 'rhythmic auditory stimulation (RAS) may be beneficial for improving gait parameters in stroke patients, including gait velocity, cadence, stride length and gait symmetry'.[49]

This research reveals an important and interesting tension within music therapy practice and research: to what degree should we as music therapists concentrate on music as a tool of rehabilitation in relation to specific medical problems and to what degree should we concentrate on the psychosocial aspects of living with medical challenges? The latter perspective is especially relevant when conditions are chronic or even deteriorating. In the next section we turn to the areas of cancer care and palliative care, highlighting the relevance of working with psychosocial aspects.

Music therapy, adult cancer care and palliative care

Music therapy in adult cancer care and palliative care has grown over the past few decades. These are challenging areas and demand much flexibility on the part of the therapist. The following example demonstrates a range of musical approaches and can be related to Yalom's 'curative factors' and Foulkes's musical analogies described earlier in the chapter.[50]

A group of six women and three men settle into comfortable chairs at the start of their regular music therapy session. The setting is a community-based centre for cancer care. The members of the group have been attending sessions for three weeks and have developed a trusting relationship with each other and the therapist. They are accustomed to using the different instruments. After an opening discussion the agreed focus for the session is to explore some of the inner resources required for living with cancer. The music therapist, who is also a trained practitioner in the Bonny Method of Guided Imagery and Music, has brought a selection of music for listening. The therapist proposes that this session should integrate relaxed listening, verbal discussion and improvising. The participants are invited, after a short relaxation induction, to imagine themselves on some kind of edge or

---

48 Bradt *et al.* (2010).
49 Ibid.: abstract: 'Main results'.
50 The example is an amalgamation of activities that can occur in this type of group experience.

threshold. Liadov's *The Enchanted Lake* is played, an evocative and atmospheric piece at a moderate tempo, with shifting harmonies and timbres that seems to float magically on the surface between water and air, yet with the grounding element of some long-sustained low sounds.[51] Where will the music take the members of the group? Images and narratives reported after the listening include soaring over water, underwater swimming, exploring a cave, meetings and dialogues with loved ones (both past and present) in places of special significance and meaning, and being presented with a gift. The therapist then invites each group member to see whether any particular instrument resonates with the images evoked by the listening. Each participant then plays a short improvisation on their chosen instrument, creating a bridge between the evoked images and the sounds now played out into the room. A general discussion follows as individuals hear strands of their own personal narratives and connections echoed in some of the music played by the other members of the group. Several common themes emerge and the group decides to explore the all-embracing theme of a journey that, after moving through some difficult and unclear territory, will reach a different location before making a return. The participants choose different instruments to represent parts of the journey. The music sounds rather chaotic and fragmented at the start, as each player begins her or his own individual journey. Gradually, small rhythmic and melodic ideas emerge and are passed between members of the group. A common pulse and direction for the music are found, with a sense of gathering momentum and collective strength. An explosive climax is reached and after one additional final crescendo the music subsides, ending with gentle, more individual bell-like sounds, reminiscent of some sounds from the Liadov piece. After the extended improvisation there are opportunities for more verbal reflection and discussion. There is now a peaceful feeling in the room after the loud struggles heard in the earlier part of the improvisation. As a way of acknowledging this calmer atmosphere, the music therapist proposes a final listening, this time to Pachelbel's well-known Canon; the constantly repeating bass pattern adds to the feelings of quiet comfort and secure support. No more words are needed as the members of the group quietly disperse.

In this session there was an almost palpable flow between words and music. The opening discussion helped the music therapist to choose the Liadov piece, which

---

51 One of the pieces from Kenneth Bruscia's GIM programme 'Pastorale'. See *Music for the Imagination* (Bruscia 1996).

appeared to match the group's agreed focus. This music feels as though it is on the edge between different spaces, and can be a liminal kind of listening experience. The group members listened to this short piece of music while being both relaxed and focused, exploring the theme of a threshold.[52] The images evoked by the music were then articulated in words and by playing out some of the feelings on the instruments. A crucial feature of this session was how individual resonances became integrated into themes that connected with other members of the group. These dynamic processes echo the shifts, as outlined by Bruscia, from *intrapersonal/musical* to *interpersonal/musical* perspectives.[53] The collective themes developed into the most extended group improvisation of the session, in which participants could play their own part yet hear how it resonated with others in the group. Inner resources clearly had both personal and group agendas. Such insights appeared to be releasing and transformative, leading to the calm and reflective end to the session.

There was no singing in this group session, but singing, and particularly songwriting, has increasingly become part of music therapy practice for people coping with cancer at different stages of the disease. Bob Heath and Jane Lings write:

> People facing death or bereavement may find themselves seeking new ways to express and understand the many feelings that may arise. The authors' experience as music therapists working in hospices is that creative song-writing in therapy can provide an opportunity to express these complex feelings within a cultural form that is both ancient yet wholly contemporary. The songs that clients create express a vulnerability that can seem profoundly intimate and yet deeply familiar.[54]

Heath and Lings identify how songwriting can be used to clarify and contain feelings as part of a life review process or as a form of legacy. A song may emerge from a moment of improvisation, verbal reflection, a sharing of feelings and thoughts or as a kind of 'creative visualisation' being transformed into the beginning of some lyrics. Different ways of supporting the creation of melodies or co-creation of harmonic or rhythmic structures are subtly negotiated with the songwriter/patient/participant. A song may be ready to be recorded at the end of

---

52 This way of listening was further discussed as a self-help tool for use outside the sessions.
53 Bruscia uses the term *intrapersonal* to categorise the relationships that 'are found within the person between any parts of the self', for example between the physical and the emotional, the aural and the visual, thoughts and feelings. *Intramusical* relationships are those 'that exist within a person's music', for example between what the patient plays melodically and rhythmically. At this level the relationships are fundamentally within the self. When considering the more *interpersonal* aspects of relationships, Bruscia explores examples such as between one person's behaviour and another's feelings, between one person's 'tone of voice' and another's 'verbal response'. When discussing more *intermusical* relationships, Bruscia explores 'those found between one person's music and the music of one or more other persons', with examples such as the relationships between a different person's rhythm or melody (1998a: 127–8).
54 Heath and Lings (2012: 106).

one session or after a series of sessions. It is something tangible to take away from a session and, depending on individual choice, to share with others.

Dileo and Courtney Parker have described how music therapy can facilitate 'the process of "dying well" . . . Helping a person restore his or her personal identity and integrity, and facilitating healing and completion of relationships with self, others and a Supreme Being is integral'.[55] In addition to using songwriting as a therapy, these therapists create 'song legacies' with their patients and talk about, improvise and play favourite songs, live and recorded, from many different genres. They offer support at the bedside while patients join in singing songs that hold precious memories and meanings.

Some different approaches to research

Songwriting was featured in a study by Clare O'Callaghan and colleagues which explored themes within the lyrics that emerged when music therapists supported parents with cancer composing songs for their children.[56] O'Callaghan was also involved in another collaborative qualitative study exploring caregivers' backgrounds to music and how they might use music as part of caring for a family member.[57] Earlier, she published a comprehensive overview in which she examined how a balance could be found between these types of qualitative studies underpinned by constructivist philosophy, and those with a more quantitative and positivist approach, as in RCTs.[58]

RCTs are included in the Cochrane Collaboration systematic literature review, 'Music interventions for improving psychological and physical outcomes in cancer patients'. This review specified thirteen music therapy interventions and seventeen that focused on listening to pre-recorded music and did not involve a trained music therapist. Four of the seven adult-based music therapy studies in this review focused on hospital-based procedures. The review indicates that music interventions may have beneficial effects on anxiety, pain, mood and quality of life for people with cancer. Because of the small number of studies, the researchers could not compare the effectiveness of music therapy interventions and the other music interventions included in the review.[59]

We conclude this section by summarising the stages of a research programme carried out at a community-based cancer care centre that used collaborative and mixed-methods approaches. The work also relates to some of the themes outlined at the beginning of the chapter. The programme began when a researcher invited participants to respond to the statement 'Music and Us' before and after six one-off group music therapy improvisation-based sessions. Two themes to emerge from the analysis were:

---

55 Dileo and Parker (2005). See also Aldridge (1999).
56 O'Callaghan *et al.* (2009).
57 O'Callaghan *et al.* (2011).
58 O'Callaghan (2009).
59 Bradt *et al.* (2011).

1   a shift from effects of the music on the individual to those on the group, for example relaxing and calming to communication and group togetherness;

2   a corresponding shift from more introspective feelings evoked by the music to more active use of the music, for example calmness and sadness to spontaneity and release.[60]

A mixed-methods approach was used for the next collaborative project. A one-off listening session to meditative music sung to a small group of nine participants produced significant increases, after the listening, in both the concentration and the secretion rates of the antibody salivary immunoglobulin (SigA), a possible biomedical marker related to immunity. The results from a standardised psychological test produced significantly reduced levels of energy and tension at the end of music listening sessions, using both live and recorded music. Conversely there was a significantly increased level of energy and sense of well-being after the participants took part in active group music therapy sessions using improvisation.[61]

The next study involved twenty-three telephone interviews carried out by the research collaborators after active group music therapy sessions. Emergent themes included 'choice and enrichment' (as opposed to the limitations imposed by a cancer diagnosis); 'power, freedom and release' (as contrasted with feelings of disempowerment); 'musical meaning and group process'; 'music and healing'; and 'creativity and creative identity', sometimes in a 'latent' and emergent form, again as related to the impact of the diagnosis and living with cancer. This study also identified participants' feelings of 'regret and loss' in their individual musical biographies, and notions of 'musical talent' and 'being musical'. Such themes accentuate the sensitive care and the potential risks involved when inviting people to improvise in group music therapy within this context.[62] Some of the themes of this third study included spiritual perspectives such as 'hope, transcendence and looking forward'.[63]

Concluding points

As in the other practice-based chapters we have been selective in the areas of practice discussed. We are conscious of omissions, such as, for example, music therapy in forensic psychiatry and for people living with HIV/AIDS.[64] We have highlighted the use of improvisation, song and songwriting when working with adults, with only brief reference to the growing use of receptive approaches, including the Bonny Method of Guided Imagery and Music (BMGIM).[65]

---

60 Bunt and Marston-Wyld (1995).
61 Burns *et al.* (2001).
62 Daykin *et al.* (2007).
63 McClean *et al.* (2012).
64 For example Compton Dickinson *et al.* (2012); Lee (1996).
65 Grocke and Wigram (2007). See also www.ami-bonnymethod.org.

Music can represent individual and group needs in a range of contexts. Music therapy can help adults find a voice when there is limited capacity to use words, take risks, confront change, reconcile crises and move forward. Music can be used to explore issues from a different perspective. However, while recognising these features and music's contribution to promoting a positive attitude to life, we are mindful that music therapy is not a panacea. Referral to another kind of creative or therapeutic intervention may be more relevant.

We have indicated how music and music therapy can be a resource for relatives and carers and for building relationships in broader community contexts. This creative flexibility contributes to music therapy's increasing relevance as a holistic resource for adult health and well-being: '[M]usic contributes to health and wellbeing in numerous ways because it interconnects with the self as a unity – as a fluid and integrated matrix of body-brain-mind-conscious-and-unconscious systems that are continuously sculpted by cultural, social and environmental processes.'[66]

---

66 Elliott and Silverman (2012: 33).

7 Music therapy and older adult health

'Crown of life' . . . nothing left to lose? Older adults and music

In 1991 the UN General Assembly adopted the United Nations Principles for Older Persons. The five key principles are Independence, Participation, Care, Self-fulfilment and Dignity. *Independence* suggests that older people should have access to food and shelter, income-generating opportunities, appropriate education and the support required to live at home for as long as possible. *Participation* suggests that older persons should remain integrated in society and have an active role in decision-making. *Care* suggests that our seniors should have access to adequate health care and be able to enjoy basic human rights even if they need institutional care. *Self-fulfilment* suggests that older adults should be able to pursue opportunities for the full development of their potential. Finally, *Dignity* suggests that people of older age should be treated fairly and with respect, and be able to live in security.[1]

This formal establishment by the United Nations of the Principles for Older Persons indicates that there are human rights violations specific to this age group. Many researchers of lifespan development argue that older people are stigmatised in many contexts, perhaps because of the often unrealistic image of older persons as unproductive, feeble and needy members of society. The fact is that many older adults are quite strong and healthy.[2] For those who need help, there is evidence that older people in many countries suffer unnecessarily as a result of under-assessment and inadequate treatment, including lack of access to decent palliative care.[3]

At about the same time as the UN Principles were established, a new under-standing of older adults as a *resource* in society was also emerging. In 1989 the historian Peter Laslett published *A Fresh Map of Life*, in which he wrote about the emergence of 'the third age', the years between retirement and 'the fourth age', which is when health problems tend to increase in number and severity. Laslett's

---

1 For a full description of the UN Principles for Older Persons and for more information on the United Nations' International Plan of Action on Ageing, see, for example, www.unescap.org/ageing/res/res46-91.htm.
2 See Hendry and Kloep (2012).
3 Davies and Higginson (2004).

analysis was naturally linked to time and place: formerly, many retired people in most societies did not usually have much good health, energy or time left, but improvements in welfare and health care have changed the situation dramatically. Laslett saw that many people nowadays experience the years after retirement as 'the crown of life'. He also developed a critique of 'ageism' (hostile and demeaning descriptions of the elderly in society).[4]

While retirement may be difficult for some people, many older adults engage in activities of various sorts, even learning new skills, for instance with the University of the Third Age (U3A). Retirement from paid work does not necessarily involve reduced activity. Sooner or later we all get feeble unless we die a sudden death, but before that, many older people are quite hardy for a number of years. They may be conscious of the possibility of growing throughout the life cycle; older persons develop in order to handle various challenges and losses, and use new possibilities for social and sexual activity.[5]

Researchers are sometimes surprised to find older persons describing themselves as healthy even though, according to medical logic, they might have several health problems. Distinctions between the terms *disease*, *illness* and *sickness* are therefore perhaps especially relevant in relation to older adults. Sometimes these terms are used interchangeably, but in the academic literature some helpful distinctions have been established. 'Disease' is the term for referring to ill health in the procedures of medicine, while 'illness' is the term used by people for referring to their own poor health, irrespective of whether they have medical diseases or not. In the literature, 'sickness' is sometimes used to refer to a group's social construction of the person's status as unhealthy.[6] If we use the terms in this way, sickness can be independent of both (medical) disease and (experienced) illness. A person could have a minor disease but feel healthy and yet be considered unhealthy by a community – because of ageism, for instance. Logically the three terms are clearly different. In real life there might be complex interactions between disease, illness and sickness.

Whatever their experience of health, older people usually pass through several transitions, for instance in relation to work and activity, health and strength, and family and relationships. Transitions are often times when a person's relationship to music changes too. Several studies suggest that music can be remarkably important for many older adults and that interest in music, and time spent on listening to music and in musical participation, often increase after retirement.[7] These findings can be seen in studies that demonstrate positive effects of creative and social activity on the health and well-being of older people.[8] It is clear that

---

4 In using the term 'third age' for the period of healthy older adulthood, Laslett (1989/1991) described adulthood as 'the second age' and placed childhood and adolescence together to form 'the first age'.
5 Hendry and Kloep (2012).
6 Boyd (2011).
7 Gembris (2008); Hays and Minichiello (2005); Laukka (2006); Pickles (2003); Saarikallio (2011); Taylor (2011).
8 Greaves and Farbus (2006); Silverstein and Parker (2002).

older persons use music both in spite of and because of various health issues. Here, 'in spite of' indicates strong interests in music 'whatever happens'; 'because of' indicates conscious uses of music as a tool for 'keeping the doctor away'.[9]

In an interview study on the use and functions of music in a lifespan perspective, Saarikallio finds that after retirement, music is a source of revival and relaxation, as it is for many throughout their adolescent and adult years. However, some other functions become salient after retirement. The older adults in Saarikallio's study underlined that music as a pastime and entertainment becomes significant in a new way, as it contributes more to meaning in everyday life than before. Listening to music and taking part in various musical activities are also tools for regulating and expressing emotions and alleviating feelings of loneliness and isolation. Several of the interviewees had started new musical hobbies after retirement, such as playing an instrument or singing in a choir. This was linked to feelings of agency and mastery. Saarikallio explains that musical hobbies provide experiences of success and capability across the lifespan but the importance of this seems to be empha-sised more when people get older.[10]

Traditionally, music therapists have mostly worked with older adults who are frail and have serious health challenges. The transition from the third to the fourth age is usually gradual, although accidents or sudden disorders might create important exceptions. Music therapists therefore need to be aware of societal tendencies and the research on music in the third age, and become interested in how they might support people's use of music as an everyday life health resource. As we will see below, some music therapists increasingly work in prevention and health promotion with people in this period of life.

Music therapy practice and research with older adults

A quick search for 'Forever Young' on YouTube reveals song classics by artists such as Alphaville, Jay-Z and Bob Dylan or, if you keep looking, a video published by the American Music Therapy Association entitled *20 Years since 'Forever Young'*. On 1 August 1991 the NAMT, one of the two music therapy organisations that merged in 1998 to form the American Music Therapy Association, had the opportunity to provide testimony on ageing at a hearing before the Senate Special Committee. The American hearing was called 'Forever Young: Music and Aging'. The video on YouTube shows music therapists, musicians, legislators, patients and physicians giving testimony in support of music therapy.[11]

In the United States the Senate hearing on music therapy and ageing provided a foundation for recognition and advocacy at state and federal level. In many other countries also, there is considerable interest in music therapy with older adults.

---

9 Clift *et al.* (2010); Zanini and Leao (2006); Stige (2010b).
10 Saarikallio (2011).
11 A transcript of the hearing was published in 1992 in *Music Therapy Perspectives*; see, for example, Sacks (1992). See also a summary celebrating the twentieth anniversary of the hearing on the AMTA's webpage: www.musictherapy.org/20th_anniversary_of_senate_hearing/

The situation is often challenging, however, as care for the elderly is frequently under-resourced and music therapy posts in this area are often few and part-time. Furthermore, music therapy is not always integrated sufficiently into health and social care services.[12] There is still a need to work for more music therapy practice and research in this field.

The range of contexts in which music therapists work with older adults is broad. Many music therapists work in nursing homes and hospitals; others work in day-care centres, home-based services or hospices. The conditions and health issues with which music therapists work vary correspondingly. They include, for example, dementia and various neurodegenerative diseases, pain, respiratory difficulties, and depression and anxiety. Broader issues and areas of work such as social isolation and quality of life are central, too, as well as the meaning of life and death in the context of palliative care.

Dementia is arguably the most common condition in music therapy practice with older adults. There are several types of dementia. The most widespread is Alzheimer's disease, which is a neurodegenerative disorder. The construct of dementia is similar in DSM and ICD, and in both diagnostic systems it is defined as a syndrome characterised by memory impairment and decline in other cognitive abilities.[13] In most countries the majority of residents in nursing homes have dementia, and cognitive impairment is 'by far the strongest health condition predictor of institutionalisation'.[14] The number of people with dementia is increasing rapidly in most countries because of demographic changes. The baby boomers of the post-Second World War generation are now ageing. Life expectancy has increased and the percentage of a cohort with dementia increases dramatically with greater age. We will focus on dementia when describing theory, research, activities and formats for music therapy with older adults, but it is important to bear in mind the broad range of contexts and conditions described above.

The orientations and theoretical perspectives that inform music therapists when working with older adults include the whole range discussed in Chapter 2. In relation to dementia, two contrasting examples will be described here, namely a cognitive-behavioural and a psychodynamic-humanistic approach.

Alicia Clair and several of her colleagues focus on a cognitive-behavioural approach in which music is understood as a stimulus event and reinforcement, mediated by cognitive processes. Within this perspective, music can be used to provide diversion, decrease symptoms, offer physical and emotional stimulation, help in the management of pain and relieve stress and tension.[15] Working in this tradition, Melissa Mercadal-Brotons maintains that a cognitive-behavioural

---

12 Myskja (2012).
13 DSM and ICD are two of the most widely used systems of diagnosis (at the time of writing with DSM–V and ICD–10 as the most recent editions). The first has been developed by the American Psychiatric Association (APA) and the second by the World Health Organization (WHO).
14 Alzheimer's Disease International (2009: 51).
15 Clair and Memmott (2008).

approach is particularly well suited to dementia patients because it enables behaviour modifications without requiring the capacity to understand and analyse events through use of meta-cognition.[16]

In contrast, Hanne Mette Ridder integrates psychodynamic and humanistic perspectives in music therapy with patients with dementia. Ridder's main orientation is informed by the person-centred approach developed by psychologist Tom Kitwood, who argues that dementia care should fulfil psychosocial needs by enhancing *personhood*. Kitwood's theory of personhood, developed in the 1990s, is based on a critique of the healthcare practices he observed, in which he argued that dementia was regarded almost solely as a biomedical phenomenon. Kitwood claimed that there is a connection between this basic assumption and a heavy reliance on control techniques such as medication and physical restraints. In Kitwood's view, such techniques can lead to a devaluation of persons with dementia. He envisioned a different culture of dementia care, one that attends to the whole person and enables each individual to remain a social being who makes the fullest possible use of his or her abilities.[17] Ridder applies these general and value-based principles and links them to an approach from which she integrates more specific elements such as 'communicative musicality', acoustic cueing techniques, musical regulatory elements and social engagement. Like Mercadal-Brotons, Ridder acknowledges the limited capacity for meta-cognition among patients with dementia, but she proposes very different implications. She understands agitation, for instance, common among many patients with dementia, not as an aspect of the disease process or as inappropriate behaviour, but as reactions to unmet psychosocial needs and as attempts to communicate these.[18]

How is music being used in music therapy with older adults? Again there is a whole gamut of possibilities, ranging from the use of songs to dance and movement, instrumental improvisation, ensemble playing, performance, music listening and conversations focusing on reminiscence. The choice would depend on theoretical orientation, client population, cultural tradition and personal preference. Differences in theoretical orientation are often reflected in practice. For example, the use of structured activities might focus on the training of functions, whereas improvisations might focus on emotional communication and interpersonal relationships. Ridder argues that therapeutic singing is a very flexible method for patients with moderate to severe dementia and is applicable also to patients who cannot play instruments because of, for instance, apraxia (the inability to perform purposeful movements).

If an aim is to establish an emotionally safe frame for patients with moderate or severe dementia, Ridder recommends frequent and short sessions, for example fifteen minutes three times a week rather than forty-five minutes once a week. When it comes to content, the principle of 'less is more' is key to good practice in

16 Mercadal-Brotons (2011: 545).
17 Kitwood (1997).
18 Ridder (2003, 2007, 2011).

dementia care. She argues that 'the therapist must be aware that for every question, comment, movement and touch that she "adds" to the therapy, it becomes a stimulus that *might* confuse or overwhelm the client, leading to misinterpretation and lack of trust'.[19]

Research on the effects of music therapy with patients with dementia is currently inconclusive. A randomised controlled study by Ridder and colleagues reports positive effects on agitation disruptiveness and the prescription of psychotropic medication,[20] but other studies have less convincing findings.[21] Before the study by Ridder and her colleagues was published, McDermott and associates performed a systematic review containing a narrative synthesis of research on music therapy in dementia, including evaluation of both process-based and outcome-based studies.[22] They found evidence for short-term improvements in behaviour and mood following music therapy. Singing featured as a medium for change in several of the studies reviewed, but the authors argue that there is too much heterogeneity in the material to develop a new theory based on this finding. The researchers found little evidence for longer-term benefits and they found no longitudinal studies investigating how and why music therapy might work in relation to dementia. They state the need for studies based on qualitative research in which older people with dementia are given the opportunity of providing their own views on quality of life and music therapy, before outcome measures are defined. The researchers conclude that future studies on music therapy in dementia need to look beyond short-term effects, use a defined theoretical model, clarify descriptions of the intervention and employ study designs that use more appropriate outcome measures.[23]

The story of Jon's first encounter with music therapy

Working in dementia care can be very rewarding, as music often brings life to a situation. It can be quite challenging too, emotionally, musically and theoretically.

Jon was a strong man. He was 74 but his gait was upbeat and his back straight as he went up and down the corridor of the nursing home, knocking on each and every door. As he knocked, he would shout, 'Can anybody help me? I need to get out! I need to get out!' Jon's language was not fluent any more but he would repeat this sentence again and again. As he grew increasingly desperate he grew aggressive too. Eventually, the nurses knew, he would end up hitting someone because

---

19 Ridder (2011: 132).
20 Ridder *et al.* (2013).
21 See, for example, Vink *et al.* (2011).
22 A narrative synthesis relies primarily on the use of words and text to summarise and explain findings of multiple research studies (qualitative and/or quantitative). See, for example, Pope *et al.* (2007: 102–6).
23 McDermott *et al.* (2012).

nobody was helping. As he had been a farmer, he knew that he should have been in the shed and that the cows were mooing loudly in pain now, because he was late for the milking.

Nothing could stop Jon from knocking and shouting, not even the sight of one of the nurses. When he was not aggressive, Jon found them very attractive and he did not usually hesitate to express this in flirtatious behaviour. When his wife, Ruth, visited, this would at times hurt her feelings but she also told the nurses that anything was better than seeing Jon in his desperate search for a way out. One day when she came for her visit, Ruth heard from one of the nurses that a music therapist would now be working on the ward two days a week. Ruth immediately asked whether Jon could be among the patients who received music therapy services. 'I don't know if he knows any music any more. Actually, he was never especially active musically. He never went to concerts or any of that stuff,' she said, 'but he used to love to dance and I think you should try everything to give him *some* good moments.'

Mark, the music therapist, was engaged by the nursing home to work on this specialist ward for patients with dementia and agitated behaviours. The ward had agreed to participate in a research project investigating the effects of music therapy on the agitated behaviour, quality of life and medication of patients with dementia. For Mark this was a new and exciting experience. He had been working as a music therapist with older adults for more than a year now, but it was usually group work that was requested by the staff at the nursing homes. He found the group work interesting and meaningful but he had often hoped for more intensive work with the patients who seemed to need it. The research project allowed this to happen. He could now work with patients individually if the patient needed this as a supplement to the group work, and he could offer sessions twice a week. At the same time he was also anxious. Would he be up to the expectations of the researchers? And would the generation of empirical material restrict him, burden him or affect the clinical work negatively in any other way?

Mark was soon informed about Ruth's wish that Jon could have music therapy. 'Are there any reasons not to prioritise Jon among the patients in this ward?', Mark asked the nurses. 'No . . . He is going to be hard work, but why not give it a try?', the nurses responded. The assessment that Mark had planned was a staged procedure involving two music therapy sessions where he would see whether he was able to engage Jon musically, combined with two simple forms that the nurses and the family would fill out, containing information about his history, challenges, resources and musical preferences.

Now Mark had prepared himself for the first encounter with Jon. Because this was a specialist ward, it was richly resourced compared to the other wards where he had worked previously. There was even an extra lounge, not often used, which was for use as a music therapy room. The nurses had recommended that he do the individual sessions in each patient's living room but he wanted to try out having every session in the lounge. He was also given the opportunity to buy a decent number of instruments, CDs and songbooks. There was not enough money to buy a good guitar but he didn't mind too much. He preferred working with his own guitar, which had served him so well for so many years. 'It would perhaps be more professional not to bring my own private guitar,' he worried to himself, 'but . . .' There was no more time to think about the guitar. He had to tune it and get ready for the session. The day before, he had spent quite some time on YouTube and other internet sites searching for and learning songs that the family had said that Jon liked. He hoped that he was prepared for a session in which he would be able to engage Jon with songs that he knew well.

The music therapist left the lounge to go and get Jon. Some minutes ago he had seen that Jon was relaxing in his own living room. Mark had promised the nurses that he would come and bring Jon to the lounge instead of having them bring him over. The nurses were always quite busy and he did not want them to feel that the new music therapy on offer would be another weight on their shoulders. He entered the long corridor and started walking towards the other end where Jon's room was located, expecting to find him there. Then he realised that he was already too late. He observed an aggressive man at the other end of the corridor and heard some loud shouting. 'Can anybody help me? I need to get out! I need to get out!' Jon was knocking on a door, shouting desperately. Mark approached him carefully, seeing how agitated he was. 'Can you help me?', Jon shouted in his face when he came close.

The music therapist did not know what to say. He realised that he was scared. Jon was very strong, very agitated and near enough to hit him. Would he strike out? In the corner of his eye Mark spotted a nurse coming down the corridor. She stopped some metres away, obviously uncertain about whether or not she should interfere. What should he do? Mark had brought his guitar with him, not because he had planned to use it much but because he wanted to show it to Jon when explaining that they could go to the music therapy room together. Before he knew what he was doing, Mark started playing the guitar. His voice trembled as the words of 'Hallelujah' came out of his mouth. What was he doing? The question circled around in his head and he looked quickly over to the nurse to see whether there was any reaction there. To his surprise he had noticed the other day that songs by Leonard Cohen were on the list of songs that the family suggested Jon would like. But 'Hallelujah' now, in the middle of this frightening situation? That did not make much sense.

It did make a difference, however. Mark observed that Jon's breathing changed. The shouting stopped and Mark noticed that Jon started to watch what he was doing. It seemed as though he was listening. The music therapist did not know what to do but kept singing the song, several times, until Jon started humming in his own fragmented way and his breathing and posture were much more relaxed. Mark was just about to ask Jon whether he wanted to join him and walk over to the music therapy room. But then he stopped himself. Why risk everything with a question that Jon probably would not understand or know how to respond to? He wanted to respect Jon's choices but, thinking it over, the invitation could be musical. He knew that Jon could respond in sound and movement. The only problem was that the corridor down to the lounge was a long one. Would the moment last? Should he perhaps instead try to lead Jon back to his living room, just a door or two away?

The story of Jon's first encounter with music therapy reveals several themes that are central when working with patients in an institution for older adults with dementia. For the music therapist there is the challenge concerning the moment of encounter: how do you best meet the older person musically and emotionally? There are other challenges: how to collaborate with nurses and other professionals? What does it mean to be professional? How can a music therapist establish that his or her role is legitimate and valuable?

Musical and emotional encounters in professional context

Mark obviously wanted to respect Jon's musical preferences. Assessment criteria and recognition of music preference are considered key features when music is used in various healthcare contexts and perhaps are especially important when it comes to work with older adults.[24] We will briefly outline three implications for music therapy practice. First, the musical preferences of each patient cannot be assumed on the basis of information such as gender, ethnicity, age group or class, but need to be assessed in each individual case.[25] Second, preferences might vary

---

24 Dileo and Bradt (2005); Ridder (2003); Myskja (2012).
25 North and Hargreaves (2007) investigated the relationship between musical preferences and socio-economic aspects among more than 2,500 informants. They found certain correlations; for instance, people who like opera and classical music had often been through higher education. However, the researchers argue that the relationships are complex and that no *simple* causal relationships between musical preference and social factors can be established. Relationships obviously vary between cohorts, countries, cultures and individuals.

over time from one situation to the next and from one activity to the other; our preferences on a good day and a bad day differ, as they do when we are resting or being active.[26] Third, expressed preferences should not be interpreted too narrowly. Certain pieces of music might be linked to strong associations and emotions but a person's relationship to music is usually more flexible than that. There might be broader genres or types of music that a person appreciates and some musical-cultural codes that are appreciated across genres. The chords of Cohen's 'Hallelujah' are not particular to this song or genre, for example. In short, musical preferences go beyond a concrete identification of which songs to use with the patient; they are more flexible and multidimensional than that.

This suggests that music therapists should not work with preferences in ways that are too narrowly focused on the past. People's history and cultural background are obviously important, but the significance of the experience of the present situation and of possibilities for learning and change should not be forgotten. We learn about facets of the other person's identity and are therefore invited to reflect upon our own identity as well. The process might involve deep and intriguing work. The music therapist's musical choice in the story above ended up being quite intuitive, while also based on information given by Jon's wife. The musical encounter cannot be fully understood as just a cognitive choice of a song to match the patient's needs and predilections; Mark used his innate yet cultivated communicative musicality in a moment of musical-emotional improvisation.[27]

The question of how to meet the older person musically cannot be separated from the question of how to meet someone emotionally. It is not just about *what* music to use but also about *how* to use it. Mark, the music therapist in our story, had been reading about this issue and, given the fact that he had agreed to take part in a research project, wanted to explore how to understand emotional encounters in music. He had read the narrative synthesis of McDermott and associates (see p. 154) and had noted that, in both the qualitative and the quantitative studies, singing appears to be associated with benefits in this area. This had inspired him to read an article by Ridder on how singing can influence social engagement for people with dementia.[28]

Ridder's article explores how singing, emotions and social engagement can be closely related. She underpins her ideas with the 'polyvagal perspective', a neuroaffective theory developed by psychiatrist Stephen Porges.[29] An evolutionary understanding of human emotions characterises this theory, which highlights how mammals, in order to survive, need not only to evaluate whether there is any danger in the immediate environment but also to engage in social communication. The myelinated vagus system (part of the tenth cranial nerve) has evolved to allow

26 Change can relate to an individual but also to age group. For example, the rapid technological development of the twentieth and twenty-first centuries has made mediated music experiences much more accessible and thus has changed the conditions for musical engagement dramatically from one decade to the next. See, for instance, Bossius and Lilliestam (2011).
27 See Malloch and Trevarthen (2009) and the discussion of communicative musicality in Chapter 4.
28 Ridder (2011).
29 Porges (2001, 2010).

social engagement, Porges argues: it 'integrates the regulation of facial muscles, cardiac output and the vocal apparatus for affective communication'.[30] Mark was not quite sure whether he was able to follow this and the detailed explanations that preceded and followed on the immobilisation system, fight and flight responses, and various circuits of the nervous system. But the clinical implications suggested by Ridder made sense to him and the recent encounter with Jon served to highlight this. Ridder writes:

> A person with severe dementia with cognitive difficulties in perception will not understand the reason for participating in music therapy. If he is occupied with other things that are meaningful to him, he might not find it meaningful to go to a music therapy room and might not understand what he will do there. If he has difficulties in processing environmental stimuli, he will be disoriented in time and place. The environment might seem unfamiliar to him, and staff and other residents may be perceived as strangers. If his feelings of safety are threatened, older circuits of the nervous system may become activated, leading to the mobilization of the flight or fight behaviors or immobilization.[31]

Informed by the polyvagal theory of Porges, Ridder develops guidelines for practice that made sense for Mark. Ridder proposes that, because of the attention and memory deficits in persons with dementia, music therapists should use acoustic cueing to establish a clear and safe frame. Instead of words and verbal instructions, specific songs can signal what is going to happen. Ridder also proposes that the music therapist should be conscious about the critical role of the voice in creating safety for patients with dementia. And she argues that entrainment of music and movements, together with careful use of structural elements such as phrases, can contribute significantly to regulation of arousal and emotions.[32]

Mark had to admit that perhaps he had been too focused on the guitar. Certainly the stringed instrument could provide rhythmic support and wonderful tonal contexts for his singing but he wondered whether he needed to be even more aware about how he communicated through voice and body. Mark also admitted that his concern about whether to return to the lounge was as much about his own safety as about Jon's needs. It was not that Jon did not need a safe frame, but perhaps Ridder was right in suggesting that acoustic cueing and use of voice and body would be the central elements in creating this. A special room and a closed door would not necessarily help Jon to start feeling safer.

These reflections led Mark to re-evaluate some of his assumptions about what it means to be a professional music therapist. Rooms and instruments can be very

---

30 Porges (2001: 126).
31 Ridder (2011: 134–5).
32 Ibid.: 136–41.

important but his thoughts were now drawn to how he could make himself helpful for each patient and the rest of the ward in the context of challenging everyday situations. He would use the music therapy room in the lounge whenever that was helpful, but he would also work in a patient's living room, or in the corridor, or wherever he could use his skills in creating musical and emotional encounters. Instead of worrying too much about where and when he should use music, he became more and more absorbed by the idea that as a professional music therapist he needed to understand how music connects people. He revisited Porges' polyvagal theory, which he found fascinating, but he still did not feel quite convinced – not that he could explain why. He started to search for literature critiquing the theory in order to see whether that would enlighten him. In one article he found a substantial critique of the basis of the polyvagal theory and the version of evolutionary theory that it subscribes to.[33] Mark wondered to himself how he was supposed to know who was right.

Mark clearly needed to develop his skills in critical appraisal of theory. He also decided that he wanted to read a very different theoretical account and studied Ansdell's book on how music helps in music therapy and everyday life. Mark would recognise themes from Ridder's writings, such as personhood and musical relationship, but Ansdell's take is ecological, with a focus on psychosocial and cultural levels, quite different from the theory of Porges.[34] 'This is probably the kind of stuff Emma should read,' Mark was thinking. 'But is it relevant for me, in my context?' Emma was one of Mark's classmates from his music therapy education. They had studied together at a university in southern Norway. After they graduated, she had decided to go up north to work in a small town. In a recent email Emma had enthusiastically described to Mark a community music therapy project she was involved in.

Aurora: the story of a senior choir

A growing number of older adults experience a 'third age' in life where they are relatively healthy. Many take part in activities that they feel enhance the quality of life. Singing is one such activity, and several music therapists now work with prevention and health promotion in community contexts:

> In the spring she graduated as a music therapist, Emma chose to apply for a music therapy position in a small town in the northernmost county of Norway. In June she was invited for an interview for the position. She arrived by plane and was struck by the beauty of the landscape. No darkness, not even a sunset, just the bright light of the sun shining on the treeless hills and the shimmering sea twenty-four hours a day. She

33 Grossman and Taylor (2007: 274).
34 Ansdell (2013).

fell in love with the place and almost forgot to ask about the job itself. The impression she had was that the position would be interesting yet also quite wide-ranging and challenging. She was a bit nervous about the fact that there are so few music therapists in this part of the country. Professionally she might get lonely. But she was also intrigued by the possibilities. The fact that the indigenous Sami population had a high profile in the town inspired her. She did not know much about Sami culture but was eager to learn. When she was offered the job, she accepted.

In August she moved up north and by November the same year, one of the exciting things in her new job was the establishment of a choir for health, focusing on the needs of older adults. By this time of the year the bright light of the summer had been replaced by a sub-polar incessant darkness that Emma found heavy, except when the northern lights came along with their fascinating dance. Perhaps the choir could bring some light too? In the very first rehearsal more than fifteen people arrived and wanted to join, which was so inspiring for everybody that they started discussing the name for the choir almost before doing anything else. Someone first suggested 'Nordlyd', playing with the Norwegian word for 'northern lights' by changing the final letter from 's' to 'd', transforming the meaning into 'northern sounds' – a constructed compound not in common use. Everybody laughed and some liked the idea but others argued that the name was too 'invented'. People would perhaps not take the choir seriously with such a funny name. Someone said, 'What about Aurora Borealis?' Everybody laughed again. The northern lights were certainly part of their identity but the long Latin name might not be taken seriously. When Emma suggested that perhaps 'Aurora' could work, many hesitated but grew more interested when they heard that the word referred not just to lights moving on the sky but also to the old Roman goddess of the dawn, who was known to renew herself every morning. Many of those who had arrived for the choir rehearsal quite liked that; to begin singing at their age was indeed some kind of new morning, they argued. So, after a bit of discussion back and forth, Aurora became the name of the choir.

A few months later there are 30 singers in Aurora, all above 65 years old. Many are in their seventies, quite a few in their eighties and some even in their nineties. Most of them live at home and are relatively healthy, but many have health concerns, for themselves and for people they care for. They come to the choir rehearsals once a week. The rehearsals are located in the public community music school in the centre of town. Some choir members live in apartments for older adults only a block away. Others live in remote areas along the fjord or in the valleys under the mountain plateau. Some of them drive for almost an hour in order to attend the rehearsals.

When a rehearsal begins, Emma calls for attention and the singers gather together. Some sit down on their respective chairs while others prefer to stand when they sing. Emma has established the practice of starting every rehearsal with some vocal and physical exercises. The singers used to singing in a choir were not surprised by this. For others it was a bit strange. There was some giggling here and there. 'Stop giggling,' one of the choir members said with indignation. 'These exercises are good. They prepare us for the singing and are helpful for our breathing and asthma problems too!' The giggling ends, for a while.

Emma announces which songs to practise before the break. She has decided to start the practice with a few songs every choir member knows well. This was the first rehearsal after a demanding concert so it would be good to use well-rehearsed material at this point, in order for everybody to take part in a relaxed way. When the choir starts singing, Emma takes notice of Mirjá, a tiny little woman in her late eighties. A few weeks ago Mirjá's husband, Mikkal, had asked Emma for a conversation and explained that his wife would probably have to move to a nursing home soon. She was so disorganised now because of her dementia that he felt that it was not safe for her to live at home much longer. Also, as her spouse he was getting more and more exhausted. Still, he tells Emma that he wants to continue to bring Mirjá to choir rehearsals. She had lost so many skills now, including much of her verbal language, but she still intensely enjoyed singing and seemed able to remember both the lyrics and the melodies of songs. While conducting, Emma sees and hears that Mirjá is able to join in with the rest of the choir most of the time but also that she gets very confused every time there is a verbal instruction or some chat in between songs. Emma also notices that the singers surrounding Mirjá keep an eye on her and make sure that she finds the right sheet of music and things she needs. Emma does not really believe that Mirjá sings from the sheets any more, but she still appreciates the efforts of her co-singers.

Just before the break, the choir committee, elected among members for one year at a time, leaves the group for a few minutes to prepare some coffee. When the break comes, the committee members invite the singers to help themselves and then initiate a plenary discussion. The chair of the committee first asks Emma to reflect upon their last performance. She says that she thinks the performance was very successful. Everybody seemed to have been well prepared and able to manage the stress of performing. She did wonder whether they should work more on how they present themselves verbally for the audience.

Perhaps one of the singers could introduce the songs and perhaps it should be a male singer? Male singers were in a minority in Aurora, but if they were more visible perhaps more male members would be recruited? A long discussion ensues before someone throws in a different yet related theme: better verbal introductions or not, their singing could not have been too bad. This choir member had heard a lot of praise of the choir from her neighbours. One neighbour had been especially impressed by the vitality that she heard in the delivery of the songs. 'I guess she was quite surprised that these grey old things could be that vital,' the singer laughs.

The issue of whether one of the male singers could introduce the songs in the choir concerts is not quite resolved but the committee members decide to proceed by introducing another issue. Proudly they announce that Aurora has been invited to perform at another concert, and not a small one either this time, but one connected to the yearly dog sledge race on the mountain plateau. This is a big event in town every winter and most choir members were delighted to hear the news. 'It is quite an honour and a real acknowledgement of Aurora,' one of them commented.

'Perhaps we could talk more about this next time?', Emma suggests. It is time to continue rehearsing and the singers make themselves ready again. After another series of warming-up exercises and a song the singers know really well, Emma announces that she has brought with her a new song. There is some excitement in her voice. 'I have found a collection of very nice compositions inspired by the Sami joik tradition and arranged for mixed choirs,' she explains. Being from southern Norway, Emma does not really know the joik, a form of song unique to the Sami people, but she knows the sound of it and she loves it. Through her head runs what she has been reading about joik lately: she knows that each joik is very personal, often spiritual in nature, and that a joik reflects a creature or place in a very direct way: in a joik you do not sing 'about' a person, you sing 'a person'. Emma finds this idea beautiful and wants Aurora to honour the tradition.

'These joik arrangements for mixed choirs are really exciting,' she tells the choir members. 'Today we could try the song "Katnihavuolle".' One of the male singers laughs and asks, 'Katt ka?' (Norwegian for 'Cat what?'). There is silence. Emma senses a sudden tension among the choir members. Immediately she realises that she feels very insecure. In all honesty she has no idea of the meaning of the Sami word 'Katnihavuolle', but that is not her main concern. There is something about the sudden tension among choir members that scares her in a way she had not anticipated. She does not quite know what to do or what to say and turns to the song by playing an introductory chord on the piano without really having any plan. All of a sudden, she hears a female voice from somewhere among the choir members, singing the tune with only a little hesitation at first and then with increasing strength. The voice is intense and raw in a beautiful way and Emma thinks for herself that this is how the song should be sung, even though she has never heard it like this before. Everybody is listening now, and Emma realises with surprise that it is Mirjá who is singing. Mirjá, who usually does not remember the name of her husband, obviously knows and remembers this song. Emma has never heard Mirjá use anything but the Norwegian language, but she can hear, from how Mirjá pronounced the Sami words of the joik, that Mirjá is now singing in her mother tongue.

When Mirjá has finished singing there is silence again, but it is a different kind of silence now. Emma nods to the singers, plays an introductory piano chord once again and invites the choir members to try out the different lines of the arrangement. The singers join in, not everybody to begin with, but after a while most of the singers take part quite actively. A few singers are still reluctant and hardly seem to be trying. This bothers Emma quite a lot, but she decides to keep the song going.

We have to leave Emma here, in the middle of a challenging situation, in order to examine some of the issues, processes and theoretical concepts that might be significant for this kind of work.

Music, care and social capital in a world of conflicts

Issues around ethnicity created substantial tension in the Aurora choir. After the rehearsal the music therapist would hear some singers endorse the Sami efforts at reclaiming their culture and community. Others were angry and would say things like 'It's a long time since these people were repressed. Today they have just too many rights. They think they own the land!' Emma realises that she has been far too naïve in her approach to the conflicts around Sami culture in the area. It is not enough to bring in a nice traditional song and expect things to work.

Using the song 'Katnihavuolle' had worked, mostly, but perhaps more by chance and Mirjá's unexpected resources than anything else.[35] Emma had recently read Cochavit Elefant's description of an action research project making previously unheard voices heard in an attempt to negotiate a shared vision for a

---

35 See, for example, Van Bruggen-Rufi and Vink (2011) for a discussion of the significance of cultural knowledge when selecting songs for music therapy with older adults with diverse cultural backgrounds.

community music therapy choir project in Israel.[36] Perhaps she could contact the Sami research centre of the neighbouring town and ask whether they would be interested in a collaborative research project with Aurora, so that the conflicting values could be articulated and negotiated? She had a vague idea that this would alter Aurora's role and function in the town too. Obviously she should not forget to discuss the idea with the singers before proceeding.

Emma identifies herself with the movement of community music therapy.[37] She is aware that not every music therapist would agree that to work with a senior choir is an appropriate task for a professional music therapist. From reading some of Stephen Clift's extensive research on singing and older people, she knows that in the United Kingdom, conductors of senior choirs would typically be community musicians and music in health practitioners.[38] 'Music therapists in no way could or should have a monopoly of practice in relation to such choirs,' she would usually respond if someone asked, 'but why should they not be part of an interdisciplinary endeavour exploring how music can be a resource for health and well-being in the community?' Emma realised that if she wanted to follow this through, she would need to develop a professional language for talking about such things. Two of the themes that interested her were self-care versus professional care and the relationship between music and various forms of social resources.

In a qualitative study of a senior choir, Stige's analysis and interpretation focus on three aspects of *care*: 'self-care', 'care for others' and 'professional care'.[39] Almost all the singers framed their choir participation in terms that may be described as 'self-care'. This includes paying attention to one's own needs and interests, and nurturing strengths. Some singers perform self-care through explicit awareness of physical needs and problems. They might describe singing as a 'remedy' and claim that they 'need to sing' because of specific challenges such as asthma or other breathing problems. Other participants reflect on the more general challenge of prophylactic self-care, where singing in a choir becomes a way of avoiding passivity and isolation.

In the same study, 'care for others' includes responsiveness within interactive events as well as more concrete acts of helping, such as driving fellow singers to rehearsals:

> Related to this is the fact that many singers talk about a strong sense of *community* and *friendships*. Choir singing, they claim, is *social*, but in a way which is quite different from just coming together over a cup of coffee. One singer that was quite new in town explains the intensity of the experience in the following way: 'I used to be new here . . . I knew nobody else, but today I would say that I think of us as a really good group of friends. Or: we are siblings; singer-siblings . . .' (female singer, 79 years old).[40]

36 Elefant (2010).
37 See, for example, Pavlicevic and Ansdell (2004), Stige *et al.* (2010) and Stige and Aarø (2012).
38 Clift *et al.* (2010).
39 Stige (2010b: 263–74).
40 Ibid.: 266.

In the choir Stige studied, the appreciation of 'self-care' and 'care for others' was intertwined with appreciation for 'professional care'. The singers talked about the importance of the music therapist (in the role of choir conductor) encouraging them with humour, attention and positive remarks. They also underlined the importance of the music therapist's capacity to provide relevant feedback when that was required. A high degree of *mutual trust* seemed to be involved. Many singers also stressed how the music therapist contributed to the collaborative efforts of producing energy, hope and direction in the work.

The interplay between self-care, care for others and professional care could be summed up in the following way:

> The professional care . . . is differentiated care, then, the conductor being credited for sensitively reading the needs and interests of each singer. This seems to be experienced as support not only by the singers in need but also by the neighbors of those in need. It also seems to make the 'intrapersonal negotiations' on how to balance self-care and care for others somewhat easier to handle.[41]

Stige suggests that a 'culture of care' is nurtured in the choir, with positive consequences for social networks, social support and capacities for coping. These terms all describe phenomena and processes that take place at personal and interpersonal levels. In addition, we can relate the work of a choir like Aurora to *social capital*, a notion that characterises larger units such as local communities.[42] Social epidemiologists Kawachi and Berkman define social capital as 'those features of social structures – such as levels of interpersonal trust and norms of reciprocity and mutual aid – which act as resources for individuals and facilitate collective action'.[43]

Political scientist Robert Putnam distinguishes between *bonding* and *bridging* as two forms of social capital. *Bonding* is defined as the social capital associated with the social networks of homogeneous groups of people. Bonding social capital may exist, according to Putnam, for example within various fraternal organisations, church-based groups or country clubs. In contrast, *bridging* is social capital associated with groups or networks that include people from diverse social interests and backgrounds. Examples, according to Putnam, are civil rights movements, many youth service groups and ecumenical religious organizations. 'Bonding social capital' may manifest as cohesion, solidarity and high levels of emotional support. 'Bridging social capital' typically means exchange of information, diffusion of information and access to external assets.[44]

A choir such as Aurora can host both forms of social capital. Members might come from the same neighbourhood or cultural group and they might know each

41 Ibid.: 268.
42 See Stige and Aarø (2012: 87–114).
43 Kawachi and Berkman (2000).
44 Putnam (2000: 22).

other well already. In the choir they can strengthen bonding social capital, which then represents an important source of emotional and social support. A multi-ethnic choir such as Aurora might involve building higher levels of bridging social capital as well. This suggests that bridging and bonding could be considered complementing and interacting aspects of a process.[45]

So how are social capital and health related? In a review, social epidemiologists Kim, Subramanian and Kawachi found quite consistent associations between trust as an indicator of social capital, and better physical health. The evidence was stronger for self-rated health than for measurable physical health outcomes, however, and stronger for differences in trust at the individual level than at the community level. Much as this is a promising area of research, the researchers call for theory development and stronger study designs.[46]

We can relate these reflections about Aurora's processes and challenges of bonding and bridging to Simon Procter's research-based examination of music therapy and social capital,[47] and also to the work of Guylaine Vaillancourt and others who work with music and conflict transformation.[48] Emma's experiences with Aurora remind us that music is often part of interpersonal and socio-cultural conflicts. Music therapists therefore must go beyond the naïve assumption that music in and of itself leads to conflict resolution. Used in the right way, however, it might be a powerful tool for conflict transformation.

Concluding points

We have seen in this chapter that music can be remarkably important for many older adults, both for adults of the 'fourth age' needing help and support and for adults of the 'third age' actively using music as a resource in everyday life. Individuals with serious health challenges such as Jon, the patient with dementia, will need professional care and individually tailored music therapy services. At the same time, awareness in society about older adults as a resource is often lacking; there is a tendency to highlight problems and there is a degree of ageism in many societies. If and when music therapists take on a socially engaged role, as Emma did, the discourse should focus not only on music as a practical tool for health enhancement but also on human rights issues such as inclusion, participation and social justice.[49]

As this chapter has tried to demonstrate, music therapy with older adults is a broad and complex field of study and practice, growing in importance in many countries. There are numerous conditions and health issues that we have not had space to discuss in this chapter. Similarly, we have not included significant professional issues that have been explored elsewhere in the music therapy

45 Stige and Aarø (2012: 214–17).
46 Kim *et al.* (2010).
47 Procter (2004, 2006, 2011).
48 Vaillancourt (2009).
49 Stige and Aarø (2012).

literature in relation to older adults: the need for services for health and well-being within home-based care, and the need to build collaboration between music therapists, other professionals, family and relatives, for example.[50] There are also several other relevant theoretical perspectives on music therapy and older adults that we have not had room to discuss, including the growing neuroscientific knowledge of music's effects on a range of processes relevant for music therapy, such as arousal, pleasure and plasticity.[51]

Mark's story, set in the traditional professional context of a nursing home, reveals several themes that are critical for the profession and discipline of music therapy today. Theory development, theory use and theory evaluation constitute one such cluster of themes. When and how is it acceptable to import theoretical ideas from other disciplines? And how do music therapists develop skills in critical appraisal of the theories they use? The challenges illuminated by his story are not unique to his context. Mark was a keen young man who happened to discover that the theory he was interested in is controversial. Any other music therapist's reading of the interdisciplinary literature would lead to discovery of critical perspectives on theories that many music therapists find useful. Not every communication researcher would subscribe to Malloch and Trevarthen's theory of communicative musicality, and not every sociologist to Putnam's notion of social capital. We do not want to suggest that the theories with which music therapists engage should never be controversial. Given the fact that music therapy is still on the margins of traditional academia, perhaps the theories music therapists find helpful often will be controversial. On the other hand, a situation where 'anything goes' is hardly useful. There is a need for reflection on what kind of critical appraisal skills are needed among music therapists as they read, develop and use theory (see Chapter 9).

Perhaps Mark and Emma could teach us something very important here. Mark initiated a conversation with Emma because he had discovered some theoretical perspectives he imagined would be relevant for her work. They then dialogued and discussed. We can imagine that Emma discovered that some of Mark's ideas about music therapy at the nursing home were also relevant for her work with the choir, such as the ideas about acoustic cueing and the suggestion that the voice can be crucial in creating safety for people with dementia. Similarly, Mark discovered some ecological ideas that he originally thought would only be relevant for Emma's community music therapy practice, but we can imagine he later found them useful for him too, when trying to understand his decision not to always work in a special music therapy room with the door closed. In a way, both Emma and Mark work with challenges of inclusion and participation. Mark realised that for a patient like Jon it is not only the ecology between socio-cultural systems that matters, but also the ecology of body, brain, actions and reactions in a musical situation.

50 Hanser (2010); Myskja (2012); Rio (2009); Schmid and Ostermann (2010).
51 Särkämö *et al.* (2012).

8 The profession of music therapy

A resource for the community

Introduction

A colourful figure in Richard Holmes's book *The Age of Wonder* is the chemist and inventor Sir Humphry Davy (1778–1829), whose explorations and discoveries had enormous scientific, practical and social implications.[1] As well as his many contributions to the discipline of chemistry, he invented a lamp that allowed miners to work safely in the presence of flammable gases. The Davy lamp prevented many destructive explosions and literally brought light into the darkest of places. Leslie Bunt heard about Davy the hard-working scientist at his grammar school in Penzance, Cornwall, where the school was named after this locally born hero. But there was not much talk of Davy's creative passion, his poetry and the more radical approaches to his work. What has the title of Holmes's book, and Humphry Davy in particular, to do with the themes for this chapter, you may well be thinking? First, we hope that readers will share with us that a sense of 'wondering' is fundamental to all scientific, artistic and practical explorations, and certainly to working as a music therapist. Second, are we not inspired by Davy's professional life lived at the cutting edge of discovery, as scientist, artist, inventor and public figure? Third, we are proposing that there are some similarities here with the responsibilities and risks of working as a professional music therapist. We feel this is certainly the case when inviting people of all ages to listen to music or to take that first courageous step of discovery into new and improvised sounds.

Naturally we will each choose different figures for our inspiration. In Bergen, many users of mental health services have been inspired by Amalie Skram, a writer who was born there in 1846 and died in Copenhagen in 1905. Her name has been given to a non-medical and user-led centre for people living with mental health challenges, Amalie Skram House. The centre offers a range of creative and social activities, including music. The inspiration arrives from Skram's anti-oppression activism and not least from her two 'asylum novels', published in English with the title *Under Observation*.[2] Skram writes about a female painter who agrees to be hospitalised for treatment of insomnia and depression. This painter expected a

---

1 Holmes (2008).
2 Skram (1895/1992).

'rest cure' but encountered an authoritarian and patriarchal culture. Every action and statement was interpreted in ways she experienced as misdiagnoses. When she reacted to these, it only confirmed the doctor's interpretations. She was branded irrational and hostile and found herself ensnared in the repressive system. Skram's critical novels received little praise in her lifetime but have since been acknowledged as heralding more democratic, user-oriented perspectives on mental health care in Scandinavia.

So with Davy's lamp and Skram's critical light as inspirations to accompany our journey, the main question we would like to explore in this chapter is: in what ways are music therapists able to keep alive what is most radical, illuminating and creative when working to foster individual and group health and well-being? We will try to answer this by exploring how the profession of music therapy is, and can be, a resource for the local community as well as society in general. We hope that Davy and Skram would approve.

We continue with an example of a day in the life of a music therapist and then proceed to consider the identity of the music therapist as a professional, noting that music therapists might choose to put on different 'hats' in different situations. Productive and problematic relationships for the professional therapist as a 'disciplined' practitioner and as a responsible member of a community and society, with knowledge of and interest in the broader picture, will be described. We will relate such questions to other contemporary challenges of the profession. After some brief reflections on how music therapists work to sustain well-established collaborative approaches with other professionals, we will expand the agenda and raise the question of how music can be a resource for health and well-being for all. We will conclude with a summary of how the profession might best fulfil its purpose in society.

A day in the life of a music therapist

What is it that is professional about a music therapist's day? There is the fact of being paid: professionals are not amateurs engaged in interesting activities in their free time. This might seem a trivial point, but complex processes of establishing music therapy education and training, associations, ethical guidelines, research activities and so on are required before it is reasonable to talk of music therapy as a profession. These processes have taken decades to establish in most countries. A professional is also educated, usually to university level. A music therapist undertakes a specific training that brings with it qualifications, privileges and certain responsibilities. Possibilities for employment or business are among the privileges, usually accompanied by access to information and a supportive infrastructure. The responsibilities are manifold and we will discuss them in more detail in the next section. To illustrate the range of the challenges, here is an example of a day in the life of a music therapist (Simon Gilbertson).[3]

---

3 We are grateful to Simon Gilbertson for supplying this example and the accompanying reflections in italics.

On the basis of experiences in a neurorehabilitation clinic in Germany, a music therapist's day commonly would consist of individual and group sessions, meetings with members of the music therapy and multi-disciplinary teams, and continuing education and documentation work. Each morning the music therapist may take part in a multidisciplinary team meeting on each ward with a team of staff including medical doctors, nurses, occupational therapists, physiotherapists, sport thera-pists, neuropsychologists, speech and language therapists, art ther-apists and social workers. These meetings may include information about newly admitted or discharged patients, a short update on any patients in critical health states and planned family visits.

During the day, a music therapist may take part or lead meetings with other professions on a range of topics that may include the develop-ment of specific technology for electronic instruments, multidisciplinary projects involving music such as memory groups, treadmill training, and advising family members on music listening. Documentation of the therapy would be carried out using the clinic's centralised computer-based records, where all information about the patient's treatment and therapy progress is stored. A working day for a music therapist in neurorehabilitation might then look like this:

08:15: Ward meeting with all staff, including information about admis-sions, discharges, infection and medication changes

08:30: Music therapy team meeting (including any students on place-ment) – referrals and planning of the day's groups

09:00: Individual music therapy session: Tim (see Chapter 6)

09:30: Individual session: Alice (see Chapter 6)

10:00: Individual session: Jean (see Chapter 6)

10:30: Meeting with a physiotherapist to talk about the creation of a prototype for an input device for an electronic music instru-ment for a patient with a limited range of movement

11:00: Group session: Patients with severe disorientation

12:00: Note writing and documentation

12:30: Lunch

13:00: Music therapy team case presentations and group peer-supervision (once a week)

14:00: Group session (see Chapter 6)

15:15: Individual session: George (see Chapter 6)

16:00: Note taking and documentation

16:30: Regular day ends

18:00: Evening concert by staff for patients and their families and visitors

Although neurological trauma or illness is one of the most dramatic and serious causes of human isolation, coming together to play music, listen or simply watch the movements of the musicians' hands reduces these extremes of isolation, positively affects neurological, psychological and physiological capabilities, and offers these individuals and their families opportunities to find sense and meaning in their lives ahead. As professionals we are interested in music as a therapeutic factor in the clinic milieu. Often music therapists also facilitate concerts (spontaneous ones during the daytime on the ward, or planned ones in the evenings, for birthdays and anniversaries, festive seasons or in memory of a patient who has passed away). There have been many reasons why concerts have been initiated, and many effects and benefits. At Christmas we have travelled up and down playing carols on a piano in the hospital lift and we have had eleven carol concerts on Christmas Eve, one on each of the two children's and nine adults' wards.

One of the many striking aspects of Gilbertson's working day is the range and flexibility required of a music therapist in this context. It demonstrates very effectively how the music therapist offers a holistic service to meet the needs of each patient and group of patients but also the broader needs of the situation. The needs of the whole person are addressed – social, emotional, aesthetic and spiritual – not just those pertaining to physical and cognitive functionality. Listening to what is needed and sensitive adapting of musical resources to each shifting situation appears fundamental, be it improvising for an individual patient or with a family group, using and creating songs in group sessions, preparing a concert or discussing plans for some new piece of musical technology.

The total picture of this day and the different ways of working can also be described as rich, or possibly confusing. Much of the progress of music therapy practice since this book's first edition has been to consolidate what Ansdell first referred to in 2002 as the 'consensus model'.[4] According to Ansdell this arose, for the most part, from an accepted premise that music therapy would take on some of the theory, aims and practices (with particular emphasis on the boundaried private therapeutic space) of psychotherapy, and similar ethical and regulatory processes.[5] In contrast, Ansdell has been working with colleagues to explore the whole notion of community in relation to music therapy.[6] This notion provides a sense of empowerment to therapists who have been working for many years within such a fluid approach but have considered that this was not strictly music therapy. How

4 Ansdell (2002).
5 Pavlicevic and Ansdell (2004: 21).
6 Pavlicevic and Ansdell (2004); Stige *et al.* (2010); Stige and Aarø (2012).

can music therapy flourish and build communities inside and outside of the more traditional settings? Simon Procter asks similar questions that also challenge the traditional concept of professional work: 'As music therapists, do we need diagnosis? Could we work without it?' Or: 'As music therapists, do we need hierarchy? Could we work without it?'[7] Such radical questions do appear to confront some well-established traditions and practices within music therapy. Are such questions a healthy challenge to the status quo?

In many ways, Gilbertson's day seems to integrate features of a medical perspective with those of community music therapy. It is important in this kind of hospital setting to be aware of diagnosis and potential risk factors, and for the music therapist to have regular input into the ongoing work of the multidisciplinary team, which includes reading and contributing to clinical notes and records. Additionally, the day's work is viewed not in isolation but as part of the culture of the ward, the whole rehabilitation unit and, importantly, the family and social and cultural context of each patient. The work seems to be in keeping with our opening question and the guiding inspiration from Davy and Skram.

The professional as responsible member of society

In the description of the day of a music therapist we can discern much diversity. Besides direct work with patients/participants needing music therapy, there are several indirect activities that build conditions for it: by engaging in meetings, note-keeping, supervision and perhaps also research and development.[8] Gilbertson does not restrict the direct work to the boundaried private therapeutic space for individual and group work but also develops performances to which family and other visitors are invited. The indirect work is not limited to contact with patients and families but includes broader developmental tasks such as supervising students, consulting colleagues and developing new technological devices. This diversity invites reflections about the identity and purpose of the profession.

A sense of identity seems crucial both 'in relation to who we are as people and to our whole motivation in becoming musicians and music therapists'.[9] In the interdisciplinary book *Musical Identities*, the editors posed a big question relating to the nature of the self, namely '[D]o we construct "core" self-concepts which are relatively unchanging across different situations and interactions, or do we adopt different selves in different contexts?'[10] We could say that trainings as both musicians and music therapists overlap 'to form a central core self-concept . . . but that certain aspects are brought more into the foreground depending on the context' – the specific intentions of the work and setting, and the 'needs and expectations' of the people with whom we work, being the central focus.[11] As Figure 8.1

7 Procter (2001).
8 There is a growing literature on various aspects of indirect work in music therapy, such as books on music therapy supervision. See Forinash (2001) and also Odell-Miller and Richards (2008).
9 Bunt (2010).
10 MacDonald *et al.* (2002: 13).
11 Bunt (2010).

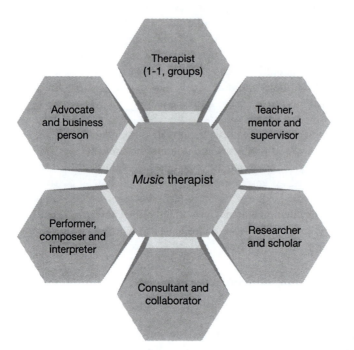

Figure 8.1 The different 'hats' of the music therapist: roles and responsibilities in
various situations.

indicates, we could imagine that a music therapist puts on different 'hats' depending upon the situation.[12] The number of 'hats' indicated by the figure is illustrative,
not comprehensive.

This figure indicates a range of possibilities for the music therapist:

- Music therapists might provide private and boundaried individual and group
  music therapy sessions; they might collaborate and work as a consultant, for
  instance in the broader community.
- They might teach and supervise music therapy students and others; they might
  act as composers, performers and interpreters of music and in that way
  maintain a strong and vital relationship to music.
- They might contribute to new knowledge through research and scholarship;
  they might advocate politically, both for the rights of the people they work
  with and for the development of the profession. The latter sometimes evolves
  into being a 'business person', promoting the idea of music therapy or actually
  selling services, for instance through the development of charities or working
  privately.

12 Bunt has been exploring this theme over time in presentations and with colleagues.

So how can we check and balance the various roles and keep some sense of integrated equilibrium, flow and authenticity whilst 'juggling different hats . . . in such diverse but in many ways subtly linked situations?'.[13]

We could say that a sense of focused and attentive listening to individual or group needs is a common feature of this list and the 'hats' in Figure 8.1, uniting many facets of facilitating and empowering others. Music is central, as indicated by the italics. There is some resonance here with Edward Said's description of Daniel Barenboim as 'an artist concerned not so much with the articulation of the self, but rather with the articulation of other selves'.[14] Whether or not music therapists see connections between their work and that of Barenboim, the words of Said could serve as a description of the music therapy ethos.

We argue that the main purpose of the music therapy profession is to promote human health and well-being, through music or as music, depending upon the theoretical perspective taken. This way of understanding the purpose requires that the term 'therapy' is understood either broadly or as a historical label that does not reflect fully the range of the present mission of the profession. Abrams puts it this way:

> Here, therapy is defined as a health promotion process – that is, the profes-sional practice of implementing a particular set of systematic interventions or other purposeful actions designed to promote health, according to any of its accepted definitions. Please note that, in the present model, 'professional' does not pertain exclusively to practices that have been codified under specific titles and can, for example, include certain practices that occur on a community or sociocultural level (provided that they are professional in nature).[15]

The openness for a range of music therapy practices that Abrams and many others propose is qualified with the addendum 'provided that they are professional in nature'. We are invited to reflect once more on what it involves to be a pro-fessional. Definitions typically point to specialised knowledge and skills in the field that one is practising, a degree of responsibility and independence, and a high standard of ethical awareness.[16] In addition, professionals are usually assumed to have an intrinsic motivation to do their job well because they are socialised during education and training to value a high-quality service for patients/participants and contributions to the development of the profession itself. Not all of these characteristics are unique to professionals, of course, and another defining feature is that professionals belong to a group of highly trained specialists who are certified or registered in some way, depending on the quality assurance within each country.[17]

---

13 Bunt (2010).
14 Barenboim and Said (2003: 11).
15 Abrams (2012: 68).
16 See Dileo (2000) on ethical thinking in music therapy.
17 Hernes (2002).

In most countries where music therapy has established itself, its practitioners have worked hard to ensure music therapy is a recognised profession. In Europe, Austria and the United Kingdom are two of the countries where at the time of writing there is state registration or law that recognises music therapy as a health profession. In the United States the website of the American Music Therapy Association (AMTA) communicates clearly the perceived importance of professionalism. The definition of music therapy presented on this website underlines that music therapy involves 'music interventions to accomplish individualized goals within a therapeutic relationship by a credentialed professional who has completed an approved music therapy program'.[18]

To support music therapy as a profession, the AMTA has developed a series of documents, such as Standards of Clinical Practice, a Code of Ethics and a list of Professional Competencies required for credentialed music therapists.[19] All of these documents seek to standardise professional conduct. The Standards of Clinical Practice include descriptions of how a music therapist should deal with referrals and acceptance, assessment, treatment planning, implementation, documentation, termination of services, continuing education and supervision. The standards are designed to assist practising music therapists as well as their employers in their efforts to provide high-quality services. Such assistance also involves regulation: 'Standards of Clinical Practice for music therapy are defined as rules for measuring the quality of services. These standards are established through the authority of the American Music Therapy Association, Inc.' And: 'Standards for each of these procedural steps are outlined herein and all Music Therapists should adhere to them in their delivery of services. Exceptions must be approved in writing by the Standards of Clinical Practice Committee.'[20]

The educated judgement of a music therapy professional is formed by such regulations. This is important and is how it needs to be if music therapy is to be recognised as a profession at all. The managers of a hospital, for instance, would argue that there has to be some kind of predictability when it comes to what procedures a professional will employ, and with what competencies. The risk is, of course, that too much control and compliance might undermine central societal values such as democracy and imaginative autonomy. Within the music therapy literature, several authors have raised this question. In the American context we can mention two examples. First, writing from a community music therapy perspective Aigen comments on the need to supplement existing ethical guidelines to accommodate new performance-oriented practices that have been identified as helpful to many clients.[21] Writing from a feminist perspective, Jennifer Adrienne argues that music therapists have taken 'a wrong turn in professionalization of our field' and that the education of music therapists does not give students the knowledge and awareness of the social functions of music that can perpetuate

18 www.musictherapy.org.
19 American Music Therapy Association (2009, 2012a, b).
20 American Music Therapy Association (2012b).
21 Aigen (2004: 212).

oppression.[22] In literature outside the discipline of music therapy even more radical critique has been offered on how professionals in contemporary societies are disciplined during education and training or participation in professional associations, as well as through various regimes presented by management and statutory bodies.[23] We return to the notion of balance, integrating the all too important legal, ethical and protective aspects of regulation and standardisation (particularly in relation to the duty of care to the public, qualified therapists and to students in training) while not overlooking the imaginative and creative potential that is so much at the heart of reflective music therapy practice.

All this suggests that to be professional involves something more than competent performance of prescribed procedures. A music therapist working with individuals and groups in different contexts will be challenged each day not to overlook 'big picture' issues such as social impact, justice and equality. In this way, what happens in a music therapy session interacts with taking responsibility for being a reflective member of the wider community. Music therapists have been addressing such responsibilities since the early days of the profession and continue to do so.

Currently there is a healthy debate on the future direction of the profession. Some members insist on a clear professional identity, for example adopting the title 'music psychotherapist'. Others promote a broader identity that includes music, health and well-being, and close collaborative relationships with other music professions. Any discussion of these issues necessarily involves value-based appraisals of the profession's body of knowledge and capacity to make a difference, as well as of the community's needs and resources.

Whatever the directions of future development, relationships to other groups working in similar areas need to be managed. We will discuss briefly some collaborative professional relationships within a traditional clinical frame before exploring the big picture issue of whether music therapists should contribute to making music available as a resource for health and well-being for all.

Sustaining collaborative cross-professional work

Many music therapists work as members of multidisciplinary teams and the way in which music and music therapy can build links is central to a great deal of the work, as observed earlier in the chapter in a day in the life of a music therapist.[24] Some opportunities and links have already been highlighted in other chapters. Three examples will be summarised here.

---

22 Adrienne (2006: 52–4).
23 See, for instance, Schmidt (2000) and his critique suggesting that professionals often serve the interests of those in power.
24 For an overview of multidisciplinary team working, including many case examples, see Twyford and Watson (2008).

Music therapy and physiotherapy

In Chapter 4 we described in Alex's story how the motivational and attentional aspects of sound and music can be used in joint interventions with physiotherapy. In this kind of combined approach with children, the music therapist can contribute with music that can motivate, establish rapport and communication, and build awareness about movements in time and space. Writing in general about this kind of combined approach with children, one physiotherapist colleague commented:

> It was noticeable that in each session: a) a better understanding of the speed of the physical activities of the children was understood by the music therapist, helping the physiotherapist; b) working with a music therapist encourages the children to obtain more physical skills themselves, music therapy stressing the self-motivation of the children rather than a requirement of therapist skills as in physiotherapy; and c) communicating with a severely disabled child is helped by music therapy; sometimes movement is stressful and upsetting to such a child and combining music therapy with physiotherapy makes movement more enjoyable and the child is happier.[25]

When music therapists and physiotherapists devise joint music and movement programmes for children and adults with severe physical disabilities, the tempo, style and timbre of the music are carefully adapted to support movements.[26] Rhythm and tempo stimulate movement; 'the melodic and harmonic content' sustains curiosity, awareness and any fluidity in a movement; 'style and timbre' support and encourage either stimulation or relaxation, depending on the context.[27] Discovering the appropriate speed for the music is crucial. Fast and stimulating music can motivate people to move very tight limbs but care needs to be taken not to over-arouse or increase tension in often already tense bodies. Such music can also over-stimulate people with involuntary movements when calmer music is needed to help focus their movements. Care is also needed to balance the level of physical response expected with the cognitive demands of the task: on some occasions a patient may be able to comprehend at a higher level of functioning than is demonstrated by the range of movements available.

Advances in computer technology have given further opportunities both for providing a regular musical stimulus for movement and to make it possible for a child or adult with even the slightest of available movements to access and have some control over musical experiences. In using the resources provided by technology, including the uses of switches and other kinds of interfaces, music therapists could work not only with physiotherapists but also with teachers, technicians and other researchers in discovering how such digital technology can improve quality of life. Music therapist Wendy Magee and music lecturer Karen

---

25 Bunt (1994: 166–7).
26 See the dual intervention approach developed by Elefant and Lotan (2004).
27 Grocke and Wigram (2007: 237).

Burland have been researching uses and limitations of technology for music therapists in several child and adult contexts.[28]

Collaboration and consultancy in educational contexts

On the basis of experiences from Norwegian educational contexts, Stige describes 'consultation-collaboration music therapy' as a practice in which direct and indirect elements interact closely. The music therapist might work with a child for a short time, in an assessment centre for instance, and then – with knowledge about the child's strengths and limitations – advise and collaborate with the child's family and teachers in order to support the mobilisation of longer-term resources in the service of the child's development.[29] Stige's experiences led him to propose a broad definition of consultation-collaboration, of potential relevance for other areas of practice:

> Consultation-collaboration music therapy would be concerned with the overall functioning of a care system supporting a client. A care system, as used here, could include didactic, medical, and psychotherapeutic components as well as nonprofessional resources such as family, neighborhood, and cultural activities in a community. The music therapist could have the role as co-ordinator and consultant, or could contribute as a node in a system coordinated by other professionals.[30]

Daphne Rickson has developed this area of consultation in educational settings, through her pioneering doctoral research in New Zealand, into the role of the music therapist when working with teachers and other staff who want to use music to help children in educational contexts.[31] This exploration of professional practices has implications for the future role of the music therapist as a resource for a community.

Collaborative approaches in mental health

We have discussed the relevance of music therapy in the field of mental health in several chapters. If we believe that confusion about words and meanings may have associations with emotional and social issues and challenges, music appears to be offering something quite different and unique in this field. Perhaps one answer lies in keeping some of these essential qualities of music in mind when setting up joint interventions in the field of mental health. We could see in the group example in

---

28 Magee and Burland (2008); see also Magee (2014).
29 In *Culture-Centered Music Therapy*, Stige (2002: 135–53) describes the ecology of consultation-collaboration in the service of a child with social problems, language challenges and learning disabilities.
30 Stige (2002: 328).
31 Rickson (2010, 2012).

Chapter 2 how the patients were beginning to explore aspects of themselves in different lights. (Here we can think again of the two opening inspirations for this chapter.) This is not to say that such moments of insight are without discomfort. The process, as in any therapy, can help people to face difficult and conflicting issues. The articulated forms of music can be viewed as the imaginative medium that brings some of these issues from the internal to the external world. The issues are often hard to translate into words; they may remain as felt bodily resonances, visual images or intangible feelings. How and where are patients/participants going to process such material?

Dialogue and collaboration can help to address this question and Helen Odell-Miller is one of many music therapists who have developed working partnerships with co-therapists within mental health care.[32] When she was working with a drama therapist, various role plays with the patients were adopted. Odell-Miller emphasises the importance of looking at what is happening in the moment within and between members of the group. Her patients are then helped to gain more insights to help themselves adapt to life outside the hospital.

Mental health is one of the many areas of practice where cross-collaborative approaches that do not include the active participation of the patients/participants have been challenged substantially. As Baines and Rolvsjord and others have advocated, music therapists need to fully embrace the existence of user-led services and acknowledge client contributions in the processes of change.[33] A non-medical notion of 'recovery' is sometimes used to communicate this perspective, and a 'recovery approach' has become influential within mental health services in many countries, based on 'principles that place the service user and their lived experience at the heart of decision making about treatment and care'.[34] The 'non-medical' quality of the recovery approach does not suggest that medical knowledge is irrelevant but rather that the principles of practice are closer to a 'contextual model' than a 'medical model'. Informed by the work of psychotherapy researcher Bruce Wampold, we use the term 'medical model' here as a generalised term for all practices (biomedical or psychosocial in orientation) that are based on the following assumptions: health problems are diagnosable conditions belonging to the patient, and the health professional is an expert whose task is to select an intervention tailored to the specific condition. Successful implementation of the intervention should then lead to the amelioration of the problem.[35] In contrast, Wampold describes contextual practices as based in perspectives that suggest a more collaborative approach in which the person's problems and resources are considered in relational terms.[36] The medical model

32 Odell (1988). See also Odell-Miller (2008) for her overview of music therapy practices in mental health.
33 Baines (2000/2003); Rolvsjord (2013).
34 McCaffrey *et al.* (2011: 186). Other music therapy references on recovery include Kooij (2009), Maguire and Merrick (2013) and Solli *et al.* (2013).
35 Wampold (2001: 14).
36 See Rolvsjord and Stige (2013).

seems to be adequate in relation to many diseases but its relevance for a multi-faceted phenomenon such as mental health is debatable. Wampold's thorough empirical analysis of the psychotherapy research corroborates the contextual model and disconfirms the medical model.[37]

The debates within the field of mental health are not necessarily transferable to all areas of music therapy practice but we will use the terms 'medical model' and 'contextual model' when we sum up the possibilities of the music therapy profession later in this chapter. The debates within mental health seem to reflect a wider debate that we have encountered several times, for instance in Chapter 2, where we discussed Buber's distinction between an 'I–It' and an 'I–Thou' relationship.[38] The idea of a 'contextual model' includes and goes beyond valuing dyadic relationships; the person's lived experience includes the experience of a world.

Promoting music as a resource for health and well-being

In this section we outline one of the most significant developments influencing the profession and discipline of music therapy, namely music for health and well-being, which has rapidly grown into a large area of practice and research.[39] Community musicians, music educators, orchestral musicians and various groups of healthcare staff all now work alongside the music therapist, offering their services. These colleagues often facilitate big groups, a cost-effective activity.[40] Research centres for music, arts and health have been able to fund research projects so that music therapists are by no means the only practitioners able to back up their work with research.[41] How does the profession relate to these developments?

The proliferation of different groups operating under an umbrella term such as 'music and health' is a complex scenario. The groups need to interact with other agencies, which in turn have their own emphases and agenda. For example, music is sometimes considered as an optional luxury, and at other times as relevant only when instrumental in effecting extra-musical and measurable physiological or psychosocial changes. Sometimes there is even the implied and rather naïve assumption that music is a kind of commodity, something that is indiscriminately used as positive and creative for all. As we have said before, music has the potential power to influence feelings and effect change, so care is needed.

---

37 Wampold (2001).
38 Buber (1958).
39 Some of the material for this section has been adapted from Bunt's keynote presentation 'Music: A Resource for Health and Wellbeing' delivered to the Music, Health and Happiness Conference at the Royal Northern School of Music, Manchester, on 7 November 2008. The presentation also incorporated the introductory reference to Davy and his lamp.
40 MacDonald *et al.* (2012).
41 For example the Sidney De Haan Research Centre for Arts and Health at Canterbury Christ Church University, led by Stephen Clift, Professor of Health Education and a protagonist in this field. See www.canterbury.ac.uk/Research/Centres/SDHR/Home.aspx.

Health sociologist and musician Norma Daykin has studied the perceived benefits of music and proposed a continuum ranging from health and well-being for individuals to wider social and cultural impacts.[42] At this point we present two hypothetical scenarios. First, we imagine the manager of a local nursing home who reads in the press about the evidence of the benefits of music, singing in particular, and responds favourably to a request from a community musician, music therapist or volunteer to bring music or music therapy into the home. Which of these might be given the contract for any work in the nursing home? Second, we can imagine an orchestral manager applying for funding of a community outreach programme in order to qualify for other funding sources that would secure a future concert season. We know that orchestral players, as part of a growing commitment to and requirement to engage in outreach work, are being expected to move out of the familiar setting of the concert hall to bring music to different audiences and into the local community: schools, hospitals, hospices and prisons, and so on, a pattern of development predicted in the earlier edition of this book. In these imagined but plausible scenarios there would be the implication that music has an inherently positive impact for community participation and engagement with music for all. In both examples there are professional and ethical issues regarding ongoing training, support and supervision. How can support mechanisms be put in place for the musicians to process the resulting experiences in a safe and confidential space and to be aware of the potential risk factors involved when working in these contexts?

The care providers themselves also seem to be experiencing confusion about the wide range of activities and musicians offering a service. As an illustration, a survey in the United Kingdom uncovered a range of musical activities being used in cancer care organisations. These included music as background or entertainment, music as adjunct to another therapy, and music therapy.[43] One of the results of the survey was that '[t]he most frequently cited activity was that of listening to recorded music'.[44] Even though 'almost two-thirds' of the organisations provided some kind of music, live or recorded, there were problems of awareness about the various personnel involved and their roles. Of the organisations offering music therapy, only around half of these reported employing a professionally registered music therapist.

National reports in the United Kingdom still express concern about another area of confusion that exists between the various practitioners. As noted in this statement from Arts Council England, 'there is, in general, a lack of understanding between arts therapists and arts in health practitioners about the unique contribution that each makes to improving and enhancing health services, and what they can learn from each other'.[45] We feel that music therapists need to acknowledge these concerns and engage in more dialogue and sharing of expertise. There need to be clearer definitions of roles and experiences between groups such as

---

42 Daykin (2007).
43 Daykin *et al.* (2006).
44 Ibid.: 407.
45 Arts Council England (2004: 6).

community musicians, musicians performing in hospitals, and music therapists. But is too much being expected of the contemporary music therapist and musician having to create mixed portfolios of work within complex healthcare arenas? A report about the work, education and training of professional musicians – *Creating a Land with Music*, published by the National Foundation for Youth Music (NFYM) – included this challenge: 'One might therefore see a genetic code for the musician comprising the four central roles of composer, performer, leader, and teacher, with linked roles relating to one or more of them.'[46]

Musicians have always needed to be flexible in developing different roles. Such adaptations are nothing new; we can think musicians working in the eighteenth century who mixed their roles of performer, composer, impresario and teacher. The contemporary healthcare musical worker or music therapist also needs to be familiar with music from different musical traditions and cultures. We can see how the contemporary music therapist is responding positively to this challenge and is very much a musician of our time. As we noted when discussing the various 'hats' (see Figure 8.1), music therapists engage in these 'central roles': there are teaching and leadership opportunities within the profession; the music therapist needs to maintain a high level of performance and practical skills; compositional opportunities exist within practice when the very act of improvising with individuals and groups has elements of composition in action. In fact, the NFYM report identifies 'developments in music therapy and healing' as an example of the professional musician redefining and extending areas of work.[47]

As community music therapy and other ecologically oriented practices have exemplified, an open and flexible understanding of the role of the professional music therapist seems to afford new opportunities for growth and service, often in collaboration with other musicians. But we must not underestimate the potential difficulties of this challenge. For the highly trained music therapist there are the pressures not only of keeping one's reflective practice alive and up to date through regular supervision and ongoing study, but also of gaining and then sustaining employment or setting up one's own work in different contexts. This often results in a peripatetic working pattern and the need for personal and organisational skills that build and sustain connections in teams of healthcare workers, especially when one is the only music therapist in that particular context.

Further challenges to the contemporary music therapist

While music therapists are understandably going to have different ideas on how the profession might evolve, first we need to celebrate the increasing acceptance of music therapy as a profession within healthcare services and clinical practices. In Chapters 4–7 there were selected examples from practice and research, documenting the visible role that music therapists can have in various specialised

46 Youth Music (2002: 27).
47 Ibid.: 17.

contexts of health care, including mental health, cancer care and neuro-rehabilitation.

Other music therapists have created services in the context of mainstream education, including bereavement work and the cultural education of immigrants and refugees.[48] This expansion of traditional areas of practice is only part of the picture. Some music therapists are interested in developing new links with other creative therapists such as art, drama and play therapists by setting up local resource centres or private enterprises. The emphasis here may be more on a shared creative base to the work. Projects could develop from this stimulating mix: art and music, drama and music, dance and music would be natural partners. In some respects such integrations remind us of the healing traditions of non-Western cultures, where divisions between these expressive modalities are less apparent. Drumming circles and other 'reinvented' traditions also include a spiritual dimension of awareness.

Some music therapists are working as part of multidisciplinary community-based teams providing local resources for people with mental health issues or learning disabilities. Former patients may have been involved in music therapy in a hospital and further music therapy may still be indicated, even if only as a temporary measure to help support and bridge the movement from living in a hospital to living outside. It is difficult for professional health workers to maintain links with patients once they have been discharged from hospital settings back into the community. An obvious problem here is the time factor. It may be impractical to continue individual sessions or to set up groups when people are living far apart. In addition to trying to see those people who could benefit from further work, a community-based therapist will also be challenged to develop a system for giving priority to the large number of people living outside the old hospitals. One challenge that may be encountered in some countries is how to fund work that is not reimbursed by insurance companies or statutory benefits.

One way to address some of the current challenges is to set up charities. Two examples from the United Kingdom will illustrate this. The change in the delivery of care for vulnerable people with long-term needs was one of the motivating factors in the late 1980s and early 1990s for the setting up of the MusicSpace Trust, a registered charity whose aim was to provide a network of spaces for music therapy practice, training, research and performance for children and adults of all ages and needs. The spaces were to be bases to where people could come in and from where therapists could go out to create other spaces in, for example, local schools, day centres, nurseries, hospices or hospitals. MusicSpace developed from its one centre in Bristol, opened in 1991, to creating, throughout the 1990s and beyond, a further six in the United Kingdom and also centres in Italy.[49] At the time of writing, the charity has moved through a period of structural reorganisation as branches outside Bristol have become new charities. This perhaps reveals one

---

48 See McFerran (2010).
49 Bunt (1994: 173–4; 2004).

characteristic of charities in that they represent highly flexible but also somewhat vulnerable tools in the development of services. The MusicSpace model can be viewed as successful in spearheading resources to answer the needs of children and adults requiring therapy within their local communities and also in providing professional and administrative support and development for groups of music therapists.

The MusicSpace project would not have been successful without the generosity of local management teams, national trustees, presidents, patrons, and local and national-based donors and volunteers. Dependency on such groups and fund-raisers is also part of the remarkable success story that is the national and international development of Nordoff Robbins Music Therapy.[50] Increasingly, as can be discovered on the Nordoff Robbins website, outreach work is developing outside the London centre in different parts of the United Kingdom. There is a well-established presence in Scotland, for example, as well as international developments in Australia, Germany and the United States. Music therapy training and research also support the provision of music therapy for children and adults.

In Norway and some other countries, community music therapy practices are to a larger degree woven into the public welfare services, the rationale being informed by the solidarity principle of human rights, specifically people's rights to health and cultural participation. The challenge for the music therapy profession is not so much to raise money directly through charity but to create public awareness and provide the research necessary to enable prioritisation of music therapy within public health initiatives.[51]

Other models and directions also provide food for thought. As changes in healthcare delivery and management occur, as recently in the United Kingdom, it may become pragmatic for music therapists to offer packages of work linked to some of the strategic priorities of a local medical practice or health centre. Blocks of sessions that focus on specific patient groups or possibilities for resource development could be offered to general practitioners, probably starting off on a trial basis followed by systematic evaluation. As medical practice begins to examine the efficacy and effectiveness of more complementary approaches and include them in treatment plans, could we predict a time when access to a community-based music therapist would become one of the many resources of your local surgery?

Possibilities of the music therapy profession

This chapter has explored three axes along which music therapists make professional choices, namely the 'what-dimension', the 'how-dimension' and the 'where-dimension'. The continuum of the first axis extends from direct work

50 See www.nordoff-robbins.org.uk and Simpson (2009).
51 Stige and Aarø (2012).

undertaken by music therapists with patients/participants to indirect work such as consultation, supervision, teaching, technology development and research. The continuum of the second extends from music therapy practices that are developed according to the logic of a medical model (broadly conceived, as presented earlier in the chapter) to those that are developed according to the more collaborative logic of contextual perspectives. The continuum of the third axis embraces the professional who works in clinical settings (contexts) and one who works in more open community contexts.

One important caveat needs to be made at this point: each of the axes should be understood as continua, not as polarities. For instance, music psychotherapy often includes elements of both a medical and a contextual model. The problem or issue is usually seen as belonging to the patient (an idea drawn from a medical model), while some forms of psychotherapeutic practice are seen as more contextual in orientation: rather than a specific intervention being taken into consideration, the whole situation of evolving relationships between people and between people and their activities is taken into account.

If we, for now, accept the 'what–how–where' of music therapy practice as convenient categorisations, not a comprehensive description but a heuristic one, we can construct a three-dimensional 'space' that illuminates possibilities for the profession in realising its purpose of promoting human health (see Figure 8.2).

While reflections on the balance between direct and indirect work are highly relevant in a small profession such as music therapy, most of the current controversies in the field relate to the how- and where-dimensions of Figure 8.2. One reading of Figure 8.2 therefore highlights four possibilities for the realisation of the profession's purpose: medical model practice in clinical contexts; medical model practice in community contexts; contextual model practice in clinical contexts; and contextual model practice in community contexts. Each of these involves consideration of the relative priority of direct and indirect work. We will briefly describe these four main possibilities, acknowledging the legitimacy of

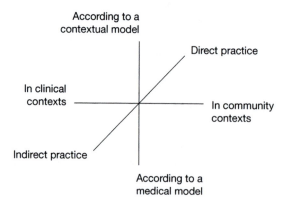

Figure 8.2 What–how–where: possibilities for the music therapy profession in realising its purpose of promoting human health.

practice based in three of them and questioning the legitimacy of medical model practice in community contexts.[52]

Medical model practice in clinical contexts

In medical model practice in clinical contexts the music therapist develops interventions to bring about change according to goals grounded in a medical diagnosis.[53] An example is Thaut's Neurologic Music Therapy (previously discussed in Chapters 2 and 6), which has developed a treatment protocol for patients living with Parkinson's disease, dementia, traumatic brain damage and other neurological conditions. Neurologic Music Therapy has been developed with specified procedures for assessment, treatment planning, intervention and evaluation, with a range of specific techniques for specific problems such as sensorimotor rehabilitation, speech and language, and cognitive rehabilitation.[54] Work in oncology is a less clear example of this professional possibility, given that assessments and interventions can change from day to day, demanding much flexibility from the therapist (see Chapter 6). A medical model perspective as a generalised way of working professionally in relation to people's problems is central to the American Music Therapy Association's Standards of Practice, in which, as we saw earlier in the chapter, music therapy is defined as the clinical and evidence-based use of music interventions to accomplish individualised goals.[55]

Medical model practice in community contexts

In medical model practice in community contexts the music therapist develops interventions to bring about change according to goals assumed to be relevant in relation to diagnosable problems. This professional possibility is less documented in the music therapy literature. A possible approach would be to make available specific musical techniques for health-related issues for the wider public. Not every person is diagnosed and treated in a clinic but the intervention is still based in the logic of the medical model. We argue that the legitimacy of exploiting this possibility – for example in producing CDs and ready-made programmes people could use for this or that condition – is debatable. Some would perhaps disagree and suggest that 'if it works, it's good'. To make music available in the service of

---

52 We defined the concepts of a medical and contextual model above. The distinction cuts across contexts of practice. For example, music therapy in a special education context can be performed according to a medical or a contextual model.

53 The caveat we made above suggests that this is a description of a prototypical approach, whereas real-life practice includes many variations and combinations, for instance when it comes to how closely goals are linked to a diagnosis and the extent to which the relationship between music therapist and patient shapes the direction of the work.

54 Thaut (2005).

55 American Music Therapy Association (2012b).

health and well-being is in many ways positive.[56] The problem here is linked to medicalisation, the process whereby an ever-increasing variety of human problems are defined in medical terms.[57] This is perhaps an area where indirect and critical work by the professional music therapist is especially important in contributing to societal awareness about both the health-promotional qualities of music and some of the potential risks.

Contextual practice in clinical contexts

In contextual practice in clinical contexts the music therapist takes part in collaborative work in which the lived experience and voice of the service-user are central in negotiations on goals and priorities. Gilbertson's description of a day in the life of a music therapist makes this clear. In the clinical context of neuro-rehabilitation this description highlights not only music's possible effects on 'neurological, psychological and physiological capabilities' but also how 'coming together to play music' might reduce the most extreme experiences of isolation and offer 'these individuals and their families opportunities to find sense and meaning in their lives ahead'.[58] Loewy's work with hospitalised infants and their parents also exemplifies this way of thinking.[59] A theoretically elaborated example in the literature is Rolvsjord's resource-oriented music therapy in mental health institutions.[60]

Contextual practice in community contexts

In contextual practice in community contexts the music therapist takes part in collaborative work in which the lived experience and voice of a group of people are central in negotiations on goals and priorities that go beyond individual change to include social change. The professional possibility of developing collaborative work in various community contexts is much more established in music therapy today than it was twenty years ago, owing to the emergence of the international discourse on community music therapy.[61] Other developments within this professional possibility include feminist and anti-oppressive perspectives.[62]

Dialogue and debate

Professional possibilities are rarely explored without debate. (We imagine that Davy and Skram would be more interested in this kind of open debate and

---

56 See Hanser (2010) and also the section 'Promoting music as a resource for health and well-being', earlier in the chapter (p. 181).
57 See Stige and Aarø (2012: 171–3) for a discussion of medicalisation and music therapy.
58 For more discussion, see Gilbertson and Aldridge (2008).
59 Loewy (2011).
60 Rolvsjord (2010).
61 See, for instance, Ansdell (2002), Pavlicevic and Ansdell (2004), Stige *et al.* (2010) and Stige and Aarø (2012).
62 See Adrienne (2006) and Baines (2013), respectively.

discovery than in a rigid reductionism.) The descriptions just given of possibilities for realisation of the profession's purpose are developed not as an attempt to categorise music therapy comprehensively but to point to some major debates and considerations within the profession. The debates include Thaut's argument that music therapy should leave its social orientation behind and focus on practice informed by neuroscience,[63] and they include Abrams' contrasting argument in favour of relational perspectives in music therapy.[64] The debates also include the question of whether community music therapy challenges the profession adversely or expands it more positively. In 2008 a special issue of the *British Journal of Music Therapy* was devoted to this question. Alison Barrington argued that the clinical standards established for the profession by statutory bodies represented expert advice and that it would be irresponsible to neglect them; development of less regulated practices such as community music therapy was therefore potentially destructive. Others argued that such practices did not represent a negative challenge; they could instead be understood as symptoms of a more general transformation instigated by social and cultural change in society at large.[65]

We need debates within the profession in order to develop awareness of what the possibilities are and how we can prepare ourselves for realising them. Such debates should include discussions on the crucial competencies of the profession, the design and development of training courses, the needs for continuing education and professional development, and so on. All of these debates are healthy and necessary in order to develop a refined understanding of how professional music therapy makes a difference in contemporary society. Such debates are helpful when music therapists listen to one another and learn from people with contrasting views, thereby avoiding falling into the trap of an entrenched position. In his lecture 'Ways of thinking in music therapy', Bruscia argues that the profession will serve clients and the community better if we can shift from 'one-way' thinking to more 'integral' thinking in which we are able to move between different possibilities depending upon the needs in each situation.[66] The sociologist Richard Sennett draws attention to how we listen dialectically or dialogically in conversations, the former where we 'come eventually to a common understanding' and the latter where there is respectful interest in uncovering difference, in which opinions are echoed in different words. Sennett draws on his musical experiences, particularly as a chamber musician, in drawing parallels with the dialogical form of exchange. During a rehearsal any comment from a fellow musician 'makes you think again about the sound and you may adjust as a result but not copy what you heard'.[67]

Bruscia's request for less 'one-way' thinking and Sennett's respectful exchange of different ideas and kinds of thinking are highly relevant. Music therapists need

---

63 Thaut (2005: 113–36).
64 Abrams (2012).
65 Barrington (2008); Ansdell and Pavlicevic (2008); Procter (2008). For a summary of this debate, see Stige and Aarø 2012.
66 Bruscia (2011).
67 Sennett (2013: 18–19).

to be able to combine possibilities flexibly. Nevertheless, some questions of priority remain, as we have indicated.

Concluding points

In this chapter we have described a day in the life of a music therapist and discussed the purpose and the possibilities of the music therapy profession. We presented two figures, one of the many 'hats' the professional music therapist can wear in various situations and another of the possibilities of the profession in realising the purpose of promoting human health. We have suggested that professionals as disciplined practitioners continue to embrace their responsibilities as members of society so that we keep asking critical questions of how the profession could best serve the broader community. General reflections on profession and processes of professionalisation, such as those we have presented here, should always be challenged by situated examinations of processes in specific contexts. As the sociologist Eliot Freidson has argued, profession is not a generic concept: it is a historic notion and one that changes over time and between places.[68]

We started the chapter with two historical figures. When Sir Humphry Davy constructed his lamp he was able to use advanced knowledge and skills to solve real-world problems. When Amalie Skram wrote her novels she was able to use art in the service of a relevant critique of her society. Are music therapists able to live up to such ideals and let the many aspects of the work – scientific and artistic, constructive and critical – complement each other? For any music therapist this is a tall order. Many would argue that it is hard enough to try to do a decent job that demands exacting standards. If we believe that music therapy contributes to the well-being of community and society, it might be necessary for the profession as a whole to ask such questions as:

- How can the profession embrace the diversity of approaches and work ranging from the most boundaried clinical work to the more blurred edges in community settings?
- Can the music therapy profession provide guidelines that embrace multiple viewpoints of practice?
- Can we give more space to creativity and imagination to balance the overriding influence of logic and systematic procedures in contemporary culture?
- How can professionals continue to dialogue, share resources, be aware of and respect role differentiation and limitations, learning from others?
- Are music therapy trainers and education centres sufficiently able to open up their courses to musicians from wide-ranging cultures, musical backgrounds, ages and experiences?

---

68 Freidson (1970/1988).

- How do we make sure that all musicians working in music and health have an adequate level of supervision, mentoring and support?
- How does the profession respond to culturally aware facilitation of music-making?

These questions are articulated in such a way as to invite an exploration of the potential of music in society. A profession that is a community of practitioners can grow in reflexivity[69] and maturity only when its visions and purposes are under debate. Values and broader visions play significant roles which are not isolated but integrated in knowledge developed within the discipline. All professions integrate and interact with the broader community as well as with the disciplines that support them. In the next chapter the discipline of music therapy will be our focus. As music therapy research continues to develop, will there be space for collaborative research in partnership with other professions as well as with patients/participants?

69 Finlay and Gough (2003). See also the next chapter.

9 The discipline of music therapy
Towards an identity of hybridity?

Introduction: Orpheus as emblem

Orpheus with his lute made trees,
And the mountain-tops that freeze,
    Bow themselves, when he did sing:
To his music plants and flowers
Ever sprung; as sun and showers
    There had made a lasting spring.

Everything that heard him play,
Even the billows of the sea,
    Hung their heads, and then lay by.
In sweet music is such art,
Killing care and grief of heart,
    Fall asleep, or, hearing, die.[1]

Orpheus is credited with exceptional gifts as a singer and poet and through his art charmed and transformed elements of the natural world; in this final chapter we use this Greek myth as a starting point to illuminate some of the tensions music therapists face in their work.[2] Orpheus was a mythical son of the sun god Apollo. His mother was said to be the muse Calliope.[3] In *Orpheus: The Song of Life*, historian and writer Ann Wroe reminds us that Calliope was known for her singing of 'epic poems', so her voice would have been one of the first sounds Orpheus heard.[4] Shakespeare's words suggest Orpheus accompanying himself on the lute, although, like his father, Apollo, he is often depicted with a lyre. In addition to these close connections to Apollo, Orpheus may, according to tradition, also have

---

1 This song from Shakespeare's *King Henry VIII* is prefaced by Queen Katharine saying to one of her women: 'Take thy lute, wench: my soul grows sad with troubles; / Sing and disperse 'em, if thou canst: leave working' (Act III, sc. i, lines 1–14).
2 Some hymns possibly inspired by the historical figure of Orpheus have survived; see Athanassakis (1977).
3 Another version of the story has Oeagrus, king of Thrace, as his father.
4 Wroe (2011: 12).

been a Dionysian priest. For ancient Greeks the god Dionysus represented unbridled energy, free instinct, all that is irrational, body- and feeling-centred. By contrast, Apollo strove for clarity of mind, rational order and control (although he did have his out-of-control moments). In the figure of Orpheus and his music we therefore have a representation of expressive energy existing within formal limits, a combination of elements of both deities. There is a mix of the sacred and profane, the rational and irrational. Wroe talks of Orpheus bridging 'the divide' between these two forces.[5] He strives for this balance between the more 'objective' demands of rational Apollo and the 'subjective' all-embracing passions of Dionysus.

In *The Masks of Orpheus*, musicologist Wilfrid Mellers echoes the Shakespeare song, reminding us that Orpheus, as shaman and healer, 'could not only through his music arouse or pacify birds and beasts . . . he could also defy natural laws, counteracting gravity and telescoping time; and could even confront the gods themselves, defying death'.[6] After the death of his beloved Eurydice, Orpheus uses the charm of his music to descend to the Underworld to rescue her, his muse and inspiration. Hades, the god of the Underworld, allows Eurydice to return to the upper world on condition that Orpheus does not look back. He fails his prescribed task and looks back to check whether Eurydice is still following on their journey to the upper air. He was a flawed hero, human after all.[7] We can view this whole descent as a regressive pull back into the primitive subconscious or we can think of it as a failure to focus on the journey itself.[8] Orpheus was keen to move up and forward, singing his way into the light of consciousness, but lacked sufficient trust not to look back.

Eurydice is summoned by Hades back to the Underworld. In one interpretation of the story, winged Hermes, the god of transition and thresholds, is present at the crucial moment of looking back when Eurydice is required to return and Orpheus has to continue upwards.[9] Orpheus loses Eurydice for a second time and cannot gain full redemption. If we look at the myth in Jungian terms, there is no integration of anima and animus.[10] Orpheus is not complete. So what of his end?

Some endings of the Orpheus myth have female followers of the god Dionysus dismembering him, and we could interpret this as Orpheus still unable to control his passions, being torn apart by them. He needed Eurydice to recover a sense of balance and equilibrium and to gather the Dionysiac passions into Apollonian

5 Ibid.: 44.
6 Mellers (1987: 3).
7 Wroe (2011: 105) points out that although Eurydice 'was never really a woman, always an allegory', she did make Orpheus human.
8 Bunt is grateful for additional insights into this myth during discussions with his supervisor, the Jungian analyst Shelagh Layet.
9 This transitional moment is captured in a bas-relief of Orpheus, Eurydice and Hermes housed in the National Archaeological Museum of Naples. See Rilke's poem of that title (1996). The moment is also captured by Cocteau in his film *Orphée* with the Hermes figure Heurtebise leading Orpheus in and out of the underworld; see Wroe (2011: 143–4).
10 'Anima' refers to the archetypal female, 'animus' the male.

form. His remains are scattered on water, yet his head carries on singing. It continued to sing and prophesy even after coming to rest in a cave sacred to Dionysus.[11] So here is the head of the son of father Apollo resting in a space sacred to the god of unbridled passions. And it is finally Apollo who, exhausted by all this singing and prophecy, stands over the head, crying, 'Cease from interference in my business: I have borne long enough with you and your singing!'[12] Silence returns. And as for the lyre, it was meant to have drifted to an island, been placed in a temple of Apollo and later positioned in the heavens as a constellation.

Monteverdi deviated from the myth to present a more joyous conclusion to his opera *Orfeo*, although this was not the case in the original text by Striggio. In the opera the *deus ex machina* figure of Apollo reclaims his son, who becomes united with his father, climbing heavenwards with him.[13] In their duet the music becomes increasingly animated as they soar, Orpheus at one point taking the higher part. There is a spiritual unification but this is not the final story. The myth presents us still with a quest: the constant struggle to unite Dionysus and Apollo, to discover the whole, to discover an 'earthly paradise'.[14] Consequently, the opera ends, as Mellers reminds us, with a repetition of this eternal pattern. The shepherds sing and dance with the same energy and freedom as at the start of the opera.

In Orpheus, music therapists have an emblem. Like Orpheus, music therapists are struggling with tensions and opposites that at times seem impossible to unite. Like Orpheus, music therapists will experience that the struggle involves risks. Music therapists often seek to bring together diverse phenomena or processes and again and again experience that their powers to do so are limited. We have noted that without Eurydice Orpheus is not whole, in essence a wounded healer, but his music is powerful and lasting. It is woven into the different pull of forces but cannot easily be ascribed to or absorbed by any one side of opposites. Like Orpheus, music therapists will hardly come across the whole truth or find an 'earthly paradise' where the tensions and contradictions are resolved. Not all the questions can be answered at once and each set of questions interconnects with the next. Each story might have several different endings.

Before we move on, a note of caution is needed. In Chapter 1, reference to Gouk warned against drawing from the ancient past to give some historical credence for the profession in the present. In relation to a mythic figure such as Orpheus she is equally cautious: 'Caught between the archetypes of rational doctor, priest and divinely (or demonically) inspired musician, the identity of the musical healer is inevitably compromised.'[15] While acknowledging this potential compromise, one can still draw on elements from Orpheus's story to re-examine many of the apparent

---

11 See Wroe (2011: 230) for description of both the placing of the head in the realms of Dionysus and the lyre with Apollo.
12 Graves (1955/1960, 1: 113).
13 The 'god out of the machine', originating from early Greek plays, relates to the sudden appearance of a god to create a solution to the narrative. For the example of Apollo's arrival, see Mellers (1987: 39, 48).
14 Mellers (1987: 40).
15 Gouk (2002: 172).

paradoxes and tensions highlighted throughout this book, such as the contradictory aspects of art and science, practice and theory. Our focus when exploring them in this chapter will be in the context of music therapy as a discipline.

The discipline as the 'invisible college' of music therapy

Music therapy is variously described as an applied, scientific, academic or practitioner practice or professional discipline.[16] Each of these terms implies some kind of bridging. For instance, if music therapy is an applied discipline, it is assumed that practitioners are able to make use of knowledge provided by researchers. Many music therapists claim that music therapy is much more practice driven than that. Others suggest that the relationships between practice and academia should be articulated in reciprocal and dynamic ways. Similar discussions occur in other disciplines that support professional practices and require judgement in context. The educationalist and poet Geoffrey Squires argues that professional disciplines (he uses medicine, law and management as examples) cannot be understood as applications of basic sciences; they use knowledge from other disciplines to inform a framework that becomes their own.[17] In this chapter the focus is on music therapy as a professional discipline, but in what way can we maintain that a distinct framework exists? We will be suggesting that what exists is hardly a ready-made framework, but there are conditions for continuous collaboration in constructing one, even if we can never envisage its being finished.

In a discussion of the values and practices that seem to unite disciplines within academia, physicist John Ziman suggests that a discipline is simply a recognised domain of organised teaching and research. As such, disciplines are institutionally based yet cut across barriers of specific institutions. Ziman contends that we could talk of disciplines as 'invisible colleges', with scholars in a discipline typically cultivating relationships with members of the same discipline across institutions, countries and cultural barriers.[18]

Ziman's understanding of academic disciplines also suggests that they are established by historical circumstance, which implies that they are differentiated somewhat arbitrarily: 'It would be quite an intellectual exercise, for example, to assign research projects correctly as between sociology, social anthropology, and social psychology.' In a similar way, music therapists will have to admit that the boundaries between, for example, music therapy, community music, music education and music psychology are not always obvious. At the same time, disciplines are 'surprisingly real', Ziman argues; they are 'tribes' (cultural subgroups) living out their particular version of a broader academic culture.[19] In a professional discipline like music therapy we could supplement the idea of an 'invisible college' of scholars with that of real or imagined communities existing

16 For instance, Davis *et al.* (2008) frequently refer to music therapy as an applied discipline or scientific discipline, while Peters (2000) often uses the term 'professional discipline'.
17 Squires (2001).
18 Ziman (2000: 46).
19 Ibid.: 47.

between practitioners and academics; what is taught and researched sits alongside a diversity of music therapy practices, each area informing the other.

In an increasing number of universities around the world, music therapy is a recognised domain of organised teaching and research. It is a discipline. As indicated by our use of the myth of Orpheus, it is nevertheless a discipline characterised by tensions and struggles. In this chapter we use Ziman's idea that a discipline could be compared to a social group with a cultural identity. Before doing so we will describe some of the tensions and contradictions that characterise music therapy as a discipline. In academic terms the ideas might be quite complex but the tensions and contradictions are not abstract or intangible; they are part of the everyday life of music therapists and students. Here is an example from music therapy student training:

> For their final projects for the MA in Music Therapy at the University of the West of England, Bristol students currently present two pieces of work. The first is a proposal for an evaluation of some music therapy practice. How would a student reply, for example, to a future request from a manager of a nursing home for a short evaluation to sustain the funding of some on-going work? Students need to become familiar with the underlying philosophies, different methodologies and methods needed to design a service review or evaluation alongside the ethical issues in proposing, for example, to carry out interviews or design questionnaires.[20] The second piece of work is a creative musical analysis, underpinned by critical theoretical and therapeutic reflection, of a short excerpt of improvised work, a songwriting process or some music used for listening as part of a receptive approach.[21]

In these two tasks the students are engaging with current issues relating to science and art, theory and practice, external impact and internal relevance. At one level we could think of these as different or contradictory dimensions of the work. Such dimensions are necessary and perhaps not problematic in themselves but, as we will see, often involve pulls in different directions.

Some tensions and contradictions

In the original edition of this book the title of the final chapter was 'Music therapy as a synthesis of art and science: Orpheus as emblem'. We are conscious that use

---

20 In accomplishing this task, students will be referring to publications that aid the emergent evaluator/researcher to use the appropriate 'evidence platform' related to context and overriding question, for example Pavlicevic *et al.* (2009). The research team at the Nordoff Robbins Centre have also produced a useful workbook focusing on ethics in preparing research in music therapy: Farrant *et al.* (2011).

21 For this, the book edited by Wosch and Wigram (2007) is instructive for the students.

of the term 'synthesis' requires careful consideration, especially given its particular uses in various academic disciplines. Generally speaking, a synthesis is a combination of two or more entities that together form something new. In chemistry, we understand synthesis to result from a combination of different elements, for example water as a synthesis of hydrogen and oxygen. When we talk about synthesis in music therapy, such smooth blends are perhaps neither possible to achieve, nor even what we should strive for. We suggest the theme of 'mixing' to be central to the possible identities of the discipline of music therapy, with processes that are multifaceted and shifting, characterised by ambiguity and contradictions. Later in the chapter we will be talking of 'hybridity', a metaphor challenging ideas of 'purity', which are often limiting and sometimes even repressing. We will be looking more to cultural theory than to chemistry in search of metaphors.

Many writers have reflected on the tensions and contradictions that seem to characterise music therapy. Bruscia writes, 'Being both art and science practiced within an interpersonal context requires the integration of many seemingly contradictory elements. Music therapy can be both objective and subjective, individual and universal, creatively unique and replicable, intrapersonal and interpersonal, collective and transpersonal.'[22] In this section we examine some apparently 'contradictory elements'. Our discussion is driven by a search for a refined understanding of the claim that music therapy is a discipline of both art and science. Neither of these terms is independent of history. Art and science, as we tend to think of them today, are terms for evolving practices.

The history that we outlined briefly in Chapter 1 suggests that modern music therapy first evolved as a practice in response to real-world needs and challenges. Impulses from art and science were obviously present, but both art and science were never uniquely individual worlds, as we also saw when referring to Davy and Skram in Chapter 8. Even if they were, the moment when these two worlds merged into the world of music therapy seems hard to detect. In other words, might the idea of music therapy as integration of contradictory elements be a misleading search? On the other hand, this idea of integration of contradictory elements seems to be a struggle not easily given up.

Music therapy as professional practice deals with a number of apparent opposites, such as outcome/process, mind/body, individual/communal, receptive/active, verbal/non-verbal, and so on. Many would argue that outcomes are what legitimise the practice, yet the process of music-making is very often what attracts participants. The discipline of music therapy needs to be able to deal with a number of opposites, including those mentioned above and many more. Here are two from research-based terminology where, in each pair, one term could be considered a potential opposite of the other, but the relationships could also be more reciprocal.

22 Bruscia (1998a: 10).

Quantity and quality

The terms 'quantity' and 'quality' introduce the possibilities of carrying out research using numerical calculations or, alternatively, verbal descriptions and interpretations. This rough distinction finds definition in labels such as quantitative and qualitative research, empirical and interpretive research, or even 'hard' and 'soft' research.[23]

Some of the projects described in Chapters 4–7 used statistics as a means of establishing any levels of significance (or not) to the numerical presentation of results. Music therapy researchers can devise specific outcome-based measures in order to indicate efficacy and change. The complex stream of behaviours and interaction of the many variables observable in music therapy sessions can be reduced to questions of a manageable size. Researchers can choose to work within existing reliable methods and measures: for example, using standardised 'before-and-after' tests, or using them in conjunction with specifically constructed outcomes such as target objectives or behaviours. There can be engagement with well-established methodologies from the behavioural and social sciences, making causal connections between a period of intervention and specific observable outcomes. In addition to numerically based outcome studies, surveys of where therapists work, training records, numbers of therapists, and so on are important.

Some of the projects reported in Chapters 4–7 adopted qualitative approaches when answering a particular question. Here researchers can focus on participants' individual experiences within a process of music therapy by employing such methods as the use of interviews or focus groups. We could think of qualitative research as 'rigorous storytelling'. As we noted with the myth of Orpheus, stories are ways of expressing, exploring and communicating human insights. In research, storytelling is rigorous if the descriptions and interpretations are given a systematic critique and evaluation.

Increasingly, researchers try to combine the tools of qualitative and quantitative research. Aldridge proposes that the case study provides a helpful opportunity for research when a behaviour or group of behaviours is observed at stages both during and outside the therapeutic intervention. 'Single case study designs are an attempt to formalise clinical stories with factors of rigorous experimental design being grafted on to the clinical process.'[24] Practising music therapists would not need to alter their current practice to any great degree to carry out such forms of observation and documentation. Many therapists are turning to the single case study as research and writing about their work without recourse to jargon, anecdote or over-interpretation.[25] As Sarah Hoskyns reminds us, such work is also economical in resources, time and personnel.[26]

It might appear that the complexity of a rich artistic process such as music therapy is reduced to almost naïve proportions by attempts to quantify results.

23 Wheeler (2005) provides an introduction to music therapy research.
24 Aldridge (1988, 2005).
25 For discussion of case study as research, see Yin (2012) and McLeod (2010).
26 Hoskyns (1988).

Nevertheless, it is possible to organise research into rigorous strategies that will not affect the musical empathy established with patients/participants. Our sensitivity in the practice of music therapy will not suffer by asking rigorous questions about the what, how, why of our work. Ethical considerations and careful attention to rigour are central. One kind of rigour is employed when an external researcher uses a standardised observational procedure or biomedical indicator to measure, for example, the effects of group music therapy on the stress levels of adults with severe depression. Some selected questions, using observable measures, would be answered by such an approach. A different kind of rigour would be necessary if another researcher were then to invite participants in the group music therapy to take part in individual interviews or a focus group, adding these more qualitative methods to the more quantitative ones. This would be rigour, stressing informed interpretation and reflexive appreciation of subjectivity in context.

There are both advantages and disadvantages to the individual case study and the control group study. On the one hand, individual studies contain rich detail and inform, but they lack a generalising effect; on the other hand, group studies gain on the generalising but lose on the rich detail. Group studies require sufficient numbers, in order to comply with requirements for statistical analysis: the notions of sufficient 'power' and 'effect size'.[27] Sufficient sample size and randomisation to the intervention condition or the control group condition are required for any results to have the potential to be generalised. In case studies, individuals are sometimes used as their own controls. It would be interesting to develop more specific studies of individual progress within a group and thereby integrate the two approaches.

Different approaches can converge in increasing our understanding of the whole picture. 'Softer' methods, such as interviews and self-evaluations, can add richness to what may appear on the surface to be 'hard' numerical information. Sometimes some quantitative elements, for example in the simple numerical presentation of a record of attendance, can be meaningfully integrated into a fundamentally more qualitative-based narrative. Such convergences occur in 'mixed methods' approaches, when the overall aim of a large research project might be broken down into a series of different objectives and questions. These emerge from different philosophical premises and result in different kinds of research methodologies and methods. Can we then move away from the notion of 'hard' or 'soft' research and begin to think more of evolving different and complementary research strategies in relation to the questions being addressed, the specific needs of research participants and contexts?

Objectivity and subjectivity

The idea that research should be objective implies that findings will reflect reality, are independent of the observer and are produced through application of tested

27 See Gold (2004) for a discussion of 'effect size' in randomised controlled studies.

procedures rather than personal judgement. This way of thinking was central to the logical positivism of the early twentieth century.[28] It has been challenged substantially more than once by scholars who suggest that any observation involves a certain amount of pre-understanding and therefore is interpretative. In contemporary science, however, objectivity is not dead. There might be less confidence in the researcher's capacity to describe things 'as they are' but impartiality is still valued, especially in quantitative research traditions, where methodological rigour is central.[29]

Qualitative research is often considered subjective in comparison. Does this suggest that qualitative research is more 'fanciful' or 'illusory'? Not necessarily. Qualitative researchers rarely try to reduce subjectivity. Instead they capitalise on human subjectivity, understood as our capacity to reflect critically on our experiences of the world. Because human lives are experiences in relationships and communities, human subjectivity is based in intersubjectivity and could be developed into 'reflexivity', the process of trying to understand our own position and perspective in relation to those of others.[30] In other words, qualitative researchers often stress how human understanding and knowledge are intersubjective and co-constructed, with patient and participant constructions often being crucial in the process of investigation.

Historically, there were moves by music therapy researchers from the mid-1980s to explore more qualitative approaches to research, thereby addressing some of the subjective, intersubjective and musical processes by which more observable and measurable therapeutic outcomes were reached. International research seminars were organised in the early 1990s and a series of texts began to address issues within qualitative research.[31] Detailed research into social-musical processes can also teach us a great deal about the musical journeys of the participants during music therapy, and contribute to our understanding of musical techniques and structures as well as to processes of meaning-making. An early example of a study of meaning-making is Dorit Amir's study of 'meaningful moments' in music therapy processes, as experienced and expressed by both music therapists and music therapy clients.[32] In Chapter 2 we highlighted the contributions of Aigen, among others, in developing a more music-centred approach to practice and research.

Some music therapy research is attempting to blend objective and subjective approaches: Apollo and Dionysus are still playing their part. For example, Ridder and Aldridge studied individual music therapy with people with frontotemporal dementia in ways that combined measurements of physiological processes and verbal representations of the experiences.[33] Subjective reporting is increasingly

28 See Ruud (2005b) for an exposition of terminology and some philosophical underpinnings to music therapy drawn from the theory of science.
29 Ziman (2000).
30 Finlay and Gough (2003).
31 Langenberg *et al.* (1996); Smeijsters 1997.
32 Amir (1992).
33 Ridder and Aldridge (2005).

becoming accepted as a means of imparting further meaning and richness to evidence, and there is a growing acceptance for 'mixed methods' in research and specifically in music therapy.[34] Patients and participants can make significant contributions to a research process; in participatory action research projects they take part in the planning, execution and interpretation of the research.[35]

Could the meeting points between apparent opposites be a source of interest? Can music therapists enjoy the creative paradoxes afforded by these crossroads? There are no simple answers to such questions. What seems clear is that tensions and contradictions are inevitable. Two debates in the discipline – on evidence-based practice (EBP) and on the challenges of representing musical processes in verbal language – have developed our understanding of this.

Reflections on the evidence-based practice debate

For a professional discipline like music therapy, relationships between research and practice have been made acute by the growing call for evidence-based practice. Since the 1990s the increased emphasis on establishing an evidence base to the work has led some music therapy researchers to explore how and where their research methodologies and methods fit within the hierarchies that have largely arisen from a medically dominated research culture. Here is one such hierarchy cited by Wigram, Pedersen and Bonde:

1 systematic review;
2 review;
3 randomised controlled trials (RCTs);
4 case control studies;
5 case series;
6 case reports/case studies;
7 qualitative studies;
8 expert opinion.[36]

This list is based on hierarchies established, for example, by the Cochrane Library and the Oxford Centre for Evidence-Based Medicine. It is in keeping with the demands originating from evidence-based medicine, which is defined as 'the conscientious, explicit and judicious use of current evidence in making decisions about the care of individual patients'.[37] In current times of limited resources, questions are being asked regarding which kind of interventions can be introduced, funded and continued in relation to the amount of sufficiently robust and reliable evidence available. There has been substantial progress in demonstrating evidence

---

34 Creswell and Plano Clark (2011); and see research using mixed methods in, for instance, the *Journal of Music Therapy* and the *Nordic Journal of Music Therapy*.
35 Stige (2002: 277–314).
36 Wigram *et al.* (2002: 261).
37 Sackett *et al.* (1996); and see www.cebm.net and www.thecochranelibrary.com.

of effective music therapy practice. We have referred in previous chapters, particularly Chapters 4–7, to the steady rise in the number of music therapy systematic literature reviews (SLRs) published on the Cochrane Collection Database (where only SLRs and meta-analyses of RCTs can pass the strict criteria for inclusion).

In spite of this rapid growth in research since the publication of the first edition of this book, purchasers of the services provided by music therapists continue to ask for evidence of potential effects. We can argue that it is the purchasers' due, as it is that of patients, parents and all interested in the developing service. There is a need to discover what is accomplished by any music therapy intervention or involvement, its impact and any specific outcomes. Positive results demonstrating successful outcomes are obviously welcome but we can also learn from inconclusive results, which in turn can help set up future questions and further investigations. We may have been asking the wrong sort of questions or using excessively gross measures or methods.

A clear piece of outcome research provides increasing external validation for the developing discipline of music therapy. Results can be published in language that is understood by members of other professions and by people outside music therapy. Such work contributes to improved professional credibility and to greater academic recognition. The outcome studies referred to in earlier chapters indicate that music therapy has an application for specific patient groups, even if only a narrow band of questions was asked.

Edwards has noted that during training, and when seeking and sustaining employment, it is important for music therapists to have a working knowledge of relevant studies, including RCTs, that support different areas of practice.[38] She also indicated some of the pitfalls in an over-reliance on the so-called gold standard of the RCT. Edwards proposes that there might be problems in recruiting the necessary large samples and securing substantial grants and resources. There are also methodological issues concerning the concept of 'blinding', in which all research participants are blind to allocation to treatment or control groups. In a music therapy intervention, staff and patients will necessarily be aware of who is taking part in the musical activity. Randomisation or matching procedures for control purposes present problems resulting from the diverse characteristics of the different populations with whom music therapists work, alongside individual responses to music and to different kinds of musical intervention. Further, the individual nature of a music therapy process, particularly one involving interactive improvisation, creates practical difficulties in applying any standard protocol or repeatable procedure.[39]

Some of the practical challenges Edwards articulates, such as recruiting sufficiently large samples, have increasingly been resolved by researchers. Other challenges address the tension between research rigour and therapeutic flexibility.

38 Edwards (2005b).
39 Ibid.: 296.

This tension creates an ethical dilemma and there are many reasons for music therapists to be interested in 'pragmatic trials' with as little distortion of everyday practice as possible.[40] In music therapy this might involve developing manuals that are based not on prescribed procedures but on principles that can guide practice in a more flexible way.[41] The legitimate request for more thorough descriptions of how music is actually used in music therapy and other health practices would then not necessarily suggest listening to prescribed music, but could embrace improvisation and other flexible approaches as well.[42]

We are still left with some questions. Is the nature of evidence limited to the methodological constraints of the randomised controlled trials and systematic literature reviews? Are there other kinds of acceptable evidence for music therapy? Awareness of the limitations of RCTs was a topical issue for Professor Sir Michael Rawlins, the then chair of the National Institute of Clinical Excellence (NICE), in an address to the Royal College of Physicians in 2008, when he questioned hierarchies and the supremacy of the RCT. Sir Michael called for a range of approaches to analyse the whole of the evidence base (including RCTs, observational and case-control studies) in order that 'decision makers' could be aware of the potential beneficial or harmful effects of therapeutic interventions. He made 'a plea to investigators to continue to develop and improve their methodologies; to decision makers to avoid adopting entrenched positions about the nature of evidence; and for both to accept that interpretation of evidence requires judgement'.[43]

Encouragement to explore alternatives to the more established methodologies is appearing from researchers in other disciplines. DeNora suggests that music therapists are well positioned to extend their search for evidence to include the local, temporal, social and cultural aspects of their practice, those features that often fall outside the confines of an RCT. She calls for a broadening of the evidence-based practice debate 'to consider features of health, illness and "treatment" that exceed narrow medical definitions of treatment and health procedure'.[44]

Music therapists need to resist being restrained or over-preoccupied by what might be inappropriate rules and regulations. Bunt's daughter provided the metaphors of selecting an appropriate scaffolding to support the work rather than that of trying to escape from the restrictions of a straitjacket. This is not to suggest that RCTs and SLRs are unimportant in music therapy, but that the idea of a hierarchy should not allow them to dominate the discipline. The hierarchy is constructed around the one question 'What works?' More sophisticated versions of this question are developed within this strong research tradition, such as 'What

40 Thorpe *et al.* (2009).
41 Rolvsjord *et al.* (2005).
42 Robb *et al.* (2011).
43 Rawlins (2008: 2159). These arguments from Edwards and Rawlins are also discussed in Bunt (2012: 177).
44 DeNora (2006: 82).

works for whom, how?' But radically different questions about how people experience and use music in different contexts require different research methods combined with broader academic pursuits of critical reflection.

Reflections on challenges of representation

As we have discussed, there are strengths and limitations to numerical representation. This suggests that qualitative research, in which verbal representation and narrative forms are commonly fundamental, should be developed as well. However, there are also strengths and limitations to verbal representation. This creates another acute challenge for a discipline that is concerned not only with health outcomes but with musical practice.

> The centipede was happy quite
> Until a toad in fun
> Said, 'Pray, which leg goes after which?'
> That worked her mind to such a pitch
> She lay distracted in a ditch
> Considering how to run.

This famous little poem about the distracted centipede is usually attributed to Katherine Craster (1841–74), although it is sometimes cited as anonymous. We can appropriate it here as an introduction to one of the central dilemmas of the discipline of music therapy, namely that many of the processes that we are studying are non-verbal and fluid while the tools we use in studying them rely heavily on language, numbers and models, all of which seem to operate on a different scale. This little poem also highlights the range of what happens in music therapy at any given moment; many legs have to be synchronised and by focusing or researching on one leg we inevitably miss the contributions of the other legs.

Working in the field of music therapy integrates many factors: practical and therapeutic aims; the setting; all the people involved; the complexities of the musical medium. Can the tools of the discipline do justice to the whole, to the richness and multiplicity of the material? Words are often highly intrusive after a deeply moving musical experience. In moments of ecstasy or intense expressive communication, we often can utter only the most elemental of sounds. The very fact that music therapists have decided to work in such a field may be based in some way on the inadequacy of language for articulating some of our deepest and most personal feelings.

We may at times be expecting too much of ourselves in the discipline of music therapy. How can we begin to translate the untranslatable? Ansdell aptly refers to the 'Music Therapist's Dilemma', 'the core problem in music therapy of having to use words and verbal logic . . . to represent complex musical processes . . . (and the therapeutic processes which are seen to occur within these)'.[45] This dilemma does

---

45 Ansdell (2001: 23).

not suggest that it is meaningless to talk about music. The media of words and music are different and while translations usually are impossible, we might still experience that words, sounds and actions make sense in relation to each other – or 'interpret each other' – in concrete situations of use. When we talk about music we are not necessarily translating meaning from one medium to the other but we might still be producing resources that enable us to use and experience music in new ways.[46]

The musical process is rich in interplay between opposites. In some ways we have come round full circle. The anecdotal descriptions typical of the early phase of the profession's development in the mid-twentieth century evolved into a period of increased rigour. There was a striving for objectivity and much borrowing from well-established research methods in the health and behavioural sciences. The development of outcome studies has been, for the most part, very much under the control of external researchers, who have based the various designs and measures within their value systems. This period has led in turn to a stage in which research rigour and interpretative sensitivity have been cultivated, sometimes in quantitative or qualitative studies, sometimes in mixed methods research.

The challenge of representing musical experiences remains. We could think more in images, metaphors, analogies and gestures rather than complex inter-pretations describing the connections between people and music. The analytical psychologist James Hillman was convinced that standard psychological language is 'impoverished, without imagination and incapable of giving good descriptions of phenomena. Clinical language had become too abstract, too professional, and is consequently less and less capable of describing sensuous experience.'[47] This call for an 'imaginative inquiry' is a tall order, being at the same time rigorous and clear, warm, sensitive and highly readable. Can our descriptive writing be multi-dimensional and non-linear, and take on multiple forms? Hillman refers to Joyce's *Ulysses*, which clearly acknowledges multiplicity. Joyce gives us much detail about the lives of some people in one city on a particular day but the writing also embraces vast and universal themes. More recent developments of arts-based research methods are being developed with similar qualities.[48] One response is 'hypertextuality', where 'series of text chunks . . . may represent an explicit alternative by offering possibilities for interactivity and multidirectional reading'.[49] This includes the presentation of music as text as well as other artistic media, such as poetry, and contemporary advances in computer technology.

Are we entering a stage in music therapy in which creative forms of repre-sentation could stress both the uniqueness of our work and the connections with other disciplines? Can we keep the music alive while still valuing a rigorous interdisciplinary approach to research, being true to ourselves both as practitioners

---

46 Consider Stige's work on music and meaning (1998, 2002), as informed by Wittgenstein's metaphor of 'language game'.
47 McNiff (1987: 290).
48 See Austin and Forinash (2005) and Barone and Eisner (2011).
49 Stige (2002: 332).

and as academics? We may not yet have discovered the appropriate language to give full value to the work but stand Janus-like on the edge, respecting the past and with tantalising glimpses of what might be.[50] And we are not talking here of the development of a general theory of music therapy, but more of the continued evolution of a body of knowledge, given the many local and interweaving complex elements involved.

Towards a culture of hybridity?

We have outlined some of the tensions and contradictions that currently characterise the discipline of music therapy. While diversity and differences in appraisal and approach characterise all disciplines, that of music therapy is especially diverse, given its dimensions within both science and arts. This is expressed both in the need for scientific evidence on the effectiveness of healthcare interventions and in the need for sensitive exploration of music as an artistic and aesthetic phenomenon. Does this suggest that the discipline is fragmented or that it needs to be so, or are there possibilities for synthesis, integration or some other constructive way of exploring the diversity?

A number of music therapy writers have been influenced by Wilber, whose theory-building tries to bridge the natural and social sciences, particularly psychology, with spiritual traditions from both East and West.[51] His conceptual model of quadrants has been influential in music therapy and reflects dimensions such as individual versus collective and interior versus exterior. Bruscia, in the second edition of *Defining Music Therapy*, builds on the concept of quadrants and Wilber's differentiation in proposing his 'Six Dynamic Models of Music Therapy'.[52] As an example, when an individual's response to the stimulus of music can be measured objectively, Bruscia positions this within the 'individual' and 'exterior' quadrant, and when one is focusing on the internal and 'subjective' experience of the music, this is then positioned within the 'individual' and 'interior' quadrant. In addition to these two possibilities, which he labels 'objective music' and 'subjective music' respectively, Bruscia uses Wilber's quadrants to describe what he calls 'universal music' (collective and external) and 'collective music' (collective and internal). Superimposed over these four models Bruscia also proposes an 'aesthetic model' and a 'transpersonal model'.

More recently, Abrams has engaged with the Wilber quadrants 'to illustrate a framework based upon four distinct epistemological perspectives on evidence-based music therapy practice that together represent an integral understanding'.[53]

---

50 Janus being the Roman god of thresholds, his name incorporated into the first month of a new year, January.

51 Wilber (1995, 2000).

52 Bruscia (1998a: chapter 15); and see this book, Chapter 2.

53 Abrams (2010: 351). Abrams also argues that the 'hierarchies' of evidence that we referred to above are based on the values of the dominant paradigm of natural science. From another point of view different questions will be asked and different methods addressed.

Bonde has also been evolving frameworks from Wilber's quadrants.[54] He places 'health musicing' at the centre of a model that incorporates the individual versus social and the polarity of body and mind.[55]

Wilber's model and its uses in music therapy remind us about a broad range of conceptual and theoretical possibilities and suggest openness for the many positions and perspectives in any field. At the same time, integral models are bound to be controversial, as is the reception and use of them in any discipline. Every academic theory is debatable within itself and there will be further controversy in any attempt to integrate theories from diverse domains. Integral models might of course be valuable and stimulating but they may not resolve tensions and contradictions.

It might be more fruitful to think in terms of 'hybridity' as a cultural project instead of ready-made integral models. In cultural theory, 'hybridity' was made prominent in postcolonial writings of the 1990s, such as in Indian literary theorist Homi Bhabha's influential book *The Location of Culture*.[56] In this work the development of the term 'hybridity' addressed issues of cultural imperialism but the term has since been used more broadly. In contemporary cultural theory, which refers to rapidly changing societies where cross-group memberships are prominent, issues of identity are often discussed in terms of a flow of cultures and their interactions. Rather than thinking about the self as having a fixed essence, identity is then conceptualised as continuously evolving from active use of mixed influences. Hybridity is understood to mean the ongoing process of something new being developed, something that had not existed in the previously established cultures.

Hybridity is only one of several terms describing cultural mixing in contemporary cultural theory. Other terms include syncretism and creolisation. Often the terms are used interchangeably or in confusing ways, and the term 'hybridity' has its critics. Some suggest it is reminiscent of 'biologised' views of identity or that it has been used to celebrate fluidity with too little interest in continuity.[57] Taking such criticisms into account, hybridity can be thought of as a term that we can use to direct 'attention toward individuals or cultural forms that are reflexively – self-consciously – mixed, that is, syntheses of cultural forms or fragments of diverse origins'.[58] To what degree could this metaphor apply to a discipline such as music therapy and how would it shed light on the challenge of diversity, tensions and contradictions in the field?

We have proposed in this chapter that a discipline is not just a body of knowledge but a culture as well, grounded in an 'invisible college' or community of collaborating (and competing) colleagues, both researchers and practitioners. Given music therapy's gradual evolution from a dependency on medicine and

54 Bonde (2011).
55 Ibid.: 122.
56 Bhabba (1994/2004).
57 Dominelli (2002: 48–50).
58 Eriksen (2007: 172).

various other disciplines to a more independent position where it has developed its own voice, it might be appropriate to borrow metaphors and ideas from post-colonial theory, where the notion of 'hybridity' was first developed. For Bhabha, hybridity is active confrontation against forces that define culture and identity as fixed. Mixing cultural elements in the face of hegemony, dissidence and ambivalence, hybridity involves a creative rethinking of established principles, which provides a space of resistance, negotiation, and articulation of new meanings.[59]

What would a culture of hybridity involve for the discipline of music therapy? It might involve going beyond defining it only in terms of more established disciplines. In this respect, music therapy is already moving towards hybridity. Attempts at assimilation into the established cultures of medicine, psychology and education were part of the early history of modern music therapy (see Chapters 1 and 2). There is today a sense that music therapy is increasingly voicing its own perspectives. It might involve embracing the tensions and contradictions we have been discussing in this chapter, instead of favouring one side and rejecting the other side of the many opposites in the field. Embracing tensions and con-tradictions is not enough, however, if there is no process of negotiation and creation of new meaning. Integral models such as the ones developed by Wilber provide us with few answers in this respect, but may perhaps help us in asking new questions. Instead of seeing such models as representations of how things are or should be, we could use them as tools in ongoing debates about how to understand and develop the identity of the discipline.

How, then, could we cultivate a culture of hybridity in music therapy? First of all, it might help to be aware of how individual music therapists, unlike Orpheus, can move beyond reliance on their own capacities for integration. Culture emerges through social interaction. Music therapists may enjoy and learn from the community of practitioner-scholars that is the profession of music therapy. This community is inhabited by people who are interested in different things. Perhaps the motto for the Tenth World Congress in Music Therapy, held in Oxford in 2002 – 'dialogue and debate' – provides us with one of the best recipes for nurturing a culture of hybridity. Dialogues present a powerful tool for exploration of how degrees of consensus could be established, while debates – if dialogical enough to keep the conversation going – help us explore differences and their implications.[60]

In order to achieve this, we need awareness of the 'dialogue-enhancing tools' of the discipline. Music therapy congresses, symposia and viva voce events already exist as possibilities that could be developed further, supplemented by contem-porary inventions such as social media. EPICURE, an agenda developed for dialogic evaluation of qualitative research, is one attempt at developing new tools.[61] New forms of reflexivity can be sought in which hybridity becomes a

59 Bhabba (1994/2004).
60 Sennett (2013); and see the subsection 'Dialogue and debate' in Chapter 8 (p. 189).
61 Stige *et al.* (2009).

conscious alternative strategy for development. This would be in contrast with attempts to assimilate music therapy into the logic of more established disciplines or to preserve its uniqueness by isolating it as its own discipline. We can now return to the idea presented earlier, where we indicated that a professional discipline such as music therapy uses knowledge from other disciplines to inform a framework that is distinctively its own. The idea of a culture of hybridity acknowledges 'indigenous' elements in this process but should help us worry less about borrowing from other disciplines. The idea of framework becomes transformed, perhaps to the degree that we could start thinking of it as a verb, referring to the continuous work we engage in on the 'scaffolding' that the discipline needs.

Developing the discipline of music therapy

In Chapter 2 we presented a range of theoretical perspectives *on* music therapy. Gradually, as the discipline has matured, what we could call perspectives *from* music therapy have also been evolving – that is, perspectives on music, music therapy, health and human (inter)action that are of relevance for other disciplines. The work of some music therapy researchers can illustrate this trend. In 2003 Odell-Miller contributed a chapter entitled 'Are words enough?' to a compilation on psychoanalytic psychotherapy, and in 2005, with her art psychotherapist colleague Joy Shaverien, a chapter on the arts therapies as part of a textbook on psychotherapy.[62] Likewise, in an international encyclopedia on adolescence, a chapter on music therapy by Gold, Saarikallio and McFerran finds its natural place.[63] In Chapter 4 we referred in the discussion on 'communicative musicality' to contributions by Pavlicevic and Ansdell to further evolution of this theory.[64] Their chapter is part of the important series of music psychology texts published by Oxford University Press, to which music therapists have contributed.[65]

In spite of these developments, several commentators have noted that music therapy as a discipline still relies too much on theories and models from other disciplines. Music therapy is 'neglecting the pursuit of its own independent foundations,' Aigen argued in 2005.[66] His argument in favour of 'indigenous' theory originating primarily from music therapy practice represents only one of several perspectives and we can take his request for theory development to reflect broader concerns relevant to contemporary music therapy. Chapters 4–7 revealed several different challenges to theory in music therapy, as exemplified by the stories of Mark and Emma in Chapter 7. We now comment briefly on notions of theory in music therapy, methods of theory development, uses of theory and criteria for evaluation of theory. Each of these areas is complex and deserves much

62 Odell-Miller (2003); Shaverien and Odell-Miller (2005).
63 Gold *et al.* (2011).
64 Pavlicevic and Ansdell (2009).
65 See also the contributions to the music series published by Ashgate.
66 Aigen (2005: 31).

more thorough treatment than can be given here, so our intention is to highlight some areas for future debate and development.

Notions of theory in music therapy

The word 'theory' is derived from Greek *theorein*, to view. In *Readings on Music Therapy Theory* Ansdell makes use of the etymology of the term when sharing a story that communicates facets of how he 'views' theory:

> After a research seminar in which a group of music therapy students was discussing what 'theory' is, a Greek student of mine came back from holiday with a photo she'd taken in her home city of Athens. In the foreground, there's a corner with a street-sign named (in Greek) 'Theory Street.' The road leads up a hill to a fine view of the Acropolis. Theory Street simply means 'View Street.' Similarly, a theory means 'view this my way for a while.' . . . Climb up from a road on the other side and the view can be quite different. Theories are necessarily perspectival, partial, and historically situated. Ideally, they are also communal and cumulative, as varying perspectives assemble a more inclusive and shared understanding of a phenomenon.[67]

A more formal definition of theory is offered by Bruscia in the second edition of *Defining Music Therapy*:

> A theory is a set of interrelated principles or constructs which have been created by a theorist in order to: (a) describe and organize a particular domain in a comprehensive and coherent manner; (b) explain or understand related facts, empirical data, and phenomena within the domain; and (c) offer a conceptual framework for decision-making in future theory, research, and practice.[68]

These two ways of describing theory complement each other for the purpose of our discussion. Bruscia's definition clarifies some of the formal components and functions of theories in music therapy: they describe and organise complex phenomena and processes in ways that make them more understandable. Ansdell's story emphasises any description or explanation as 'perspectival' and 'partial', and suggests that the continuing efforts of a (critical) community are usually constructive in the development of theoretical thinking. We could perhaps suggest that Bruscia's definition favours the image of theory as constructed by a single thinking subject confronting an external world, while Ansdell's reflections favour the idea of theory as the discourse of a community collaborating in exploring a perspective on selected aspects. These differences make it clear that there is more

---

67 Ansdell (2012: 213).
68 Bruscia (1998a: 243).

than one theory in music therapy and more than one way of understanding the nature of theory.

Methods of theory development in music therapy

In a chapter on theory development in music therapy, Bruscia highlights five possible methods, namely explication, integration, philosophical analysis, empirical analysis and reflective synthesis.[69] *Explication* involves identifying, clarifying and organising understandings that already exist within music therapy, for instance as identified through a review of the literature.[70] *Integration* involves relating descriptions of music therapy to concepts developed in another field.[71] *Philosophical analysis* involves relating philosophical concerns, such as reflections on the nature of reality, to the practice, research and theory of music therapy.[72] *Empirical analysis* involves articulating theory based on the analysis of research data.[73] Finally, *reflective synthesis* involves articulating theory on the basis of one's own experiences by relating them to existing ideas within philosophy or other disciplines.

Bruscia's overview of methods of theory development is simple yet also inclusive. In many academic disciplines the focus is almost exclusively on empirical analysis, although we would add that elements of integration and philosophical analysis are inevitable, as few theoretical ideas are unrelated to interdisciplinary or philosophical debates. The interdisciplinary nature of music therapy (as discussed earlier in this chapter) and its close relationship to practice (as discussed in Chapter 8) constitute two of the reasons why an inclusive approach to theory development might be helpful. Reflective synthesis, for instance, might appear idiosyncratic and speculative in the eyes of scholars geared towards empirical analysis, but might be critical in generating insights based on the wisdom of experienced practitioners.

Uses of theory in music therapy

In some academic contexts a theory is almost exclusively understood as a body of fundamental principles underlying scientific practice (research).[74] Music therapy,

---

69 Bruscia (2005: 541–5).
70 Some of Bruscia's previous contributions to music therapy theory have been of this type, such as his articulation of sixty-four clinical techniques in improvisational music therapy; see Bruscia (1987: 533–58).
71 Bruscia (2005) explains that the method of integration is necessarily interdisciplinary and he gives examples that draw upon disciplines such as sociology, psychology and neuroscience.
72 Bruscia argues that there are two approaches, one starting from philosophy, one from music therapy.
73 Here Bruscia distinguishes between analysis based in quantitative and qualitative research approaches.
74 The classic debates within philosophy of science – between scholars such as Popper, Kuhn and Lakatos – are to a large degree based in the relationship between theory and research; see Ziman (2000).

a professional discipline, needs a broader understanding of the uses of theory. Aigen offers a useful overview of the role of theory in contemporary music therapy. He particularly stresses as productive the use of theory, by practitioners and qualitative researchers, which goes beyond the traditional scientific approach referred to above. Aigen suggests that theories 'provide the foundation for treatment', 'advance and disseminate the skills and knowledge of practitioners', 'create directions for research' and 'establish links with other disciplines'.[75]

Each of these uses of theory is complex and multifaceted and can be understood in different ways. Aigen sees music therapy as a musical, creative and inter-personal process and so a 'foundation for treatment' will not necessarily be a prescription for concrete actions:

> Instead, theory provides a foundation for treatment through a variety of other functions: It creates a post-hoc rationale for actions; it dictates the components of academic and professional training programs by suggesting the skills necessary to practice in a given domain; it creates a common language for discourse among practitioners in a domain; it provides an overall world view, value system, and set of standard procedures that define interventions in a given domain. In short, theory makes possible the professional education of practitioners as it provides the rational basis for interventions. It is a necessary component of the social structure that defines a profession and differentiates it from other forms of social relationship.[76]

The broad uses of theory in music therapy, as exemplified by Aigen's reflections, illustrate that theories in a professional discipline are not selected merely for their intrinsic truth value. Equally, or more so, they are chosen because of their use-fulness (their perceived match with existing practice) and their heuristic value (their capacity to generate new ideas and developments). This makes the question of how to evaluate theories in music therapy both acute and complex.

Evaluation of theory in music therapy

The literature on the evaluation of theory in music therapy is surprisingly sparse. One of the few contributions is a short list of evaluation criteria proposed by Bruscia in his introduction to *Readings on Music Therapy Theory*. First, he stresses that

> [o]ne must start with the notion that a theory is a 'way of thinking' that the theorist 'constructs' about what we do or what we know. As such, it may or may not be a statement of fact, it may or may not be completely true, and it may or may not be verifiable.[77]

---

75 Aigen (2005: 13–17).
76 Ibid.: 14–15.
77 Bruscia (2012: 17).

Second, Bruscia proposes these five evaluation criteria:

1) Coherence: How well organized is the theory? Are the ideas sequenced in an understandable way? Are parts of the theory logically related to one another? Is there a hierarchy of ideas?
2) Clarity: Are basic premises of the theory stated in the simplest possible way, and are all important terms and concepts clearly defined? How well-written is the theory?
3) Comprehensiveness: Does the theory deal thoroughly with the topic or question under scrutiny? Does it address all issues related to the main topic or question?
4) Relevance: Does the theory provide pertinent and relevant answers to the most important topics or questions under scrutiny?
5) Usefulness: Does the theory provide any new and valuable insights? Can the theory guide one in decision-making? Does this 'way of thinking' actually facilitate practice and research?[78]

Bruscia's list should be a helpful starting point for dialogue and debate on the evaluation of theories in music therapy. We may remember from Mark's story in Chapter 7 that doubts about the correctness and relevance of theory are not just interesting academic questions. For a practitioner they may be experienced as acute, and perhaps overwhelming, in ways that can create insecurity about one's own professional competence. This suggests the need for at least two areas of development. As the discipline of music therapy grows and matures, the request for solid scholarship that can support the training of practitioners should be taken very seriously. There is also a need for enhancing the practitioners' own skills in using and evaluating theories, as in ongoing supervision of practice.

As we have seen, development of the discipline of music therapy will necessarily include theory development and critique. The metaphor of 'hybridity' reminds us, however, that discipline must relate to a broad range of cultural values and practices. While there are academic challenges linked to theory development, it is crucial to remember that music therapy knowledge is more than academic knowledge. Creative musicianship and sensitive interpersonal communication, skills and competencies that traditionally have been developed in practice are constitutive elements in music therapy knowledge. A culture of hybridity therefore will involve continuous striving towards reflective integration of theory and practice.

Concluding points

We began this chapter with reference to the mythic story of Orpheus and the manner in which his music transcended boundaries of space and time. This is a

---

78 Ibid.: 17.

story that has inspired a large number of artists for centuries. We quoted lines from a song from Shakespeare's *King Henry VIII* and we described how Monteverdi in his opera *Orfeo* played with the myth to present a more joyous conclusion. Indeed, there are several ways to tell the myth and several ways to understand it. Myths do not offer answers to specific questions so much as offer ways of beginning to think about answers, or even ways of beginning to ask new questions.[79]

In contemporary popular culture the myth of Orpheus continues to stimulate creativity. In 'The Lyre of Orpheus', Nick Cave and the Bad Seeds have developed a song that retells the myth in an ironic and rather free way that plays on perennial themes of problematic gender relationships. In the concept album *Hadestown*, American folk singer Anaïs Mitchell has developed a personal yet socially engaged universe based on the myth. If, as we were suggesting, music therapists use Orpheus as an emblem, they can feel free to play with the myth, to try out twists and endings that inspire in new ways.

As we approach the end of this chapter and of this book we return to a suggestion in the myth of Orpheus that reality is not as fixed as we tend to think. Orpheus made trees bow. Perhaps this aspect of the myth does not seem too remote from the major changes in how physicists view the world. To the classical physicist, nature was objective; time was linear; matter, energy and space were absolute. To the modern, post-Einstein physicist, nature is not entirely objective; time is not just linear; matter, energy, space and time are not absolute. There are the mind-baffling notions of matter being wave and particle at one and the same time, and the observer influencing what is observed. At the sub-atomic level, cause and effect are no longer fundamental. If we think about music therapy from the viewpoint of the determinism and causality of a rigid approach to behaviour therapy, then maybe we keep alive an earlier fixed position. Charles Eagle was among the first to suggest that perhaps music therapy could begin to move into the uncharted waters of non-linear space-time.[80]

The ever-changing, open-ended, connected and interactive nature of artistic processes has much that is complementary with these new constructs. There is a multiplicity of connections in musical transactions. We make music in a space-time continuum, using a highly subjective art form that gains meaning through the translation of inner impulses into recognisable pattern, objective form and structure (Dionysus and Apollo at play again?). Can we imagine processes where there is no mind and body split but a dance-like interplay between mechanistic and non-mechanistic patterns, influencing mind, body and spirit? Such attitudes can be seen in the recent apparent thirst for and appreciation of the more spiritual qualities of music, within and outside music therapy. A piece such as John Tavener's *The Protecting Veil* has become very popular and the rather mystical compositions of Arvo Pärt, for example, are performed to large audiences. There is a growing interest in the ancient healing traditions that use music as a central core, as was

79 McLeish (1996: 11).
80 Eagle (1991).

mentioned in the opening chapter.[81] It seems that interest in such self-healing potential of sound and music is part of a deeper search for meaning and a sense of belonging. Alternatives to a fast, hectic lifestyle are being sought by some.

Music and music-making can be a focus of real beauty and transformation, helping us to define our humanity and all that is vibrant in living to our creative potential. Music can contribute to making life possible and liveable, if sometimes only for a moment. There may well be dance-like movement at the quiet centre of the revolving world, to paraphrase Eliot.[82] At the source of the dance, we may then find resonating and rhythmic vibration. And according to the Sufi master Hazrat Inayat Kahn, 'The whole of life in all its aspects is one single music; and the real spiritual attainment is to tune oneself to the harmony of this perfect music.'[83]

Some music therapists find such ideas inspiring, while some find them close to an impossible dream of finding solutions to all of our problems or final answers to our largest questions.[84] Others might refer to myth, as we have done with the story of Orpheus and how it points to opposites and struggles to unite seemingly disparate roles. In some ways he succeeded but as a hero he failed: he could not bring Eurydice all the way back from Hades. If we allow ourselves to play with the myth we might imagine Orpheus encouraging Eurydice to sing or play herself. He would have known that she was there and the music and soul of Eurydice would have been more present in the world. There could be some new and surprising endings to the story.[85]

81 In addition to the compilations by Gouk and Horden referred to in Chapter 1, see also, for example, Boyce-Tillman (2000) and McClellan (1991).
82 Eliot (1944).
83 Khan (1988: 129).
84 For a critique of New Age ideas on music, see Summer with Summer (1996).
85 It has not escaped our notice that two male music therapists have selected Orpheus as an emblem; we hope that listening to our male anima makes up for the lack of female representation.

Epilogue

Music therapy: an art beyond words?

As described in the Introduction, this book is the result of years of collegial contact and months of intense collaborative writing. As part of this collaboration, Leslie travelled to Norway to visit Brynjulf in Brandal on the western coast of the country. We would write and discuss most of the time, except for our daily walk in the countryside and the day off when we went to Ålesund, the major town in the area. This town has a fine collection of Art Nouveau buildings as well as an interesting Art Nouveau centre. On the next day we were back to the discipline of writing but, of course, there would always be some time for more free-floating conversations and reflections, especially in the evenings. We have written this epilogue as a dialogue constructed from the many conversations we had together during these days. You can imagine the two of us sitting in front of the fire one evening, trying to sum up our thoughts about the book and the writing process.

BRYNJULF: I remember very well when the first edition of the book came out, one of the things I noticed was the subtitle: *An Art beyond Words*. I liked it but also found it a bit romantic and one-sided. Music therapy is more than art, so when art was highlighted in the subtitle I assumed that it communicated a priority or preference, or perhaps more probably a broader concept of art. Were you highlighting music therapy as a *doing*, requiring craft, as when we talk about 'the art of' something?

LESLIE: In 1994 I did want to emphasise that music therapy has artistic roots in music and the humanities. I suppose this is closely connected with the tradition in the United Kingdom of musicians being secure in their musical identities before training as music therapists. This has continued to be a focus in the intervening years but with increasing emphasis and celebration on what musicians from many different backgrounds can bring to the profession, with songwriters, jazz musicians, orchestral players, music teachers and solo performers bringing so much variety of experience to the trainings and potential work. This inclusivity also applies to how music therapy is practised, like you say 'as a *doing*'. Another reason for this earlier focus on the 'art' of music therapy is because as therapists we make the practice available to people of all ages who have wide-ranging healthcare needs and might benefit. I'm reminded of the phrase attributed to William Morris that caught our attention when we visited the Art Nouveau centre in Ålesund, which referred to art being for all and finding art in 'all things'. So there is an element of craft and hard work implied and, as you say, a broad concept of art. This introduces the theme of everyone having access to all kinds of music, and a further role of the professional music therapist is to be aware of these cultural and political implications.

BRYNJULF: I'm also interested in the phrase 'beyond words'. Some music therapists suggest that words are not necessary, others that music alone does not suffice, but I would like to suggest something a bit more dynamic and interactive than that. Words, sounds and actions often interpret each other in music therapy, don't you think?

LESLIE: Words are a necessary part of music therapy practice but often can be redundant or get in the way of allowing the music to have its full therapeutic impact. I agree that there are dynamic and interactive connections between words and the musical actions in music therapy, and increasingly I tend to view everything that happens in a session as belonging to music therapy, be they simple sound forms, complex musical interactions or verbal discussions of the more psychological and dynamic processes involved. We can listen to the music and then there are the musical elements, shapes and contours behind all the words and sounds within the therapy room, as music flows from and into words. I do not want to imply any arbitrary division. Words go beyond music: music goes beyond words. There is this transcendent potential of moving beyond, yet music-making is also grounded in the physical. We seem to be able to hold these apparently paradoxical tensions in balance. I am increasingly drawn to the non-dual nature of our work: not the binary preoccupations of, for example, body *or* mind, science *or* art, words *or* music but *both . . . and . . .* So should we be playful and add a question mark at the end of the subtitle?

BRYNJULF: Well, yes, that's something to think about for the third edition . . . Questions invite dialogue, so it's not a bad idea. I think we both consider dialogue as central to the practice of music therapy but maybe also we should think about dialogue more in relation to how we develop the profession and discipline? When we hear and read colleagues, perhaps the central thing is not always whether we think they are right or wrong but whether they could make us think again?

LESLIE: In the Introduction we referred to dialogue as a starting point for our collaboration and I think it has been a feature of how we have worked systematically: we have maintained some of the elements of the earlier edition, with its emphasis on telling stories and different psychological processes, while opening up the dialogue to include other perspectives, particularly those with a more cultural and ecological emphasis. In 1994 I raised the question, as others had done, as to whether music therapists continue to refer to other disciplines to underpin their practice or begin to have more confidence in developing theories from within the discipline. I think we have seen moves towards this, with so much happening in the twenty years between these two editions. I hope our readers will also be aware of the increasingly wide range of practices and perspectives. Hopefully, we have achieved our intention of not privileging any one approach or theory but have left it open to readers to explore areas that resonate with them and to which they are drawn. There have been considerable worldwide developments of the profession in these past twenty years and we can only wonder where the next twenty years will take both the profession and discipline of music therapy.

BRYNJULF: Hmm ... another twenty years ... In Chapter 1 we referred to Kenny's use of a lifespan framework to describe the evolution of music therapy. In some countries music therapy is many decades old now, so there might be signs not only of maturity but even of midlife crises. In other countries there is still the restless energy typical of a young age. In all countries it would be helpful to search for possibilities to re-evaluate the past and look for new meanings and directions. Perhaps in twenty years our professional discipline will be more reflexive in this way, with a tradition of critical research on our own historical development.

LESLIE: Yes, we mentioned in the first chapter that there is still a dearth of historical research, given the focus, in the early stages of a practice-based profession, on developing skills, creating work, building public awareness, setting up research and building theoretical knowledge. I recall that in your 2002 book you considered music therapy at a stage of being 'in search of a discipline'. I'm wondering how you view that phrase today and whether you would consider music therapy to have reached a more confident stage in its development?

BRYNJULF: Music therapy has gradually grown more noticeable as a discipline with an audible voice in society and in interdisciplinary discourse. However, this does not settle the identity of the discipline, but accentuates the need to reflect on its nature. And, as we have been talking about, our capacity to 'mix' seems to be key.

LESLIE: Yes, and as we suggest in the final chapter, the metaphor of hybridity might be helpful for a discipline that is part science, part art, and I don't want to underestimate the science part.

BRYNJULF: I feel like telling a story that invites us to play with that metaphor. It is a story from my childhood when I sometimes used to travel from my little home town down to Bergen, the main city of western Norway. We would always take the boat along the coast. On one of the many stops on the eighteen-hour boat trip there was a village store with a shopkeeper who was different from any shopkeeper I had met before. He was always busy talking – which is already kind of striking in Norway, you know – and he would tell the most wonderful stories in a high-pitched voice, full of fun. The most fascinating thing, however, was how he would use his old-style balance. You could ask for two apples, an orange and a banana. The shopkeepers in my hometown would have used the balance three times to find the weight of each, probably 'just because' but also for the practical reason that the price of each item would be different. Not this shopkeeper. He would put all those things on the balance together, glance at the weight and suggest a price. He was using a logic that I could not decode. It was a bit bewildering. The rational ideals of the Enlightenment have certainly put its mark on European culture; we train our children thoroughly when it comes to categories. I was a trained child too but here was a man who didn't care about categories in the same way as the others. I was not sure what to make of it but I certainly made sure that I went to this shop every time I took this boat. After some visits, I would be tempted to see how far he would stretch the mixing of categories.

LESLIE: 'Three potatoes and some grapes, please . . .'?

BRYNJULF: Yes, something like that. I will stop the story here and play with it to suggest a version of the hybridity metaphor that might be relevant for the mixing that we need to do in music therapy. Let's start with the potatoes and the grapes. Science and art are probably as different as that, don't you think? If we just put them on the balance together without actually *doing* anything else with them, the result will be unusual but not very interesting over time. If we use the melting-pot strategy and cook everything into one integrated thing . . . , well, I don't know, the result might be disgusting. But we could cook the potatoes and cut them up, slice the grapes, and perhaps throw in some walnuts and other nice things. Everything would be recognisable as individual ingredients but they would be transformed and would also be in contact with each other in ways that would give us something new and different. And a salad like this is usually best if we have some dressing, not just because we then have a medium for connecting the ingredients but also because it brings out their juices and flavours.

LESLIE: A salad where we recognise the bits but actively bring them in contact with each other; that could be an image for hybridity in music therapy, yes, I agree . . . It would be an ever-evolving salad, I guess. We could eat and take nourishment from it and throw in new bits as we grow and learn how to do things.

BRYNJULF: It could become quite a mix but we wouldn't want to throw in whatever in whatever way at whatever point. We need to cultivate our creativity but also some sort of critical awareness.

LESLIE: And the dressing that . . .

BRYNJULF: . . . connects it all and brings out the juices?

[Both authors' collaborative note: At this point in the conversation there is no more of the customary turn-taking that characterises verbal interaction. We both realised something at the same time, partly talking at the same time as well. This is impossible to capture in lines on paper but we will allude to it here through use of short and incomplete sentences. In addition, you will have to imagine the non-verbal participation of the person not speaking.]

LESLIE: It's music, isn't it? The music that connects . . .

BRYNJULF: . . . people and places and . . .

LESLIE: ... promise and hope. Yes, but we might need to elaborate on our salad image and think of the dressing as where we start and not as an add-on ...

BRYNJULF: Exactly! Hybridity applies to this rich mixing of music in music therapy practice. We return here to some of the themes of our Introduction ...

LESLIE: ... that people of all ages make unique connections to music ...

References

Abrams, B. (2002) 'Transpersonal dimensions of the Bonny Method', in K.E. Bruscia and D.E. Grocke (eds) *Guided Imagery and Music: The Bonny Method and Beyond*, Gilsum, NH: Barcelona Publishers.

—— (2010) 'Evidence-based music therapy practice: an integral understanding', *Journal of Music Therapy*, 47, 4: 351–79.

—— (2012) 'A relationship-based theory of music therapy: understanding processes and goals as being-together-musically', in K.E. Bruscia (ed.) *Readings on Music Therapy Theory*, Gilsum, NH: Barcelona Publishers.

Adrienne, J. (2006) 'A feminist sociology of professional issues in music therapy', in S. Hadley (ed.) *Feminist Perspectives in Music Therapy*, Gilsum NH: Barcelona Publishers.

Ahonen-Eerikäinen, H. (2007) *Group Analytic Music Therapy*, Gilsum, NH: Barcelona Publishers.

Aigen, K. (1991) 'The roots of music therapy: towards an indigenous research paradigm', unpublished PhD thesis, New York University.

—— (1998) *Paths of Development in Nordoff-Robbins Music Therapy*, Gilsum, NH: Barcelona Publishers.

—— (2004) 'Conversations on creating community: performance as music therapy in New York City', in M. Pavlicevic and G. Ansdell (eds) *Community Music Therapy*, London: Jessica Kingsley Publishers.

—— (2005) *Music-Centered Music Therapy*, Gilsum, NH: Barcelona Publishers.

—— (2014) *The Study of Music Therapy: Current Issues and Concepts*, New York: Routledge.

Ainlay, G.W. (1948) 'The place of music in military hospitals', in D.M. Schullian and M. Schoen (eds) *Music and Medicine*, New York: Henry Schuman.

Aldridge, D. (1988) 'The single case in clinical research', in *The Case Study as Research: Proceedings of the Fourth Music Therapy Day Conference*, London: City University.

—— (1995) 'Spirituality, hope, and music therapy in palliative care', *The Arts in Psychotherapy*, 22, 2: 103–9.

—— (1996) *Music Therapy Research and Practice in Medicine: From Out of Silence*, London: Jessica Kingsley Publishers.

—— (1999) *Music Therapy in Palliative Care: New Voices*, London: Jessica Kingsley Publishers.

—— (2005) *Case Study Designs in Music Therapy*, London: Jessica Kingsley Publishers.

Aldridge, D. and Fachner, J. (eds) (2010) *Music Therapy and Addiction*, London: Jessica Kingsley Publishers.

Altshuler, I.M. (1954) 'The past, present, and future of music therapy', in E. Podolsky (ed.) *Music Therapy*, New York, Philosophical Library.

Alvin, J. (1975) *Music Therapy*, London: Hutchinson.

—— (1977) 'The musical instrument as an intermediary object', *British Journal of Music Therapy*, 8, 2: 7–13.

Alzheimer's Disease International (2009) *World Alzheimer report*, available at: www.alz.co.uk/research/world-report#2009 (accessed 11 June 2013).

American Music Therapy Association (2004) 'Music therapy quantitative and qualitative foundations' (CD-ROM, 1964–2003).

—— (2009) 'AMTA professional competencies', available at: www.musictherapy.org/about/competencies (accessed 1 March 2013).

—— (2012a) 'AMTA code of ethics', available at: www.musictherapy.org/about/ethics (accessed 1 March 2013)

—— (2012b) 'AMTA standards of clinical practice', available at: www.musictherapy.org/about/standards/ (accessed 1 March 2013)

Amir, D. (1992) 'Awakening and expanding the self: meaningful moments in music therapy process as experienced and described by music therapists and music therapy clients', unpublished PhD thesis, New York University.

Ansdell, G. (1995) *Music for Life: Aspects of Creative Music Therapy with Adult Clients*, London: Jessica Kingsley Publishers.

—— (2001) 'Musicology: misunderstood guest at the music therapy feast?', in D. Aldridge, G. Di Franco and T. Wigram (eds) *Music Therapy in Europe*, Rome: ISMEZ/Onlus.

—— (2002) 'Community Music Therapy and the winds of change – a discussion paper', *Voices: A World Forum for Music Therapy*, 2, 2, available at: https://normt.uib.no/index.php/voices/article/view/83/65 (accessed 23 February 2011).

—— (2004) 'Rethinking music and community: theoretical perspectives in support of Community Music Therapy', in M. Pavlicevic and G. Ansdell (eds) *Community Music Therapy*, London: Jessica Kingsley Publishers.

—— (2005a) 'Being who you aren't; doing what you can't: Community Music Therapy and the paradoxes of performance', *Voices: A World Forum for Music Therapy*, 5, 3, available at: https://normt.uib.no/index.php/voices/article/view/229/173 (accessed 24 February 2011).

—— (2005b) 'Musicing, time and transcendence: theological themes for music therapy', *British Journal of Music Therapy*, 19, 1: 20–8.

—— (2010a) 'Where performing helps: processes and affordances of performance in community music therapy', in B. Stige, G. Ansdell, C. Elefant and M. Pavlicevic, *Where Music Helps: Community Music Therapy in Action and Reflection*, Farnham, UK: Ashgate.

—— (2010b) 'Belonging through musicing: explorations of musical community', in B. Stige, G. Ansdell, C. Elefant and M. Pavlicevic, *Where Music Helps: Community Music Therapy in Action and Reflection*, Farnham, UK: Ashgate.

—— (2012) 'Steps toward an ecology of music therapy: a reader's guide to various theoretical wanderings, 1990–2011', in K.E. Bruscia (ed.) *Readings on Music Therapy Theory*, Gilsum, NH: Barcelona Publishers.

—— (2013) *How Music Helps – in Music Therapy and Everyday Life*, Farnham, UK: Ashgate.

Ansdell, G. and Meehan, J. (2010) '"Some light at the end of the tunnel": exploring users' evidence for the effectiveness of music therapy in adult mental health settings', *Music and Medicine*, 2, 1: 29–40.

Ansdell, G. and Pavlicevic, M. (2005) 'Musical companionship, musical community: music therapy and the process and value of musical communication', in D. Miell, R. MacDonald and D.J. Hargreaves (eds) *Musical Communication*, Oxford: Oxford University Press.

—— (2008) 'Responding to the challenge: between boundaries and borders (response to Alison Barrington)', *British Journal of Music Therapy*, 22, 2: 73–6.

Antonovsky, A. (1979) *Unraveling the Mystery of Health: How People Manage Stress and Stay Well*, San Francisco: Jossey-Bass.

Arrington, G.E. (1954) 'Music in medicine', in E. Podolsky (ed.) *Music Therapy*, New York: Philosophical Library.

Arts Council England (2004) 'The arts, health and wellbeing: a strategy for partnership', draft for consultation, November.

Assagioli, R. (1965/1990) *Psychosynthesis: A Manual of Principles and Techniques*, Wellingborough, UK: Aquarian Press.

Athanassakis, A.N. (1977) *The Orphic Hymns: Text, Translation, and Notes*, Missoula, MT: Society of Biblical Literature.

Austin, D. (2008) *The Theory and Practice of Vocal Psychotherapy: Songs of the Self*, London: Jessica Kingsley Publishers.

Austin, D. and Forinash, M. (2005) 'Arts-based research', in B.L. Wheeler (ed.) *Music Therapy Research*, 2nd edn, Gilsum, NH: Barcelona Publishers.

Baines, S. (2000/2003) 'A consumer-directed and partnered community mental health music therapy program: program development and evaluation', *Canadian Journal of Music Therapy*, 7, 1: 51–70. Republished in *Voices: A World Forum for Music Therapy*, 3, 3, available at: https://normt.uib.no/index.php/voices/article/view/137/113 (accessed 26 January 2011).

—— (2013) 'Music therapy as an anti-oppressive practice', *The Arts in Psychotherapy*, 40: 1–5.

Baker, F. (2011) 'Facilitating neurological reorganization through music therapy: a case of modified Melodic Intonation Therapy in the treatment of a person with aphasia', in A. Meadows (ed.) *Developments in Music Therapy Practice: Case Study Perspectives*, Gilsum, NH: Barcelona Publishers.

Baker, F. and Tamplin, J. (2006) *Music Therapy Methods in Neurorehabilitation: A Clinician's Manual*, London: Jessica Kingsley Publishers.

—— (2011) 'Coordinating respiration, vocalization, and articulation: rehabilitating apraxic and dysarthric voices of people with neurological damage', in F. Baker and S. Uhlig (eds) *Voicework in Music Therapy: Research and Practice*, London: Jessica Kingsley Publishers.

Baker, F. and Uhlig, S. (eds) (2011) *Voicework in Music Therapy: Research and Practice*, London: Jessica Kingsley Publishers.

Baker, F. and Wigram, T. (eds) (2005) *Songwriting: Methods, Techniques, and Clinical Applications for Music Therapy Clinicians, Educators and Students*, London: Jessica Kingsley Publishers.

Barenboim, D. and Said, E.W. (2003) *Parallels and Paradoxes: Exploration in Music and Society*, London: Bloomsbury.

Baron-Cohen, S., Tager-Flusberg, H. and Cohen, D.J. (1993) *Understanding Other Minds: Perspectives from Autism*, Oxford: Oxford University Press.

Barone, T.E. and Eisner, E.W. (2011) *Arts Based Research*, Thousand Oaks, CA: Sage.

Barrington, A. (2008) 'Challenging the profession', *British Journal of Music Therapy*, 22, 2: 65–72.

Bateman, A., Brown, D. and Pedder, J. (2010) *Introduction to Psychotherapy: An Outline of Psychodynamic Principles and Practice*, 4th edn, Hove, UK: Routledge.

Bateson, M.C. (1979) 'The epigenesis of conversational interaction: a personal account of research development', in M. Bullowa (ed.) *Before Speech: The Beginnings of Interpersonal Communication*, Cambridge: Cambridge University Press.

Begbie, J.S. (2005) *Theology, Music and Time*, Cambridge: Cambridge University Press.

Behne, K.-E. (1997) 'The development of "Musikerleben" in adolescence: how and why young people listen to music', in I. Deliège and J. Sloboda (eds) *Perception and Cognition of Music*, Hove, UK: Psychology Press.

Benenzon, R.O. (1981) *Music Therapy Manual*, Springfield, IL: Charles C. Thomas.

Berger, D.S. (2002) *Music Therapy, Sensory Integration and the Autistic Child*, London: Jessica Kingsley Publishers.

Berlyne, D.E. (1971) *Aesthetics and Psychobiology*, New York: Appleton-Century-Crofts.

Bernatzky, G., Presch, M., Anderson, M. and Panksepp, J. (2011) 'Emotional foundations of music as a non-pharmacological pain management tool in modern medicine', *Neuroscience and Biobehavioral Reviews*, 35: 1989–99.

Bhabha, H.K. (1994/2004) *The Location of Culture*, New York: Routledge.

Bion, W.R. (1962) *Learning from Experience*, London: Heinemann.

Bispham, J. (2009) 'Music's "design features": musical motivation, musical pulse, and musical pitch', *Musicæ Scientiæ*, special issue: 2009–10, 'Music and Evolution': 41–61.

Blacking, J. (1973) *How Musical Is Man?* Seattle: University of Washington Press.

Blacking, J. (1987) *'A Commonsense View of All Music': Reflections on Percy Grainger's Contribution to Ethnomusicology and Music Education*, Cambridge: Cambridge University Press.

Blackman, D.E. (1980) 'Images of man in contemporary behaviourism', in A.J. Chapman and D.M. Jones (eds) *Models of Man*, Leicester: British Psychological Society.

Blair, D. (1964) 'Arts in society: music therapy', *New Society*, 30 January: 26.

Bonde, L.O. (2001) 'Steps towards a meta-theory of music therapy? An introduction to Ken Wilber's integral psychology and a discussion of its relevance for music therapy', *Nordic Journal of Music Therapy*, 10, 2: 176–87.

—— (2011) 'Health musicing – music therapy or music and health? A model, empirical examples and personal reflections', *Music and Arts in Action*, 3, 2: 121–40.

Bossius, T. and Lilliestam, L. (2011) *Musiken och jag. Rapport från forskningsprosjektet 'Musik i Människors Liv'* [The Music and Me. Report from the Research Project 'Music in People's Life'], Gothenburg: Bo Ejeby Förlag.

Bowlby, J. (1988) *A Secure Base: Clinical Applications of Attachment Theory*, London: Routledge.

Boxill, E.H. (1997) *The Miracle of Music Therapy*, Gilsum, NH: Barcelona Publishers.

Boyce-Tillman, J. (2000) *Constructing Musical Healing: The Wounds that Sing*, London: Jessica Kingsley Publishers.

Boyd, K.M. (2011) 'Disease, illness, sickness, health, healing and wholeness: exploring some elusive concepts', *Journal of Medical Ethics*, 26: 9–17.

Bradt, J., Magee, W.L., Dileo, C., Wheeler, B.L. and McGilloway, E. (2010) 'Music therapy for acquired brain injury', *Cochrane Database of Systematic Reviews*, issue 7, art. no.: CD006787. doi:10.1002/14651858.CD006787.pub2 (accessed 11 January 2013).

Bradt, J., Dileo, C., Grocke, D. and Magill, L. (2011) 'Music interventions for improving psychological and physical outcomes in cancer patients', Cochrane Database of

Systematic Reviews, issue 8, art. no.: CD006911. doi:10.1002/14651858.CD00 6911.pub2 (accessed 11 January 2013).

Bretherton, I. (1992) 'The origins of attachment theory: John Bowlby and Mary Ainsworth', *Developmental Psychology*, 28: 759–75.

British Broadcasting Corporation (1983) 'Music as therapy: Part 2 of *The Music Child*', a television documentary produced by Keith Alexander for BBC Scotland.

Bronfenbrenner, U. (1979) *The Ecology of Human Development. Experiments by Nature and Design*, Cambridge, MA: Harvard University Press.

Brook, W. (2007) 'Pragmatics of silence', in N. Losseff and J. Doctor (eds) *Silence, Music, Silent Music*, Aldershot, UK: Ashgate.

Bruscia, K.E. (1987) *Improvisational Models of Music Therapy*, Springfield, IL: Charles C. Thomas.

—— (1989) *Defining Music Therapy*, Spring City, PA: Spring House Books.

—— (ed.) (1991) *Case Studies in Music Therapy*, Gilsum, NH: Barcelona Publishers.

—— (ed.) (1996) *Music for the Imagination* (10 CDs), Gilsum, NH: Barcelona Publishers.

—— (1998a) *Defining Music Therapy*, 2nd edn, Gilsum, NH: Barcelona Publishers.

—— (ed.) (1998b) *The Dynamics of Music Psychotherapy*, Gilsum, NH: Barcelona Publishers.

—— (2002) Foreword to B. Stige, *Culture-Centered Music Therapy*, Gilsum, NH: Barcelona Publishers.

—— (2004) Foreword to T. Wigram, *Improvisation: Methods and Techniques for Music Therapy Clinicians, Educators and Students*, London: Jessica Kingsley Publishers.

—— (2005) 'Developing theory', in B.L. Wheeler (ed.) *Music Therapy Research*, 2nd edn, Gilsum, NH: Barcelona Publishers.

—— (2011) 'Ways of thinking in music therapy' [the William W. Sears Distinguished Lecture Series, American Music Therapy Association 13th Annual Conference, Atlanta, Georgia], available at: http://amtapro.musictherapy.org/?p=797 (podcast accessed 5 March 2013).

—— (ed.) (2012) *Readings on Music Therapy Theory*, Gilsum, NH: Barcelona Publishers.

Bruscia, K.E. and Grocke, D.E. (eds) (2002) *Guided Imagery and Music: The Bonny Methods and Beyond*, Gilsum, NH: Barcelona Publishers.

Buber, M. (1958) *I and Thou*, trans. R.G. Smith, New York: Macmillan.

Bullowa, M. (ed.) (1979) *Before Speech: The Beginning of Interpersonal Communication*, Cambridge: Cambridge University Press.

Bunt, L. (1985) 'Music therapy and the child with a handicap: evaluation of the effects of intervention', unpublished PhD thesis, City University, London.

—— (1994) *Music Therapy: An Art beyond Words*, London: Routledge.

—— (2001) 'Music therapy', in S. Sadie (ed.) *The New Grove Dictionary of Music and Musicians*, vol. 17, London: Macmillan.

—— (2002) 'Music therapy', in A. Latham (ed.) *The Oxford Companion to Music*, Oxford: Oxford University Press.

—— (2003) 'Music therapy with children: a complementary service to music education?', *British Journal of Music Education*, 20, 2: 179–95.

—— (2004) 'Music, space and health: the story of MusicSpace', in M. Pavlicevic and G. Ansdell (eds) *Community Music Therapy*, London: Jessica Kingsley Publishers.

—— (2007) 'Making space for silence', *Voices: A World Forum for Music Therapy*, available at: http://testvoices.uib.no/?q=colbunt130807 (accessed 16 October 2012).

—— (2008) Book review: N. Losseff and J. Doctor (eds) *Silence, Music, Silent Music*, *British Journal of Music Therapy*, 22, 2: 102–4.

—— (2010) 'On juggling of different hats', *Voices: A World Forum for Music Therapy*, available at: http://testvoices.uib.no/?q=colbunt190410 (accessed 5 March 2013).

—— (2012) 'Music therapy: a resource for creativity, health and well-being', in O. Odena (ed.) *Musical Creativity: Insights from Music Education Research*, Farnham, UK: Ashgate.

Bunt, L. and Hoskyns, S. (eds) (2002) *The Handbook of Music Therapy*, Hove, UK: Brunner-Routledge.

Bunt, L. and Marston-Wyld, J. (1995) 'Where words fail music takes over: a collaborative study by a music therapist and counsellor in the context of cancer care', *Music Therapy Perspectives*, 13, 1: 46–50.

Bunt, L. and Pavlicevic, M. (2001) 'Music and emotions: perspectives from music therapy', in P. Juslin and J. Sloboda (eds) *Music and Emotion: Theory and Research*, Oxford: Oxford University Press.

Bunt, L., Pike, D. and Wren, V. (1987) 'Music therapy in a general hospital's psychiatric unit: an evaluation of a pilot eight week programme', *Journal of British Music Therapy*, 1987, 1, 2: 3–6.

Burnard, P. (2006) 'The individual and social worlds of children's musical creativity', in G.E. McPherson (ed.) *The Child as Musician: A Handbook of Musical Development*, Oxford: Oxford University Press.

Burns, S.J.L, Harbuz, M.S., Hucklebridge, F. and Bunt, L. (2001) 'A pilot study into the therapeutic effects of music therapy at a cancer help center', *Alternative Therapies in Health and Medicine*, 7, 1: 48–56.

Carr, C. and Wigram, T. (2009) 'Music therapy with children and adolescents in mainstream schools: a systematic review', *British Journal of Music Therapy*, 23, 1: 3–18.

Centre for Human Rights (1994) *Human Rights and Social Work: A Manual for Schools of Social Work and the Social Work Profession*, Geneva: United Nations.

Clair, A.A. and Memmott, J. (2008) *Therapeutic Uses of Music with Older Adults*, 2nd edn, Silver Spring, MD: American Music Therapy Association.

Clarkson, P. (1994) 'The psychotherapeutic relationship', in P. Clarkson and M. Pokorny (eds) *The Handbook of Psychotherapy*, London: Routledge.

Clift, S., Hancox, G., Morrison, I., Hess, B., Kreutz, G. and Stewart, D. (2010) 'Choral singing and psychological wellbeing: quantitative and qualitative findings from English choirs in a cross-national survey', *Journal of Applied Arts and Health*, 1, 1: 19–34.

Compton Dickinson, S., Odell-Miller, H. and Adlam, J. (eds) (2012) *Forensic Music Therapy: A Treatment for Men and Women in Secure Hospital Settings*, London: Jessica Kingsley Publishers.

Condon, W.S. and Sander, L.W. (1974) 'Synchrony demonstrated between movements of the neonate and adult speech', *Child Development*, 45, 2: 456–62.

Cook, N. (1998) *Music: A Very Short Introduction*, Oxford: Oxford University Press.

Copland, A. (1952) *Music and Imagination*, Cambridge, MA: Harvard University Press.

Creswell, J.W. and Plano Clark, V.L. (2011) *Designing and Conducting Mixed Methods Research*, 2nd edn, Thousand Oaks, CA: Sage.

Critchley, M. and Henson, R. (1977) *Music and the Brain*, London: Heinemann.

Cross, I. and Morley, I. (2009) 'The evolution of music: theories, definitions, and the nature of evidence', in S. Malloch and C. Trevarthen (eds) *Communicative Musicality*, Oxford: Oxford University Press.

Csikszentmihalyi, M. (2008) *Flow: The Psychology of Optimal Experience*, New York: Harper Perennial Modern Classics.

Curtis, S.L. and Mercado, C.S. (2004) 'Community music therapy for citizens with developmental disabilities', *Voices: A World Forum for Music Therapy*, 4, 3, available at: https://normt.uib.no/index.php/voices/article/view/185/144 (accessed 24 February 2011).

Darnley-Smith, R. and Patey, H.M. (2003) *Music Therapy*, London: Sage.

Darrow, A.-A. (2008) *Introduction to Approaches in Music Therapy*, 2nd edn, Silver Spring, MD: American Music Therapy Association.

Davies, E. and Higginson, I.J. (2004) *Better Palliative Care for Older People*, Copenhagen: World Health Organization.

Davis, W.B. (1988) 'Music therapy in Victorian England', *Journal of British Music Therapy*, 2, 1: 10–17.

Davis, W.B. and Gfeller, K.E. (2008) 'Music therapy: historical perspective', in W.B. Davis, K.E. Gfeller and M.H. Thaut (eds) *An Introduction to Music Therapy Theory and Practice*, 3rd edn, Silver Spring, MD: American Music Therapy Association.

Davis, W.B., Gfeller, K.E. and Thaut, M.H. (eds) (2008) *An Introduction to Music Therapy Theory and Practice*, 3rd edn, Silver Spring, MD: American Music Therapy Association.

Daykin, N. (2007) 'Context, culture and risk: towards an understanding of the impact of music in health care settings', in J. Edwards (ed.) *Music: Promoting Health and Creating Community in Healthcare Contexts*, Newcastle upon Tyne: Cambridge Scholars Publishing.

Daykin, N., Bunt, L. and McClean, S. (2006) 'Music and healing in cancer care: a survey of supportive care providers', *The Arts in Psychotherapy*, 33: 402–13.

Daykin, N., McClean, S. and Bunt, L. (2007) 'Creativity, identity and healing: participants' accounts of music therapy in cancer care', *Health: An Interdisciplinary Journal for the Social Study of Health, Illness and Medicine*, 11, 3: 349–70.

Del Olmo, M.J., Garrido, C.R. and Tarrío, F.R. (2010) 'Music therapy in the PICU: 0-to 6-Month-Old Babies', *Music and Medicine*, July, 2, 3: 158–66.

Demos, J. and Demos, V. (1969) 'Adolescence in historical perspective', *Journal of Marriage and Family*, 31, 4: 632–8.

DeNora, T. (2000) *Music in Everyday Life*, Cambridge: Cambridge University Press.

—— (2006) 'Evidence and effectiveness in music therapy', *British Journal of Music Therapy*, 20, 2: 81–93.

—— (2010) 'Emotion as social emergence: perspectives from music sociology', in P.N. Juslin and J. Sloboda (eds) *Handbook of Music and Emotion: Theory, Research, Applications*, Oxford: Oxford University Press.

Dileo, C. (ed.) (1999) *Music Therapy and Medicine: Theoretical and Clinical Applications*, Silver Spring, MD: American Music Therapy Association.

—— (2000) *Ethical Thinking in Music Therapy*, Cherry Hill, NJ: Jeffrey Books.

—— (2007) Foreword to D. Grocke and T. Wigram, *Receptive Methods in Music Therapy: Techniques and Clinical Applications for Music Therapy Clinicians, Educators and Students*, London: Jessica Kingsley Publishers.

Dileo, C. and Bradt, J. (2005) *Medical Music Therapy: A Meta-analysis of the Literature and an Agenda for Future Research*, Cherry Hill, NJ: Jeffrey Books.

Dileo, C. and Parker, C. (2005) 'Final moments: the use of song in relationship completion', in C. Dileo and J.W. Loewy (eds) *Music Therapy at the End of Life*, Cherry Hill, NJ: Jeffrey Books.

Dimitriadis, T. and Smeijsters, H. (2011) 'Autistic spectrum disorder and music therapy: theory underpinning practice', *Nordic Journal of Music Therapy*, 20, 2: 108–22.

228 *References*

Doctor, J. (2007) 'The texture of silence', in N. Losseff and J. Doctor (eds) *Silence, Music, Silent Music*, Aldershot, UK: Ashgate.

Dominelli, L. (2002) *Anti-oppressive Social Work: Theory and Practice*, Basingstoke, UK: Palgrave Macmillan.

Drake, T. (2008) 'Back to basics: community-based music therapy for vulnerable young children and their parents', in A. Oldfield and C. Flower (eds) *Music Therapy with Children and Their Families*, London: Jessica Kingsley Publishers.

Dryden, W. and Branch, R. (eds) (2012) *The CBT Handbook*, London: Sage.

Eagle, C.T. (1991) 'Steps towards a theory of quantum therapy', *Music Therapy Perspectives*, 9: 56–60.

Edwards, J. (2005a) 'Developments and issues in music therapy research', in B.L. Wheeler (ed.) *Music Therapy Research*, 2nd edn, Gilsum, NH: Barcelona Publishers.

—— (2005b) 'Possibilities and problems for evidence-based practice in music therapy', *The Arts in Psychotherapy*, 32, 4: 293–301.

—— (2007) 'Antecedents of contemporary uses for music in healthcare contexts: the 1890s to the 1940s', in J. Edwards (ed.) *Music: Promoting Health and Creating Community in Healthcare Contexts*, Newcastle upon Tyne: Cambridge Scholars Publishing.

—— (2011a) 'A music and health perspective on music's perceived "goodness"', *Nordic Journal of Music Therapy*, 20, 1: 90–101.

—— (2011b) 'Music therapy and parent–infant bonding', in J. Edwards (ed.) *Music Therapy and Parent–Infant Bonding*, Oxford: Oxford University Press.

Elefant, C. (2010) 'Giving voice: participatory action research with a marginalized group', in B. Stige, G. Ansdell, C. Elefant and M. Pavlicevic, *Where Music Helps: Community Music Therapy in Action and Reflection*, Aldershot, UK: Ashgate.

Elefant, C. and Lotan, M. (2004) 'Rett Syndrome: dual intervention – music and physical therapy', *Nordic Journal of Music Therapy*, 13, 2: 172–82.

Eliot, T.S. (1944) 'Burnt Norton', in *Four Quartets*, New York: Faber & Faber.

Elliott, D.J. and Silverman, M. (2012) 'Why music matters: philosophical and cultural foundations', in R.A.R. MacDonald, G. Kreutz and L. Mitchell (eds) *Music, Health and Wellbeing*, Oxford: Oxford University Press.

Eriksen, T.H. (2007) 'Creolization in anthropological theory and in Mauritius', in C. Stewart (ed.) *Creolization: History, Ethnography, Theory*, Walnut Creek, CA: Left Coast Press.

Erkkilä, J., Punkanen, M., Fachner, J., Ala-Ruona, E., Pöntiö, I., Tervaniemi, M., Vanhala, M. and Gold, C. (2011) 'Individual music therapy for depression: randomised controlled trial', *British Journal of Psychiatry*, 199: 132–9.

Erkkilä, J., Ala-Ruona, E., Punkanen, M. and Fachner, J. (2012) 'Creativity in improvisational, psychodynamic music therapy', in D. Hargreaves, D. Miell and R. MacDonald (eds) *Musical Imaginations: Multidisciplinary Perspectives on Creativity, Performance and Perception*, Oxford: Oxford University Press.

Eschen, J. (ed.) (2002) *Analytical Music Therapy*, London: Jessica Kingsley Publishers.

Farrant, C., Pavlicevic, M. and Tsiris, G. (2011) *A Guide for Music Therapy and Music and Health Practitioners, Researchers and Students*, available from: www.nordoff-robbins.org.uk.

Feder, E. and Feder, B. (1981) *The 'Expressive' Arts Therapies: Art, Music and Dance as Psychotherapy*, Englewood Cliffs, NJ: Prentice-Hall.

Finlay, L. and Gough, B. (eds) (2003) *Reflexivity: A Practical Guide for Researchers in Health and Social Sciences*, Oxford: Blackwell.

Fleshman, B. and Fryrear, J.L. (1981) *The Arts in Therapy*, Chicago: Nelson-Hall.

Forinash, M. (ed.) (2008) *Music Therapy Supervision*, Gilsum, NH: Barcelona Publishers.

Fouché, S. and Torrance, K. (2005) 'Lose yourself in the music, the moment, Yo! Music therapy with an adolescent group involved in gangsterism', *Voices: A World Forum for Music Therapy*, 5, 3, available at: https://normt.uib.no/index.php/voices/article/view/232/176 (accessed 24 February 2011).

Fraisse, P. (1982) 'Rhythm and tempo', in D. Deutsch (ed.) *The Psychology of Music*, London: Academic Press.

Freidson, E. (1970/1988) *Profession of Medicine: A Study of the Sociology of Applied Knowledge*, Chicago: University of Chicago Press.

Gabrielsson, A. (2011) *Strong Experiences with Music*, Oxford: Oxford University Press.

Gardner, H. (1984) *Frames of Mind*, London: Heinemann.

Gardstrom, S. (2008) 'Music therapy as noninvasive treatment: who says?', *Nordic Journal of Music Therapy*, 17, 2: 142–54.

Garred, R. (2006) *Music as Therapy: A Dialogical Perspective*, Gilsum, NH: Barcelona Publishers.

Gaston, E.T. (1968) *Music in Therapy*, New York: Macmillan.

Gembris, H. (2008) 'Musical activities in the third age: an empirical study with amateur musicians', *Proceedings of the Second European Conference on Developmental Psychology of Music, 10–12 September,* London: University of Roehampton.

Giddens, A. (1984) *The Constitution of Society: Outline of the Theory of Structuration*, Cambridge: Polity Press.

Gilbertson, S. (2008) 'The silent epidemic of road traffic injury: what can music therapists do about it?', *Voices: A World Forum for Music Therapy*, 8, 1, available at: https://normt.uib.no/index.php/voices/article/view/448/366 (accessed 9 January 2013).

—— (2013) 'Music therapy and stroke', in J. Allen (ed.) *Guidelines for Music Therapy Practice: Medical Care of Adults*, Gilsum, NH: Barcelona Publishers.

—— (in press) 'Music therapy and traumatic brain injury', in J. Edwards (ed.), *Oxford Handbook of Music Therapy*, Oxford: Oxford University Press.

Gilbertson, S. and Aldridge, D. (2008) *Music Therapy and Traumatic Brain Injury: A Light on a Dark Night*, London: Jessica Kingsley Publishers.

Godwin, J. (1986) *Music, Mysticism and Magic: A Sourcebook*, London: Routledge.

Gold, C. (2004) 'The use of effect sizes in music therapy research', *Music Therapy Perspectives*, 22: 91–5.

Gold, C., Voracek, M and Wigram, T. (2004) 'Effects of music therapy for children and adolescents with psychopathology: a meta-analysis', *Journal of Child Psychology and Psychiatry*, 45: 1054–63.

Gold, C., Wigram, T. and Elefant, C. (2006) 'Music therapy for autistic spectrum disorder', *Cochrane Database of Systematic Reviews*, issue 2, art. no.: CD004381. doi:10.1002/14651858.CD004381.pub2

Gold, C., Saarikallio, S. and McFerran, K. (2011) 'Music therapy', in R.J.R. Levesque (ed.) *Encyclopedia of Adolescence,* New York: Springer.

Gomez, L. (1997) *An Introduction to Object Relations*, London: Free Association Books.

Goodman, K.D. (2011) *Music Therapy Education and Training*, Springfield, IL: Charles C. Thomas.

Gouk, P. (ed.) (2000) *Musical Healing in Cultural Contexts*, Aldershot, UK: Ashgate.

Gourlay, K.A. (1984) 'The non-universality of music and the universality of non-music', *The World of Music*, 26, 2: 25–39.

Graves, R. (1955/1960) *The Greek Myths* I, London: Penguin.

Greaves, C.J. and Farbus, L. (2006) 'Effects of creative and social activity on the health and well-being of socially isolated older people: outcomes from a multi-method observational study', *Journal of the Royal Society for the Promotion of Health*, 26, 3: 134–42.

Grocke, D. and Wigram, T. (2007) *Receptive Methods in Music Therapy: Techniques and Clinical Applications for Music Therapy Clinicians, Educators and Students*, London: Jessica Kingsley Publishers.

Grof, S. (1979) *Realms of the Human Unconscious*, London: Souvenir Press.

Grossman, P. and Taylor, E.W. (2007) 'Toward understanding respiratory sinus arrhythmia: relations to cardiac vagal tone, evolution and biobehavioral functions', *Biological Psychology*, 74: 263–85.

Hadley, S. (2003) *Psychodynamic Music Therapy: Case Studies*, Gilsum, NH: Barcelona Publishers.

—— (2007) *Feminist Perspectives in Music Therapy*, Gilsum, NH: Barcelona Publishers.

Hadley, S. and Yancy, G. (eds) (2012) *Therapeutic Uses of Rap and Hip-Hop*, New York: Routledge.

Hall, G.S. (1904) *Adolescence: Its Psychology and Relations to Physiology, Anthropology, Sociology, Sex, Crime, Religion and Education*, vol. 2, New York: D. Appleton.

Hamel, P.M. (1978) *Through Music to the Self*, Shaftesbury: Element Books.

Hanser, S. (2010) 'Music, health and well-being', in P.N. Juslin and J. Sloboda (eds) *Handbook of Music and Emotion: Theory, Research, Applications*, Oxford: Oxford University Press.

Harford, F.K. (2002a) 'Music in illness', *Nordic Journal of Music Therapy*, 11, 1: 43–4 (reprinted from the *Lancet*, 1891, 4 July: 43).

—— (2002b) 'The Guild of St. Cecilia', *Nordic Journal of Music Therapy*, 11, 1: 45–6 (reprinted from *British Medical Journal*, 1891, 26 September: 714).

—— (2002c) 'Is exhilarating or soft music best for invalids?', *Nordic Journal of Music Therapy*, 11, 1: 46–7 (reprinted from *British Medical Journal*, 1891, 3 October: 770).

Hargreaves, D.J. (1986) *The Developmental Psychology of Music*, Cambridge: Cambridge University Press.

Hays, T. and Minichello, V. (2005) 'The meaning of music in the lives of older people: a qualitative study', *Psychology of Music*, 33, 4: 437–51.

Heath, B. and Lings, J. (2012) 'Creative songwriting in therapy at the end of life and in bereavement', *Mortality: Promoting the Interdisciplinary Study of Death and Dying*, 17, 2, 106–18, available at: http://dx.doi.org/10.1080/13576275.2012.673381 (accessed 9 February 2013).

Helsedirektoratet (2013) *Nasjonal faglig retningslinje for utredning, behandling og oppfølging av personer med psykoselidelser* [National Guidelines for the Assessment, Treatment, and Follow-up of People with Psychotic Disorders], Oslo: Helsedirektoratet.

Hendry, L.B. and Kloep, M. (2012) *Adolescence and Adulthood: Transitions and Transformations*, Basingstoke, UK: Palgrave Macmillan.

Hernes, H. (2002) 'Perspektiver på profesjoner' [The professions in perspective]. in B. Nylehn and A.M. Støkken (eds) *De profesjonelle* [The Professionals], Oslo: Universitetsforlaget.

Hill, E.L. and Frith, U (2003) 'Understanding autism: insights from mind and brain', *Philosophical Transactions of the Royal Society, London B*, 358, 1430: 281–9.

Hitchen, H., Magee, W.L. and Soeterik, S. (2010) 'Music therapy in the treatment of patients with neuro-behavioural disorders stemming from acquired brain injury', *Nordic Journal of Music Therapy*, 19, 1: 63–78.

Hobson, R.F. (1985/2000) *Forms of Feeling: The Heart of Psychotherapy*, London: Routledge.

Holck, U. (2004) 'Turn-taking in music therapy with children with communication disorders', *British Journal of Music Therapy*, 18, 2: 45–54.

Holmes, D. (2012) 'Music therapy's breakthrough act', *Lancet Neurology*, 11, 6: 486–7. doi:10.1016/S1474-4422(12)70126-6 (accessed 7 July 2013).

Holmes, R. (2008) *The Age of Wonder: How the Romantic Generation Discovered the Beauty and Terror of Science*, London: Harper.

Horden, P. (ed.) (2000) *Music as Medicine: The History of Music Therapy since Antiquity*, Aldershot, UK: Ashgate.

Horesh, T. (2010) 'Drug addicts and their music: a story of a complex relationship', in D. Aldridge and J. Fachner (eds) *Music Therapy and Addiction*, London: Jessica Kingsley Publishers.

Hoskyns, S. (1988) Introduction to *The Case Study as Research: Proceedings of the Fourth Music Therapy Day Conference*, London: City University.

Huizinga, J. (1955) *Homo Ludens: A Study of the Play Element in Culture*, Boston: Beacon Press.

Jellison, J.A. (1973) 'The frequency and general mode of inquiry of research in music therapy, 1952–72', *Council for Research in Music Education Bulletin*, 35, 3: 114–29.

Juslin, P.N. and J. Sloboda (eds) (2001a) *Music and Emotion: Theory and Research*, Oxford: Oxford University Press.

—— (2001b) 'Psychological perspectives on music and emotion', in P.N. Juslin and J. Sloboda (eds) *Music and Emotion: Theory and Research*, Oxford: Oxford University Press.

—— (eds) (2010) *Handbook of Music and Emotion: Theory, Research, Applications*, Oxford: Oxford University Press.

Kawachi, I. and Berkman, L. (2000) 'Social cohesion, social capital, and health', in L. Berkman and I. Kawachi (eds) *Social Epidemiology*, Oxford: Oxford University Press.

Keil, C. (1994) 'Participatory discrepancies and the power of music', in C. Keil and S. Feld, *Music Grooves*, Chicago: University of Chicago Press.

Kenny, C. (1982/1988) *The Mythic Artery: The Magic of Music Therapy*, Atuscadero, CA: Ridgeview.

—— (1988) Conference presentation, Atlanta: NAMT.

—— (1989) *The Field of Play. A Guide for the Theory and Practice of Music Therapy*, Atascadero, CA: Ridgeview.

—— (2006) *Music and Life in the Field of Play*, Gilsum, NH: Barcelona Publishers.

Kern, P. (2012) 'Autism spectrum disorders primer: characteristics, causes, prevalence, and intervention', in P. Kern and M.E. Humpal (eds) *Early Childhood Music Therapy and Autism Spectrum Disorders: Developing Potential in Young Children and their Families*, London: Jessica Kingsley Publishers.

Khan, H.I. (1988) *The Music of Life*, New York: Omega Press.

Kim, J., Wigram, T. and Gold, C. (2009) 'Emotional, motivational and interpersonal responsiveness of children with autism in improvisational music therapy', *Autism*, 13, 4: 389–409.

Kim, D., Subramanian, S.V. and Kawachi, I. (2010) 'Social capital and physical health: a systematic review of the literature', in I. Kawachi, S.V. Subramanian and D. Kim (eds) *Social Capital and Health*, New York: Springer.

Kitayama, S. and Cohen, D. (eds) (2007) *Handbook of Cultural Psychology*, New York: Guilford Publications.

Kitwood, T. (1997) *Dementia Reconsidered: The Person Comes First*, Buckingham, UK: Open University Press.

Koelsch, S., Fritz, T., Yves v. Cramon, V., Müller, K. and Friederici, A.D. (2006) 'Investigating emotion with music: an fMRI study', *Human Brain Mapping*, 27: 239–50.

Kokoktsaki, D. and Hallam, S. (2011) 'The perceived benefits of participative music making for non-music university students: a comparison with music students', *Music Education Research*, 13, 2: 149–72.

Kooij, C. (2009) 'Recovery themes in songs written by adults living with serious mental illnesses', *Canadian Journal of Music Therapy*, 15, 1: 37–58.

Krüger, V. (2012) Musikk – fortelling – fellesskap. Musikkterapi i en barnevernsinstitusjon [Music – narrative – community. Music therapy in a child welfare institution], unpublished PhD thesis, Grieg Academy, University of Bergen.

Krüger, V. and Stige, B. (in press -a) 'Music as a structuring resource: a perspective from community music therapy', in H. Klempe (ed.) *Cultural Psychology of Music Experiences*, Charlotte, NC: IAP: Information Age Publications.

—— (in press -b) 'Between rights and realities: music as a structuring resource in the context of child welfare aftercare: a qualitative study', *Nordic Journal of Music Therapy*.

Laiho, S. (2004) 'The psychological functions of music in adolescence', *Nordic Journal of Music Therapy*, 13, 1: 47–59.

Lakoff, G. and Johnson, M. (1980) *Metaphors We Live By*, Chicago: University of Chicago Press.

Langenberg, M., Aigen, K. and Frommer, J. (eds) (1996) *Qualitative Music Therapy Research: Beginning Dialogues*, Gilsum, NH: Barcelona Publishers.

Laslett, P. (1989/1991) *A Fresh Map of Life: The Emergence of the Third Age*, Cambridge, MA: Harvard University Press.

Laukka, P. (2006) 'Uses of music and psychological well-being among the elderly', *Journal of Happiness Studies*, 8: 215–41. doi:10.1007/s10902-006-9024-3

Lecanuet, J.-P. (1996) 'Prenatal auditory experience', in I. Deliège and J. Sloboda (eds) *Musical Beginnings: Origins and Developments of Musical Competence*, Oxford: Oxford University Press.

Lecourt, E. (1991) 'Off-beat music therapy: a psychoanalytic approach to autism', in K.E. Bruscia (ed.) *Case Studies in Music Therapy*, Phoenixville, PA: Barcelona Publishers.

Lee, C. (1996) *Music at the Edge: The Music Therapy Experiences of a Musician with AIDS*, London: Routledge.

—— (2000) 'A method of analyzing improvisations in music therapy', *Journal of Music Therapy*, 37, 2: 147–67.

—— (2003) *The Architecture of Aesthetic Music Therapy*, Gilsum, NH: Barcelona Publishers.

Levitin, D.J. (2006) *This Is Your Brain on Music: The Science of a Human Obsession*, New York: Dutton/Penguin.

Licht, S. (1946) *Music in Medicine*, Boston: New England Conservatory of Music.

Loewy, J. (2011) 'Music therapy for hospitalized infants and their parents', in J. Edwards (ed.) *Music Therapy and Parent–Infant Bonding*, Oxford: Oxford University Press.

Loewy, J.V. and Spintge, R. (2011) 'Music soothes the savage breast', *Music and Medicine*, 3, 2: 69–71.

McAdams, S. and Giordano, B.L. (2009) 'The perception of musical timbre', in S. Hallam, I. Cross and M. Thaut (eds) *The Oxford Handbook of Music Psychology*, Oxford: Oxford University Press.

McCaffrey, T., Edwards, J. and Fannon, D. (2011) 'Is there a role for music therapy in the recovery approach in mental health?', *The Arts in Psychotherapy*, 38: 185–9.

McClean, S., Bunt, L. and Daykin, N. (2012) 'The healing and spiritual properties of music therapy at a cancer care centre', *Journal of Alternative and Complementary Medicine*, 18, 4: 402–7.

McClellan, R. (1991) *The Healing Forces of Music: History, Theory, and Practice*, Shaftesbury, UK: Element Books.

McDermott, O., Crellin, N., Ridder, H.M.O. and Orrell, M. (2012) 'Music therapy in dementia: a narrative synthesis systematic review', *International Journal of Geriatric Psychiatry*, 28, 8: 781–94. doi:10.1002/gps.3895

MacDonald, R.A.R., Hargreaves, D.J. and Miell, D. (eds) (2002) *Musical Identities*, Oxford: Oxford University Press.

MacDonald, R.A.R., Kreutz, G. and Mitchell, L. (eds) (2012) *Music, Health and Wellbeing*, Oxford: Oxford University Press.

McFerran, K. (2010) *Adolescents, Music and Music Therapy: Methods and Techniques for Clinicians, Educators and Students*, London: Jessica Kingsley Publishers.

—— (2012) 'Music and adolescents', in N.S. Rickard and K. McFerran (eds) *Lifelong Engagement with Music: Benefits for Mental Health and Well-Being*, New York: Nova Science Publishers.

McFerran, K.S. and Saarikallio, S. (in press) 'Depending on music to feel better: being conscious of responsibility when appropriating the power of music', *The Arts in Psychotherapy*.

McGlashan, A. (1976) *Gravity and Levity*, London: Chatto & Windus.

McGuire, M.G. (ed.) (2004) *Psychiatric Music Therapy in the Community: The Legacy of Florence Tyson*, Gilsum, NH: Barcelona Publishers.

McLaughlin, T. (1970) *Music and Communication*, London: Faber.

McLeish, K. (1996) Editor's introduction, in R. Graves, *The Greek Myths*, London: Folio Society.

McLeod, J. (2010) *Case Study Research in Counselling and Psychotherapy*, London: Sage.

McNiff, S. (1987) 'Research and scholarship in the creative arts therapies', *The Arts in Psychotherapy*, 14: 285–92.

McPherson, G.E. (ed.) (2006) *The Child as Musician: A Handbook of Musical Development*, Oxford: Oxford University Press.

Madsen, C.K., Cotter, V.M. and Madsen, C.H. (1968) 'A behavioral approach to music therapy', *Journal of Music Therapy*, 5, 3: 69–71.

Magee, W.L. (2002) 'Disability and identity in music therapy', in R. MacDonald, D. Hargreaves and D. Miell (eds) *Musical Identities*, Oxford: Oxford University Press.

—— (2014) *Music Technology in Therapeutic and Health Settings*, London: Jessica Kingsley Publishers.

Magee, W. and Burland, K. (2008) 'Using electronic music technologies in music therapy: opportunities, limitations and clinical indicators', *British Journal of Music Therapy*, 22, 1: 3–15.

Maguire, A. and Merrick, I. (2013) 'Walking the line: music therapy in the context of the recovery approach in a high secure hospital', in S.C. Dickinson, H. Odell-Miller and J. Adlam (eds) *Forensic Music Therapy. A Treatment for Men and Women in Secure Hospital Settings*, London: Jessica Kingsley Publishers.

Malloch, S. (1999) 'Mothers and infants and communicative musicality', *Musicæ Scientiæ*, special issue 1999–2000, 3: 29–57.

Malloch, S. and Trevarthen, C. (2009) 'Musicality: communicating the vitality and interests of life', in S. Malloch and C. Trevarthen (eds) *Communicative Musicality: Exploring the Basis of Human Companionship*, Oxford: Oxford University Press.

Malloch, S., Shoemark, H., Črnčec, R., Newnham, C., Campbell, P., Prior, M., Coward, S. and Burnham, D. (2012) 'Music therapy with hospitalized infants: the art and science of communicative musicality', *Infant Mental Health Journal*, 334, 4: 386–99.

Maratos, A., Gold, C., Wang, X. and Crawford, M. (2008) 'Music therapy for depression', *Cochrane Database of Systematic Reviews*, issue 1, art. no.: CD004517. doi:10.1002/14651858.CD004517.pub2.

Martineau, J. (2008) *The Elements of Music: Melody, Rhythm and Harmony*, Glastonbury, UK: Wooden Books.

Maslow, A. (1968) *Toward a Psychology of Being*, New York: Van Nostrand Reinhold.

May, E. (1983) *Musics of Many Cultures*, Berkeley: California University Press.

May, R. (1975) *The Courage to Create*, New York: W.W. Norton.

Meadows, A. (ed.) (2011) *Developments in Music Therapy Practice: Case Study Perspectives*, Gilsum, NH: Barcelona Publishers.

Mellers, W. (1987) *The Masks of Orpheus*, Manchester: Manchester University Press.

Mercadal-Brotons, M. (2011) 'Music therapy and dementia: a cognitive-behavioral approach', in A. Meadows (ed.) *Developments in Music Therapy Practice: Case Study Perspectives*, Gilsum, NH: Barcelona Publishers.

Meyer, L.B. (1956) *Emotion and Meaning in Music*, Chicago: University of Chicago Press,

Michel, D.E. (1976) *Music Therapy: An Introduction to Therapy and Special Education through Music*, Springfield, IL: Charles C. Thomas.

Miranda, D. and Claes, M. (2009) 'Music listening, coping, peer affiliation and depression in adolescence', *Psychology of Music*, 37, 2: 215–33.

Mithen, S. (2006) *The Singing Neanderthals: The Origins of Music, Language, Mind and Body*, London: Phoenix, Orion Books.

Molnar-Szakacs, I. and Heaton, P. (2012) 'Music: a unique window into the world of autism', *Annals of the New York Academy of Sciences*, 1252, 1: 318–24.

Moog, H. (1976) *The Musical Experience of the Pre-school Child*, London: Schott.

Moreno, J. (1988) 'The music therapist: creative arts therapist and contemporary shaman', *The Arts in Psychotherapy*, 15, 4: 271–80.

Mössler, K. (2011) 'I am a psychotherapeutically oriented music therapist: theory construction and its influence on professional identity formation under the example of the Viennese School of Music Therapy', *Nordic Journal of Music Therapy*, 20, 2: 155–84.

Mössler, K., Chen, X., Heldal, T.O. and Gold, C. (2011) 'Music therapy for people with schizophrenia and schizophrenia-like disorders', *Cochrane Database of Systematic Reviews*, issue 12, art. no.: CD004025. doi:10.1002/14651858.CD004025.pub3.

Moustakas, C.E. (1970) *Psychotherapy with Children: The Living Relationship*, New York: Ballantine Books.

Myskja, A. (2012) 'Integrated music in nursing homes: an approach to dementia care', unpublished PhD thesis, Grieg Academy, University of Bergen.

NICE (2009) *Schizophrenia: Core Interventions in the Treatment and Management of Schizophrenia in Adults in Primary and Secondary Care*, NICE clinical guideline 82. Available at www.nice.org.uk/CG82 [NICE guideline] (accessed 2 January 2011).

Nicholson, J.M., Berthelsen, D., Abad, V., Williams, K. and Bradley, J. (2008) 'Impact of music therapy to promote positive parenting and child development', *Journal of Health Psychology*, 13, 2: 226–38.

Nöcker-Ribaupierre, M. (2004) *Music Therapy for Premature and Newborn Infants*, Gilsum, NH: Barcelona Publishers.

—— (2011) 'When life begins too early: music therapy in a newborn intensive care unit', in A. Meadows (ed.) *Developments in Music Therapy Practice: Case Study Perspectives*, Gilsum, NH: Barcelona Publishers.

Nordoff, P. and Robbins, C. (1971) *Therapy in Music for Handicapped Children*, London: Gollancz.

—— (2007) *Creative Music Therapy: A Guide to Fostering Clinical Musicianship*, 2nd edn, Gilsum, NH: Barcelona Publishers.

North, A. and Hargreaves, D. (2007) 'Lifestyle correlates of musical preference, 3: Travel, money, education, employment and health', *Psychology of Music*, 35, 3: 473–97.

—— (2009) *The Social and Applied Psychology of Music*, New York: Oxford University Press.

North, A.C., Hargreaves, D.J. and O'Neill, S.A. (2000) 'The importance of music to adolescents', *British Journal of Education Psychology*, 70: 255–72.

O'Callaghan, C. (2009) 'Objectivist and constructivist music therapy research in oncology and palliative care: an overview and reflection', *Music and Medicine*, July, 1: 41–60. doi:10.1177/1943862109337135

O'Callaghan, C., O'Brien, E., Magill, L. and Ballinger, E. (2009) 'Resounding attachment: cancer inpatients' song lyrics for their children in music therapy', *Supportive Care in Cancer*, 17, 9: 1149–57.

O'Callaghan, C., Hudson, P., McDermott, F. and Zalcberg, J.R. (2011) 'Music among family carers of people with life-threatening cancer', *Music and Medicine*, January, 3: 47–55. doi:10.1177/1943862110390821

Ockelford, A. (2013) *Applied Musicology: Using Zygonic Theory to Inform Music Education, Therapy, and Psychology Research*, Oxford: Oxford University Press.

Odell, H. (1988) 'A music therapy approach in mental health', *Psychology of Music*, 16, 1: 52–62.

Odell-Miller, H. (2003) 'Are words enough?', in L. King and R. Randall (eds) *The Future of Psychoanalytic Psychotherapy*, London: Whurr.

—— (2008) 'The practice of music therapy for adults with mental health problems: the relationship between diagnosis and clinical method', unpublished PhD thesis, University of Aalborg. Available at: http://vbn.aau.dk/en/publications/the-practice-of-music-therapy-for-adults-with-mental-health-problems-the-relationship-between-diagnosis-and-clinical-method(2239c78b-df66-434d-99f6-5b992e90caf9).html (accessed 11 February 2013).

Odell-Miller, H. and Richards, E. (ed.) (2008) *Supervision of Music Therapy: A Theoretical and Practical Handbook*, London: Routledge.

O'Donohue, J. (2003) *Divine Beauty: The Invisible Embrace*, London: Bantam Press.

Oldfield, A. (2006a) *Interactive Music Therapy: A Positive Approach: Music Therapy at a Child Development Centre*, London: Jessica Kingsley Publishers.

—— (2006b) *Music Therapy in Child and Family Psychiatry: Clinical Practice, Research and Teaching*, London: Jessica Kingsley Publishers.

Ostwald, P.F. (1990) 'Music and emotional development in children', in F.R. Wilson and F.L. Roehmann (eds) *Music and Child Development*, St Louis, MO: Magnamusic-Baton.

Overy, K. and Molnar-Szakacs, I. (2009) 'Being together in time: musical experience and the mirror neuron system', *Music Perception*, 26, 5: 489–504.

Parncutt, R. (2006) 'Prenatal development', in G.E. McPherson (ed.) *The Child as Musician: A Handbook of Musical Development*, Oxford: Oxford University Press.

—— (2009) 'Prenatal development and the phylogeny and ontogeny of music', in S. Hallam, I. Cross and M. Thaut (eds) *The Oxford Handbook of Music Psychology*, Oxford: Oxford University Press.

Patel, A.D. (2008) *Music, Language and the Brain*, Oxford: Oxford University Press.

Pavlicevic, M. (1997) *Music Therapy in Context: Music, Meaning and Relationship*, London: Jessica Kingsley Publishers.

—— (2001) 'A child in time and health', *British Journal of Music Therapy*, 15, 1: 14–21.

—— (ed.) (2005) *Music Therapy in Children's Hospices: Jessie's Fund in Action*, London: Jessica Kingsley Publishers.

Pavlicevic, M. and Ansdell, G. (eds) (2004) *Community Music Therapy*, London: Jessica Kingsley Publishers.

—— (2009) 'Between communicative musicality and collaborative musicing: a perspective from community music therapy', in S. Malloch and C. Trevarthen (eds) *Communicative Musicality: Exploring the Basis of Human Companionship*, Oxford: Oxford University Press.

Pavlicevic, M., Ansdell, G., Procter, S. and Hickey, S. (2009) *Presenting the Evidence*, 2nd edn, available as a download from: www.nordoff-robbins.org.uk/content/what-we-do/research-and-resources-8.

Pawlby, S.J. (1977) 'Imitative interaction', in H.R. Schaffer (ed.) *Studies in Mother–Infant Interaction*, London: Academic Press.

Pellitteri, J. (2009) *Emotional Processes in Music Therapy*, Gilsum, NH: Barcelona Publishers.

Pepper, S.C. (1942) *World Hypotheses*, Berkeley: University of California Press.

Peretz, I. and Zatorre, R. (eds) (2003) *The Cognitive Neuroscience of Music*, Oxford: Oxford University Press.

Perls, F.S. (1969) *Gestalt Therapy Verbatim*, Moab, UT: Real People Press.

Peters, J.S. (2000) *Music Therapy: An Introduction*, 2nd edn, Springfield, IL: Charles C. Thomas.

Pickles, V. (2003) 'Music and the third age', *Psychology of Music*, 31, 4: 415–23.

Podolsky, E. (1954) *Music Therapy*, New York: Philosophical Library.

Pope, C., Mays, N. and Popay, J. (2007) *Synthesizing Qualitative and Quantitative Health Evidence: A Guide to Methods*, Maidenhead, UK: Open University Press.

Porges, S.W. (2001) 'The polyvagal theory: phylogenetic substrates of a social nervous system', *International Journal of Psychophysiology*, 42, 2: 123–46.

—— (2010) 'Music therapy and trauma: insights from the polyvagal theory', in K. Stewart (ed.) *Symposium on Music Therapy and Trauma: Bridging Theory and Clinical Practice*, New York: Satchnote Press.

Priestley, M. (1975/2012) *Music Therapy in Action*, 2nd edn, Gilsum, NH: Barcelona Publishers.

—— (1994) *Essays on Analytical Music Therapy*, Phoenixville, PA: Barcelona Publishers.

Procter, S. (2001) 'Empowering and enabling', *Voices: A World Forum for Music Therapy*, 2, 2, available at https://normt.uib.no/index.php/voices/article/view/58/46 (accessed 12 November 2012).

—— (2004) 'Playing politics: community music therapy and the therapeutic redistribution of musical capital for mental health', in M. Pavlicevic and G. Ansdell (eds) *Community Music Therapy*, London: Jessica Kingsley Publishers.

—— (2006) 'What are we playing at? Social capital and music therapy', in R. Edwards, J. Franklin and J. Holland (eds) *Assessing Social Capital: Concept, Policy and Practice*, Newcastle upon Tyne: Cambridge Scholars Publishing.

—— (2008) 'Premising the challenge (response to Alison Barrington)', *British Journal of Music Therapy*, 22, 2: 77–82.

—— (2011) 'Reparative musicing: thinking on the usefulness of social capital theory within music therapy', *Nordic Journal of Music Therapy*, 20, 3: 242–62.

Punkanen, M. and Ala-Ruona, E. (2012) 'Contemporary vibroacoustic therapy: perspectives on clinical practice, research and training', *Music and Medicine*, 4: 128–35.

Putnam, R. (2000) *Bowling Alone: The Collapse and Revival of American Community*, New York: Simon & Schuster.

Racker, H. (1965) 'Psychoanalytic considerations on music and the musician', *Psychoanalytic Review*, 52: 75–94.

Rawlins, M. (2008) 'Harveian Oration *De testimonio*: on the evidence for decisions about the use of therapeutic interventions', *Lancet*, 372: 2152–61.

Richards, E. (2007) '"What bit of my head is talking now?" Music therapy with people with learning disability and mental illness', in T. Watson (ed.) *Music Therapy with Adults with Learning Disabilities*, Hove, UK: Routledge

Rickson, D. (2010) 'Music therapy school consultation: a literature review', *New Zealand Journal of Music Therapy*, 8: 59–91.

—— (2012) 'Music therapy school consultation: a unique practice', *Nordic Journal of Music Therapy*, 21, 3: 268–85.

Ridder, H.M.O. (2003) 'Singing dialogue: music therapy with persons in advanced stages of dementia. a case study research design', unpublished PhD thesis, University of Aalborg, available at: www.mt-phd.aau.dk/digitalAssets/15/15019_ridder-2003.pdf (accessed 13 December 2013).

—— (2007) 'En integrativ terapeutisk anvendelse af sang med udgangspunkt i neuropsykologiske, psykofysiologiske og psykodynamiske teorier' [Singing applied in an integrated therapeutic model based on neuropsychological, psychophysiological and psychodynamic theories], in L.O. Bonde (ed.) *Psyke & Logos*, Copenhagen: Dansk Psykologisk Forlag.

—— (2011) 'How can singing in music therapy influence social engagement for people with dementia? Insights from the polyvagal theory', in F. Baker and S. Uhlig (eds) *Voicework in Music Therapy: Research and Practice*, London: Jessica Kingsley Publishers.

Ridder, H.M.O. and Aldridge, D. (2005) 'Individual music therapy with persons with frontotemporal dementia: singing dialogue', *Nordic Journal of Music Therapy*, 14, 2: 91–106.

Ridder, H.M.O., Stige, B., Qvale, L.G. and Gold, C. (2013) 'Individual music therapy for agitation in dementia: an exploratory randomized controlled trial', *Aging and Mental Health*, 17, 6: 6667–78. doi:10.1080/13607863.2013.790926

Rilke, R.M. (1996) *Poems*, trans. J.B. Leishman (1960, 1964), London: Everyman's Library.

Rio, R. (2009) *Connecting through Music with People with Dementia: A Guide for Caregivers*, London: Jessica Kingsley Publishers.

Robb, S.L. (2003) *Music Therapy in Pediatric Healthcare: Research and Evidence-Based Practice*, Silver Spring, MD: American Music Therapy Association.

Robb, S.L., Burns, D.S. and Carpenter, J.S. (2011) 'Reporting guidelines for music-based interventions', *Journal of Health Psychology*, 16, 2: 342–52. doi:10.1177/13591053 10374781

Robbins, C. and Robbins, C. (eds) (1998) *Healing Heritage: Paul Nordoff Exploring the Tonal Language of Music*, Gilsum, NH: Barcelona Publishers.

Rogers, C. (1951/2003) *Client-Centred Therapy*, London: Constable.

—— (1961/1976) *On Becoming a Person*, London: Constable.

Rolvsjord, R. (2010) *Resource-Oriented Music Therapy in Mental Health Care*, Gilsum, NH: Barcelona Publishers.

—— (2013) 'Music therapy in everyday life: with "the organ as the third therapist"', in L.O. Bonde, E. Ruud, M. Skånland and G. Trondalen (eds) *Music and Health Narratives*, Oslo: NMH-publikasjoner, Skriftserie fra Senter for musikk og helse.

Rolvsjord, R. and Stige, B. (2013) 'Concepts of context in music therapy', *Nordic Journal of Music Therapy*. doi:10.1080/08098131.2013.861502

Rolvsjord, R., Gold, C. and Stige, B. (2005) 'Therapeutic principles for resource-oriented music therapy: a contextual approach to the field of mental health' (appendix to 'Research rigour and therapeutic flexibility: rationale for a therapy manual developed for a randomized controlled trial'), *Nordic Journal of Music Therapy*, 14, 1: 15–32.

Rose, G.J. (2004) *Between Couch and Piano: Psychoanalysis, Music, Art and Neuroscience*, Hove, UK: Brunner-Routledge.

Rowan, J. (1993) *The Transpersonal: Psychotherapy and Counselling*, London: Routledge.

—— (1998) *The Reality Game: A Guide to Humanistic Counselling and Psychotherapy*, 2nd edn, London: Routledge.

Ruud, E. (1978/1980) *Music Therapy and its Relationship to Current Treatment Theories*, St Louis, MO: Magnamusic-Baton.

—— (1980) *Hva er musikkterapi?* [What Is Music Therapy?], Oslo: Gyldendal.

—— (1987/1990) *Musikk som kommunikasjon og samhandling. Teoretiske perspektiv på musikkterapien* [Music as Communication and Interaction. Theoretical Perspectives on Music Therapy], Oslo: Solum.

—— (1998) *Music Therapy: Improvisation, Communication and Culture*, Gilsum, NH: Barcelona Publishers.

—— (2005a) Foreword to F. Baker and T. Wigram (eds) *Songwriting: Methods, Techniques, and Clinical Applications for Music Therapy Clinicians, Educators and Students*, London, Jessica Kingsley Publishers.

—— (2005b) 'Philosophy and theory of science', in B.L. Wheeler (ed.) *Music Therapy Research*, 2nd edn, Gilsum, NH: Barcelona Publishers.

—— (2010) *Music Therapy: A Perspective from the Humanities*, Gilsum, NH: Barcelona Publishers.

Saarikallio, S. (2011) 'Music as emotional self-regulation throughout adulthood', *Psychology of Music*, 39, 3: 307–27.

Saarikallio, S. and Erkkilä, J. (2007) 'The role of music in adolescents' mood regulation', *Psychology of Music*, 35, 1: 88–109.

Sackett, D.L., Rosenberg, W.M.C., Gray, J.A.M., Haynes, R.B. and Richardson, W.S. (1996) 'Evidence-based medicine: what it is and what it isn't', *British Medical Journal*, 312: 71–2.

Sacks, O. (1991) *Awakenings*, revised edn, London: Pan.

—— (1992) 'Hearing before the Senate Special Committee on Aging', *Music Therapy Perspectives*, 10, 1: 60.

—— (2007) *Musicophilia: Tales of Music and the Brain*, London: Picador.

Salkeld, C.E. (2008) 'Music therapy after adoption: the role of family music therapy in developing secure attachment in adopted children', in A. Oldfield and C. Flower (eds) *Music Therapy with Children and Their Families*, London: Jessica Kingsley Publishers.

Sameroff, A.J. and MacKenzie, M.J. (2003) 'Research strategies for capturing transactional models of development: the limits of the possible', *Development and Psychopathology*, 15: 613–40.

Särkämö, T. and Sotto, D. (2012) 'Music listening after stroke: beneficial effects and potential neural mechanisms', *Annals of the New York Academy of Sciences*, vol. 1252: *The Neurosciences and Music IV: Learning and Memory*, April : 266–81.

Särkämö, T., Tervaniemi, M., Laitinen, S., Forsblom, A., Soinila, S., Mikkonen, M., Autti, T., Silvennoinen, H.M., Erkkila, J., Laine, M., Peretz, I. and Hietanen, M. (2008) 'Music listening enhances cognitive recovery and mood after middle cerebral artery stroke', *Brain*, 131, 3: 866–76.

Särkämö, T., Laitinen, S., Tervaniemi, M., Numminen, A., Kurki, M. and Rantanen, P. (2012) 'Music, emotion, and dementia: insight from neuroscientific and clinical research', *Music and Medicine*, 4, 3: 153–62.

Saville, R. (2007) 'Music therapy and autistic spectrum disorder' in T. Watson (ed.) *Music Therapy with Adults with Learning Disabilities*, Hove, UK: Routledge.

Schapira, D. (2003) 'Last sounds of the shipwreck: aspects of the plurimodal method in the treatment of psychosis', *Nordic Journal of Music Therapy*, 12, 2: 163–72.

Schaverien, J. and Odell-Miller, H. (2005) 'The arts therapies', in G. Gabbard, J. Beck and J. Holmes (eds) *Oxford Textbook of Psychotherapy*, Oxford: Oxford University Press.

Scherer, K.R. and Zentner, M.R. (2001) 'Emotional effects of music: production rules', in P.N. Juslin and J. Sloboda (eds) *Music and Emotion: Theory and Research*, Oxford: Oxford University Press.

Schmid, W. and Ostermann, T. (2010) 'Home-based music therapy: a systematic overview of settings and conditions for an innovative service in healthcare', *BMC Health Services Research*, 10: 291–300. doi:10.1186/1472-6963-10-291

Schmidt, J. (2000) *Disciplined Minds: A Critical Look at Salaried Professionals and the Soul-Battering System that Shapes Their Lives*, Lanham, MD: Rowman & Littlefield.

Schore, A.N. (1994) *Affect Regulation and the Origin of the Self: The Neurobiology of Emotional Development*, Hillsdale, NJ: Lawrence Erlbaum.

—— (2012) *The Science of the Art of Psychotherapy*, New York: W.W. Norton.

Schullian, D.M. and Schoen, D. (1948) *Music and Medicine*, New York: Henry Schuman.

Schumacher, K. and Calvet-Kruppa, C. (1999) 'The "AQR": an analysis system to evaluate the quality of relationship during music therapy', *Nordic Journal of Music Therapy*, 8, 2: 188–91.

Schwartz, F.J. (2004) 'Medical music therapy for the premature baby: research review', in M. Nöcker-Ribaupierre, *Music Therapy for Premature and Newborn Infants*, Gilsum, NH: Barcelona Publishers.

Scott, M.J. (2011) *Simply Effective Cognitive Behaviour Therapy: A Practitioner's Guide*, London: Routledge.

Sears, M.S. (ed.) (2007) *Music: The Therapeutic Edge. Readings from William W. Sears*, Gilsum, NH: Barcelona Publishers.

Sennett, R. (2013) *Together: The Rituals, Pleasure and Politics of Cooperation*, London: Penguin Books.

Shoemark, H. (2004) 'Family-centred music therapy for infants with complex medical and surgical needs', in M. Nöcker-Ribaupierre, *Music Therapy for Premature and Newborn Infants*, Gilsum, NH: Barcelona Publishers.

Silverman, M. J. (2003) 'Music therapy and clients who are chemically dependent: a review of literature and pilot study', *The Arts in Psychotherapy*, 30: 273–81.

—— (2011) 'Effects of music therapy on change readiness and craving in patients on a detoxification unit', *Journal of Music Therapy*, 48, 4: 509–31.

Silverstein, M. and Parker, M.G. (2002) 'Leisure activities and quality of life among the oldest old in Sweden', *Research on Aging*, 24, 5: 528–47.

Simpson, F. (2009) *The Nordoff-Robbins Adventure: Fifty Years of Creative Music Therapy*, London: James & James.

Simpson, K. and Keen, D. (2011) 'Music interventions for children with autism: narrative review', *Journal of Autism and Developmental Disorders*, 41: 1507–14.

Sinason, V. (1992) *Mental Handicap and the Human Condition: New Approaches from the Tavistock*, London: Free Association Books.

Skille, O. and Wigram, T. (1995) 'The effect of music, vocalisation and vibration on brain and muscle tissue: studies in vibroacoustic therapy', in T. Wigram, B. Saperston and R. West (eds) *The Art and Science of Music Therapy: A Handbook*, Chur, Switzerland: Harwood Academic Publishers.

Skram, A. (1895/1992) *Under Observation*, trans. J. Hanson and J. Messick, Seattle: Women in Translation.

Sloboda, J. (1985) *The Musical Mind*, Oxford: Oxford University Press.

Small, C. (1998) *Musicking: The Meanings of Performing and Listening*, Hanover, NH: Wesleyan University Press.

Smeijsters, H. (1997) *Multiple Perspectives: A Guide to Qualitative Research in Music Therapy*, Gilsum, NH: Barcelona Publishers.

—— (2005) *Sounding the Self: Analogy in Improvisational Music Therapy*, Gilsum, NH: Barcelona Publishers.

Soibelman, D. (1948) *Therapeutic and Industrial Uses of Music: A Review of the Literature*, New York: Columbia University Press.

Solli, H.P., Rolvsjord, R. and Borg, M. (2013) 'Toward understanding music therapy as a recovery-oriented practice within mental health care: a meta-synthesis of service-users' experiences', *Journal of Music Therapy*, 50, 4: 244–73.

Solomon, A.L. (2005) 'Historical research in music therapy', in B.L. Wheeler (ed.) *Music Therapy Research*, 2nd edn, Gilsum, NH, Barcelona Publishers.

Spintge, R. and Droh, R. (1992) *Music Medicine*, St Louis, MO: Magnamusic-Baton.

Squires, G. (2001) 'Management as a professional discipline', *Journal of Management Studies*, 38: 4: 473–87.

Stainsby, T. and Cross, I. (2009) 'The perception of pitch', in S. Hallam, I. Cross and M. Thaut (eds) *The Oxford Handbook of Music Psychology*, Oxford: Oxford University Press.

Standley, J. (1991) *Music Techniques in Therapy, Counseling, and Special Education*, St Louis, MO: Magnamusic-Baton.

Steele, P. (1988) Foreword, *Journal of British Music Therapy*, 2, 2.

Stensæth, K. (2008) *Musical Answerability. A Theory on the Relationship between Music Therapy Improvisation and the Phenomenon of Action*, Oslo: Norges musikkhøgskoles publikasjoner, 1.

Stern, D.N. (1985/1998) *The Interpersonal World of the Infant*, paperback edn, London: Karnac Books.

—— (2004) *The Present Moment in Psychotherapy and Everyday Life*, New York: W.W. Norton.

—— (2010) *Forms of Vitality: Exploring Dynamic Experience in Psychology, the Arts, Psychotherapy, and Development*, Oxford: Oxford University Press.

Stige, B. (1998) 'Perspectives on meaning in music therapy', *British Journal of Music Therapy*, 12, 1: 20–8.

—— (2002) *Culture-Centered Music Therapy*, Gilsum, NH, Barcelona Publishers.

—— (2003/2012) *Elaborations toward a Notion of Community Music Therapy*, Gilsum, NH: Barcelona Publishers.

—— (2006) 'On a notion of participation in music therapy', *Nordic Journal of Music Therapy*, 15, 2: 121–38.

—— (2010a) 'Musical participation, social space, and everyday ritual', in B. Stige, G. Ansdell, C. Elefant and M. Pavlicevic, *Where Music Helps: Community Music Therapy in Action and Reflection*, Farnham, UK: Ashgate.

—— (2010b) 'Practicing music as mutual care', in B. Stige, G. Ansdell, C. Elefant and M. Pavlicevic, *Where Music Helps. Community Music Therapy in Action and Reflection*, Farnham, UK: Ashgate.

—— (2011) 'The doors and windows of the dressing room: culture-centered music therapy in a mental health setting', in A. Meadows (ed.) *Developments in Music Therapy Practice: Case Study Perspectives*, Gilsum, NH: Barcelona Publishers.

—— (2012) 'Health musicking: a perspective on music and health as action and performance', in R. MacDonald, G. Kreutz and L. Mitchell (eds) *Music, Health and Wellbeing*, New York: Oxford University Press.

Stige, B. and Aarø, L.E. (2012) *Invitation to Community Music Therapy*, New York: Routledge.

Stige, B. and Rolvsjord, R. (2009) 'Pionerer i mer enn femti år: om brudd og kontinuitet i musikkterapiens historie i Bergen' [Pioneers for more than fifty years: on change and continuity in the history of music therapy in Bergen], *Musikkterapi*, no. 2/09: 6–24.

Stige, B., Malterud, K. and Midtgarden, T. (2009) 'Towards an agenda for evaluation of qualitative research', *Qualitative Health Research*, 19, 10: 1504–16.

Stige, B., Ansdell, G., Elefant, C. and Pavlicevic, M. (2010) *Where Music Helps: Community Music Therapy in Action and Reflection*, Farnham, UK: Ashgate.

Sting (1998) 'Music and silence', *Resurgence*, November/December, 191: 32–3.

Storr, A. (1973/1991) *Jung*, New York: Routledge.

—— (1989/2001) *Freud: A Very Short Introduction*, Oxford: Oxford University Press.

Strehlow, G. (2009) 'The use of music in treating sexually abused children', *Nordic Journal of Music Therapy*, 18, 2: 167–83.

Summer, L. with Summer, J. (1996) *Music. The New Age Elixir*, Amherst, NY: Prometheus Books.

Sutton, J. (2002a) '"The pause that follows" . . . Silence, improvised music and music therapy', *Nordic Journal of Music Therapy*, 11, 1: 27–38.

—— (ed.) (2002b) *Music, Music Therapy and Trauma: International Perspectives*, London: Jessica Kingsley Publishers.

—— (2006) 'Hidden music: an exploration of silence in music and music therapy', in I. Deliège and G. Wiggins (eds) *Musical Creativity: Multidisciplinary Research in Theory and Practice*, Hove, UK: Psychology Press

—— (2007) 'The air between two hands: silence, music and communication', in N. Losseff and J. Doctor (eds) *Silence, Music, Silent Music*, Aldershot, UK: Ashgate.

Swanwick, K and Tillman, J. (1986) 'The sequence of musical development: a study of children's composition', *British Journal of Music Education*, 3, 3: 305–39.

Taylor, A. (2011) 'Older amateur keyboard players learning for self-fulfilment', *Psychology of Music*, 39, 3: 345–63.

Thaut, M.H. (2000) *A Scientific Model of Music in Therapy and Medicine*, St Louis, MO: MMB Music.

—— (2005) *Rhythm, Music, and the Brain: Scientific Foundations and Clinical Applications*, New York: Routledge.

Thaut, M.H. and Wheeler, B.L. (2010) 'Music therapy', in P.N. Juslin and J. Sloboda (eds) *Handbook of Music and Emotion: Theory, Research, Applications*, Oxford: Oxford University Press.

Thaut, M.H., Leins, A.K., Rice, R.R., Argstatter, H., Kenyon, G.P., McIntosh, G.C., Bolay, H.V. and Fetter, M. (2007) 'Rhythmic auditory stimulation improves gait more than NDT/Bobath training in near-ambulatory patients', *Neurorehabilitation Neural Repair*, 21: 455–9. doi:10.1177/1545968307300523.

Thorpe, K.E, Zwarenstein, M., Oxman, A.D., Treweek, S., Furberg, C.D., Altman, D.G., Tunis, S., Bergel, E., Harvey, I., Magid, D.J. and Chalkidou, K. (2009) 'A pragmatic explanatory continuum indicator summary (PRECIS): a tool to help trial designers', *Journal of Clinical Epidemiology*, 62, 5: 464–75. doi:10.1016/j.jclinepi.2008.12.011

Tomaino, C. (2012) 'Effective music therapy techniques in the treatment of nonfluent aphasia', *Annals of the New York Academy of Sciences*, vol. 1252: *The Neurosciences and Music IV: Learning and Memory*, April: 312–17. doi:10.1111/j.1749-6632.2012.06451.x

Trainor, L.J. and Trehub, S.E. (1994) 'Key membership and implied harmony in Western tonal music: developmental perspectives', *Perception and Psychophysics*, 56: 125–32.

Trehub, S.E. (2003) 'Musical predispositions in infancy: an update', in I. Peretz and R. Zatorre (eds) *The Cognitive Neuroscience of Music*, Oxford: Oxford University Press.

—— (2006) 'Infants as musical connoisseurs', in G.E. McPherson (ed.) *The Child as Musician: A Handbook of Musical Development*, Oxford: Oxford University Press.

Trevarthen, C. (1995) 'The child's need to learn a culture', *Children and Society*, 9, 1: 5–19.

—— (1999) 'Musicality and the intrinsic motive pulse: evidence from human psychobiology and infant communication', *Musicæ Scientiæ*, special issue 1999–2000, 3, 1: 155–215.

—— (2003) 'Neuroscience and intrinsic psychodynamics: current knowledge potential for therapy', in J. Corrigall and H. Wilkinson (eds) *Revolutionary Connection. Neuroscience and Psychotherapy*, London: Karnac Books.

Trevarthen, C. and Malloch, S. (2000) 'The dance of wellbeing: defining the musical therapeutic effect', *Nordic Journal of Music Therapy*, 9, 2: 3–17.

Trondalen, G. (2003) '"Self-listening" in music therapy with a young woman suffering from anorexia nervosa', *Nordic Journal of Music Therapy*, 12, 1: 3–17.

Tuastad, L. and O'Grady, L. (2013) 'Music therapy inside and outside prison – a freedom practice?', *Nordic Journal of Music Therapy*, 22, 3. doi:10.1080/08098131.2012.752760

Turry, A. (2005) 'Music psychotherapy and community music therapy: questions and considerations', *Voices: A World Forum for Music Therapy*, 5, 1, available at: https://normt.uib.no/index.php/voices/article/view/208/152 (accessed 6 November 2012).

Twyford, K. and Watson, T. (eds) (2008) *Integrated Team Working: Music Therapy as Part of Transdisciplinary and Collaborative Approaches*, London: Jessica Kingsley Publishers.

Tyler, H.P. (2002) 'Frederick Kill Harford – dilettante dabbler or man of our time?', *Nordic Journal of Music Therapy*, 11, 1: 39–42.

United Nations (2009) Rights of the child (CRC), Resolution adopted by the General Assembly, A/RES/64/146, December.

Unkefer, R.F. and Thaut, M.H. (eds) (2005) *Music Therapy in the Treatment of Adults with Mental Disorders: Theoretical Bases and Clinical Interventions*, Gilsum, NH: Barcelona Publishers.

Vaillancourt, G. (2009) 'Mentoring apprentice music therapists for peace and social justice through community music therapy: an arts-based study', unpublished PhD thesis, Antioch University, Santa Barbara, CA.

Van Bruggen-Rufi, M. and Vink, A. (2011) 'Home is where the heart is', in A. Meadows (ed.) *Developments in Music Therapy Practice: Case Study Perspectives*, Gilsum, NH: Barcelona Publishers.

Van de Wall, W. (1936) *Music in Institutions*, New York: Russell Sage Foundation.

Vink, A., Bruinsma, M. and Scholten, R. (2011) 'Music therapy for people with dementia (review), Cochrane Collaboration. doi:10.1002/14651858.CD003477.pub2

Wakao, Y. (2002) 'John Cage and therapeutic silence', *Voices: A World Forum for Music Therapy*, 2, 3. Available at https://normt.uib.no/index.php/voices/article/view/99/76 (accessed 9 November 2012).

Wallin, D.J. (2007) *Attachment in Psychotherapy*, New York: Guilford Press.

Wallin, N.L., Merker, B. and Brown, S. (eds) (2000) *The Origins of Music*, Cambridge, MA: MIT Press.

Wampold, B. (2001) *The Great Psychotherapy Debate: Models, Methods, and Findings*, Mahwah, NJ: Lawrence Erlbaum.

Warner, C. (2007) 'Challenging behaviour: working with the blindingly obvious', in T. Watson, *Music Therapy with Adults with Learning Disabilities*, Hove, UK: Routledge.

Watson, T. (ed.) (2007) *Music Therapy with Adults with Learning Disabilities*, Hove, UK: Routledge.

Weller, C.M. and Baker, F.A. (2011) 'The role of music therapy in physical rehabilitation: a systematic literature review', *Nordic Journal of Music Therapy*, 20, 1: 43–61.

Wenger, E. (1998) *Communities of Practice: Learning, Meaning and Identity*, New York: Cambridge University Press.

Wermke, K. and Mende, W. (2009) 'Musical elements in human infants' cries: in the beginning is the melody', *Musicæ Scientiæ*, special issue 2009–10, 'Music and Evolution': 151–175.

Wheeler, B.L. (ed.) (2005) *Music Therapy Research*, 2nd edn, Gilsum, NH: Barcelona Publishers.

Whipple, J. (2012) 'Music therapy as an effective treatment for young children with autism spectrum disorders: a meta-analysis', in P. Kern and M.E. Humpal (eds) *Early Childhood Music Therapy and Autistic Spectrum Disorders: Developing Potential in Young Children and Their Families*, London: Jessica Kingsley Publishers.

Wigram, T. (2004) *Improvisation: Methods and Techniques for Music Therapy Clinicians, Educators and Students*, London: Jessica Kingsley Publishers.

Wigram, T. and De Backer, J. (eds) (1999) *Clinical Applications of Music Therapy in Psychiatry*, London: Jessica Kingsley Publishers.

Wigram, T. and Gold, C. (2006) 'Music therapy in the assessment and treatment of autistic spectrum disorder: clinical application and research evidence', *Child: Care, Health and Development*, 32, 5: 535–42.

Wigram, T., Rogers, P. and Odell-Miller, H. (1993) 'Music therapy in the United Kingdom', in C.D. Maranto (ed.) *Music Therapy International Perspectives*, Pipersville, PA: Jeffrey Books.

Wigram, T., Pedersen, I.N. and Bonde, L.O. (2002) *A Comprehensive Guide to Music Therapy*, London: Jessica Kingsley Publishers.

Wilber, K. (1995) *Sex, Ecology, Spirituality*, Boston: Shambhala Publications.
—— (2000) *Integral Psychology: Consciousness, Spirit, Psychology, Therapy*, Boston: Shambhala Publications.
Winnicott, D.W. (1971) *Playing and Reality*, London: Tavistock.
World Federation of Music Therapy (2002) *Proceedings of the 10th World Congress of Music Therapy*, Oxford, 23–28 July, available at: http://www.wfmt.info/WFMT/2011_World_Congress_files/Proceedings%20Oxford_2002.pdf (accessed 12 January 2013).
Wosch, T. and Wigram, T. (eds) (2007) *Microanalysis in Music Therapy: Methods, Techniques and Applications for Clinicians, Researchers, Educators and Students*, London: Jessica Kingsley Publishers.
Wright, K. (2009) *Mirroring and Attunement: Self-Realization in Psychoanalysis and Art*, Hove, UK: Routledge.
Wroe, A. (2011) *Orpheus: The Song of Life*, London: Jonathan Cape.
Yalom, I.D. and Leszcz, M. (2005) *The Theory and Practice of Group Psychotherapy*, 5th edn, New York: Basic Books.
Yin, R.K. (2012) *Applications of Case Study Research*, London: Sage.
Youth Music (2002) *Creating a Land with Music: The Work, Education, and Training of Professional Musicians in the 21st Century* [Report commissioned by the Higher Education Funding Council for England], London: Youth Music, available at: www.youthmusic.org.uk/assets/files/HEFCEreport1.pdf (accessed 13 December 2010).
Zanchi, B. (2002) 'Style and identity: "being in the world" as a musical form: a clinical story', *Proceedings of the 10th World Congress of Music Therapy*, Oxford, 23–28 July, available at: http://www.wfmt.info/WFMT/2011_World_Congress_files/Proceedings%20Oxford_2002.pdf (accessed 12 January 2013)
—— (2011) 'La musicoterapia in semiresidenza: un approccio espressivo alla relazione terapeutica', in G. Rigon, L. Zucchi and E. Cocever (a cura di) *Sofferenza psichica e cambiamento in adolescenza. Intervento integrato: approccio clinico e educativo* [Psychic Suffering and Change in Adolescence: An Integrated Intervention with a Clinical and Education Approach], Trento: Centro Studi Erickson.
Zanini, C.R. de Oliveira and Leao, E. (2006) 'Therapeutic choir: a music therapist looks at the new millennium elderly', *Voices: A World Forum for Music Therapy*, available at: https://normt.uib.no/index.php/voices/article/view/249/193 (accessed 13 December 2013).
Ziman, J. (2000) *Real Science: What It Is, and What It Means*, Cambridge: Cambridge University Press.
Zuckerkandl, V. (1956) *Sound and Symbol: Music and the External World*, Princeton, NJ: Princeton University Press.

Name index

Subject index

offender 23

older adults: activity 150; health issues 150–1, 161; institutionalisation 152; music therapy with 152; relation to music 151; retirement 150–1; as a resource 149; third age 149–50, 160; *see also* United Nations Principles for Older Persons, University of the Third Age

organisation: of sounds relative to pulse 70; of vocal sounds 33; of walking 65–6, 72; *see also* melody, rhythm

Pachelbel's *Canon* 144

pain: caused by discords 105; control 39

palliative care 46, 128, 143–6, 149, 152

parenting 90

Parkinsonism 66–7

participation 11, 42, 47–8, 68, 76, 79, 88, 99, 109, 122–4, 126, 131–2, 139, 149, 167–8, 182, 185

pause *see* duration of sounds

performance 21–2, 75, 78, 114, 123, 133, 153, 162, 173, 176–7

permission: to explore instruments 59; to make loud sounds 64

perspective *see* theoretical perspective

philosophy 15; of dialogue 45, 51; of recognition 45

physical disorders 108; living with HIV/AIDS 147; neuropathy 141; *see also* cancer, disabilities, stroke

physiotherapy exercises 83–4; movement pattern supported by rhythmic pulse 83; reflected by vocal phrases 83

pitch 55, 58, 60–2, 73–5; associated with tension/relaxation 61, 75; audible range 61, 80; of babies' cries 81; causing distress 60; discordant intervals 74; effect of harmonic context 61; effect of tone quality 61; intervals 73–4, 77; overtones 76–7; physical responses to 60; 'privileged'/reference pitch 73; relation to loudness 61, 64; range 32; sequences of 73; standards 61; therapeutic use of 75; tuning systems 61; *see also* melody, harmony, scale

plainsong 73

play: imaginative 81–2; imitative 81,100; interactive 31, 33, 70, 85; music as play 54, 76, 98; solitary 91; social 90

pleasure 40, 42, 51, 81, 133

position: foetal 128; side-by-side 93

pre-composed music 108

pre-school: assessment centre 29–30; children 54, 90, 102–3; tuning into the child 85

prevention 151, 160; *see also* health promotion

prisons 21, 182

professional competence 7

professionalisation 10, 176, 190

psychoanalysis 41; defences 43; ego 42–3, 45–6; use of improvisation 43

psychodynamic perspective of music therapy 37, 41–3, 88, 108, 119; use of term 'objects' 118–9

psychosynthesis 45–6

public health 185

pulse *see* rhythm

Radiohead 112; 'Paranoid Android' 112

randomized controlled trials (RCTs) *see* research

recorded music: listening to in music therapy sessions 111–2, 144, 146–7; lullabies used to reduce stress 89; used to increase babies' weight 89; use of music transcribed from sessions 91; use of tape recorder in sessions 146

recovery (a non-medical notion of) 133, 180

reflexivity 200

rehabilitation 16; centres 107; use of music 28, 39, 52, 75, 127–8, 137–9

reinforcement 40–1, 51

relationships 15–16, 83, 119, 200; client–therapist 42–3, 45, 62; developing through music 17, 46, 51, 92–3, 121; with environment 48, 55–6; family 87; in groups 68–9; infant–caretaker 45, 81, 83, 87–9, 119; interpersonal 106–7, 145, 153; intrapersonal/musical 145; with music 110–19, 125; music structure– experience 50, 55; with others 109, 116, 119, 121; with parent/foster parent 83, 87–88; transpersonal 45–7, 56; within and between disciplines 195; *see also* therapeutic relationship, music therapy profession

repetition 42, 144

research: assessment procedures 7, 198–9; design of studies 38–40, 99–101, 120, 135, 154, 198–9; ethical considerations 196, 199; evidence-based 101–2, 120, 196; focus group 198–9; group study